Churchill's White Rabbit

Churchill's White Rabbit

THE TRUE STORY OF A REAL-LIFE JAMES BOND

SOPHIE JACKSON

First published 2012

The History Press
The Mill, Brimscombe Port
Stroud, Gloucestershire, GL5 2QG
www.thehistorypress.co.uk

British Library Cataloguing in Publication Data.
A catalogue record for this book is available from the British Library.

ISBN 978 0 7524 6748 1

Typesetting and origination by The History Press
Printed in Great Britain

Contents

– Author's Note –

TWO PREVIOUS WORKS ON Forest Yeo-Thomas have significantly helped in this revision of his history. *The White Rabbit* by Bruce Marshal first appeared in 1952 and is the closest that can be come to an autobiography from Forest. It suffered from Marshal's rather awkward prose and heavy-handed similes and was not entirely well received.

The second work, *Bravest of the Brave* by Mark Seaman, appeared in 1997 and delved into Forest's personal papers to give a better understanding of the man and above all followed him post-war, which Marshal failed to do.

Both works, however, were inevitably one-sided due to restrictions on official SOE papers, which meant that they had to rely on Forest's own words (recorded in unpublished memoirs) or the words of those who were closest to him.

Over the last decade the National Archives have gradually released SOE documents, in particular those relating to Forest's missions and his personnel file, along with other papers, which enable a greater insight into this amazing man. New research has revealed more about his closest companions, such as Henri Peulevé, as well as opening doors into the Nazi regime. In particular the work of researchers to catalogue and publish the personnel files of the SS has enabled characters that Forest mentioned briefly to be fleshed out.

Among this new research was the discovery of a letter by Ian Fleming, never before published, that indicated his involvement with Forest.

This book could not have happened without the work of many others who have performed their own researches into the Second World War and published insightful accounts. It aims to take the efforts of Marshal and Seaman and build upon them to create a truly 3D image of a remarkable man. There is probably still much more to know about Forest, along with the many men and women who served with him, and only time will tell what new revelations will emerge from the archives.

1

Beware the Agent
who isn't Punctual

IT IS MARCH 1944 in Paris. SOE agent Shelley takes the familiar steps up to Passy Métro station ready to catch a train to Rennes. He is due to make a last contact with *agent de liaison* 'Antonin' to pass on last-minute instructions and an encoded message. The Métro station is the ideal place for a casual rendez-vous. Since the Nazi occupation of 1940, cars have been virtually non-existent in Paris; aside from a ban on civilian motorists, most of the petrol stores were blown up in the invasion and what fuel is left has been secured for German use. Parisian citizens have had to fall back on other forms of transportation – the bicycle has seen a tremendous surge in popularity. But longer distances require faster transport and the Métro serves this purpose. The Nazis know that Paris cannot be brought to a standstill forever, so they ensure that the Métro runs smoothly and frequently. As Shelley saunters into Passy station bustling crowds instantly surround him. The platform is a hub of activity, filled with all kinds of passengers, and it affords solid cover for a clandestine meeting.

For the obsessively discreet Shelley, this is the perfect meeting point. He is a stickler for security. As part of his work in France developing the various resistance movements and coordinating them with British efforts, he often infuriates his espionage colleagues by drumming into them the need for strict protocol and utmost secrecy. He has come close to capture due to the reckless-ness of a resistance agent more than once. Others have died at Gestapo hands and whole resistance cells have been annihilated through the carelessness of a single individual. But as he calmly heads up the Passy steps that spring morning, he is unaware that his cover has already been blown – the last minutes of Shelley's freedom are numbered.

Shelley has his last day in Paris perfectly mapped out. He leaves his apartment at 9 a.m. for an 11 a.m. meeting with Antonin, then he plans to have lunch with two women – 'Maud' Bauer and Jacqueline Rameil, secretaries to journalist and resistance member Pierre Brossolette. Brossolette has recently been arrested, though the Germans are ignorant of his identity and importance. Shelley is planning a rescue mission, and his visit to Rennes, where Brossolette is in custody, is part of this operation. At lunch with the ladies, he will discuss news of Brossolette, as 'Maud' is in close contact with the prisoner, masquerading as his mistress in order to get access to him in prison.

With his plans organised down to the last detail, Shelley is feeling confident as he arrives at the steps of the Métro, looking forward to a brief spell away from the constant and disturbing gaze of the Paris Gestapo.

Shelley walks nonchalantly up the station steps. His meeting with Antonin will appear to be by pure chance. Antonin has been instructed to signal that the coast is clear to Shelley by having his hands in his pockets – any deviation will mean that the encounter is called off. In the last few weeks Shelley has been tailed more than once, has seen ill-disguised Germans loitering outside his rooms and has even had to accost a contact who had failed to realise he had two Germans following him to a meeting. It is imperative that Antonin respects the danger they are in and acts accordingly.

Stopping by a newspaper kiosk, Shelley pretends to browse the few 'patriotic' papers and magazines. He is uncomfortably aware that 11 a.m. is rapidly passing with no sign of Antonin. Punctuality is another part of the 'Shelley code' – a late contact is a worrying sign. With any other agent, Shelley would have argued that the meeting should be aborted there and then, but at that crucial moment he finds himself torn with indecision.

Heading down the far side of the Métro station he pauses to consider his options: his principles tell him he should abort the contact and flee the station, but the information he is to pass to Antonin is so important that he is loath to give up so easily. Besides, he is due to be in Rennes for several days and he doesn't like the idea of leaving without passing on vital instructions. The final nail in his coffin is the over-confidence that has been growing in Shelley since his first successes in France. He has outwitted the Gestapo on several occasions with the most audacious schemes, and lost tails and taken risks with seeming impunity. Right at that moment it seems as though Shelley has luck on his side, so he turns around and walks back into the station.

Glancing up the steps there is still no sign of Antonin, but Shelley heads upstairs anyway, and back to the kiosk, his contact point. The arrival of a train, which disgorges a large party of passengers, encourages him, and the commotion seems a good mask for his own clandestine activities.

Shelley is still on the stairs when, suddenly, five men break from the new arrivals and grab him. In seconds the stunned Shelley has his hands wrenched behind his back and handcuffed, while all around him train passengers scurry past and pretend not to notice. As his captors rifle through his pockets, Shelley spots the missing Antonin being escorted away between two Gestapo men. His heart sinks as he realises his hasty decision has led him straight into a trap.

Around him the Germans are yelling at the crowd to keep moving and threaten to shoot anyone who tries to intervene. The warning is hardly necessary as most Parisians are familiar with Gestapo tactics and are quick to avert their eyes from the scene. Shelley's last hope is that he has only fallen into a security check, albeit a serious one, and that his captors have no real idea who is in their hands. But his hopes are dashed when elated Germans begin congratulating each other on the capture of 'Shelley', one of the top names on the Gestapo most-wanted list. As Shelley is forced through the Métro to a waiting car, his heart sinks further. He knows the game is up.

At SOE headquarters back in London, news of Shelley is slow in arriving and when it does come it is laced with misinformation and outright lies. It is not until May that dribbles of news, leaked from less-than-reliable sources, filter down the corridors in London. By that point, unbeknown to the SOE team, Shelley has already endured torture and is sitting in a prison cell wondering when he will be shot.

Early news suggests that Shelley is already dead. Rumours have it that on 21 March a tall Englishman with a moustache took poison while in German custody and the Germans tried to pump his stomach, but failed. Whoever this Englishman is SOE don't believe it is Shelley based on the rather flimsy theory that he would have poisoned himself with cyanide (all agents carry the infamous death pills) and the Germans would have known it was futile to use a stomach pump with such a poison. Besides, they argue, Shelley is 'fairly short'.

But other stories circulate that differ from the truth even more bizarrely. On the same cyanide report is another suggesting that Shelley had been on a mission to meet a woman called Brigitte. This was Brigitte Friang, secretary to Clouet des Pesrusches, another resistance operative. During this supposed meeting between Shelley and Brigitte, the secretary was supposedly shot by the Germans when she put her hand in her bag, as they assumed she was reaching for a gun. This was all said to have happened on the Passy Métro stairs, after which Shelley simply vanished.

In fact this story is a muddled rendition of two truths. Brigitte *had* been attending a meeting when she was shot in the stomach by Germans, however the meeting was not with Shelley, but with Antonin. It was later believed that the Brigitte meeting, held at the Trocadero, was what finally turned the tables on Shelley. At the meeting four Germans approached the pair, shot Brigitte and searched and interrogated Antonin. On him they found a document that broke yet another golden rule: it stated 'Shelley Passy 11' and told the Germans everything they needed to know about the planned rendezvous. How ecstatic they must have been to stumble onto a way of trapping the infamous Shelley so easily! They dragged the terrified Antonin to the Métro station and forced him to point out the man he least wanted to betray.

Even worse than the rumours and lies is the SOE's misunderstanding of Shelley's mission. Communication between agents and headquarters is notoriously difficult, as direction-finding vans operated by the Germans regularly scan for wireless telegraph (W/T) transmissions in France. The Germans have the great advantage of being in charge of Paris and are able to switch off the power to housing blocks whenever they choose; by doing this they can isolate a transmission and wait until it is abruptly stopped due to power failure to confirm where it is coming from. Then the search vehicles are sent out to find the errant transmitter.

In this hunted atmosphere agents are supposed to keep messages short and move their W/T sets to new locations frequently. Added to that complication is the need for personalised codes for agents based on letter replacement or the alteration of key words, with special false codes involving deliberate misspellings or the use of prearranged warning words in case of capture, and the arduousness of keeping London abreast of every development becomes apparent. SOE headquarters inevitably find themselves in the dark most of the time and such is the case with Shelley – they only have a vague idea of what he was doing on the Passy Métro stairs.

Some of their information comes from Shelley's former secretaries. One cleared out his apartment after hearing that Brigitte had been shot and was puzzled to find no money; she assumed he had taken it in his suitcase to Rennes for the purpose of bribing people.

A second secretary received a typewritten note reading '*CHEVAL est a FRESNES*': Cheval is at Fresnes. Cheval is an unofficial codename of Shelley's used for secret communications with his secretaries, and Fresnes is a prison. Whoever sent the message is a mystery. It is unlikely to have been Shelley himself, but at least it goes some way to confirming his capture and where he is. His secretaries live in hope that the Germans are ignorant of Shelley's real identity and that he has avoided the hardships of Gestapo interrogation.

Time, however, reveals the truth. An SOE agent, who is a close friend of Shelley's and had seen him only four days before his arrest, arrives in England in May, going by the name of Polygone. He is interviewed by SOE and is able to give an accurate account of what has become of Shelley. British hearts despair as they hear that Shelley was arrested by the same Gestapo men who had shot another agent, Galiene II, quashing hopes that he had been picked up by accident. Polygone is damning of his friend's security precautions and describes him as indiscreet. He carried a revolver in a holster at all times, which Polygone deemed unwise. Furthermore he had the dangerous habit of frequenting the same restaurants, but to allay the British disappointment at finding their best agent so fallible, Polygone assures them that on the whole Shelley's security was good and he rarely carried important documents on his person unless absolutely necessary.

Unfortunately Polygone also knows that the Gestapo have raided Shelley's apartment and it is widely thought that they have taken a microphotograph of Shelley's mission orders and another document that includes a sketch of Shelley's railway sabotage plans. Polygone is also concerned that at least thirty coded telegrams Shelley had sent to England have apparently gone astray; what has become of them no one seems to know, but with the Gestapo breathing down resistance necks, the missing messages are cause for grave concern.

SOE finally know most of the truth about Shelley's disappearance. He is in the hands of the Gestapo, being held at Fresnes and more than likely enduring the worst kinds of interrogation the Germans can mete out. Rescue is an unlikely option as SOE takes the pragmatic view that they could easily lose more good men trying to regain one lost agent, and they simply do not have the resources for such high costs. Instead they begin to try to unravel where the blame for Shelley's loss might lie. In any secret organisation betrayal is always at the back of people's minds.

Polygone is of the firm opinion that there is an informer in their midst. He finds it highly alarming, let alone suspicious, that three *agents de liaison* have vanished at the same time as Shelley was arrested. One reappeared a month later but the other two remain unaccounted for. Then there is Antonin, who Polygone knows is missing but is unaware that he has been arrested with Shelley by the Gestapo. Lastly, a fifth *agent de liaison* who worked between Shelley and another important resistance member has vanished without a trace. Polygone cannot imagine that all these disappearances are pure coincidence and now SOE fear that they have a mole in their network.

This is not the first time that SOE's French operations have been so badly compromised. Two of their resistance networks dealing with the introduction of Allied agents have in fact been completely infiltrated by the Germans and at least one has been operated and run by the Gestapo pretending to be a resistance network. On other occasions agents have been caught and forced to transmit false messages back to the British; sometimes this is spotted, but on many other occasions it is not.

Damage limitation is now key: whatever contacts Shelley made, whatever arrangements, need to be protected. SOE know that even the hardest of agents will break under the intensity of interrogation; there is a reason that the Gestapo use torture, even if it is considered a fallible system by more conscientious interrogators. The assumption has to be made that Shelley has been broken, and the relevant security precautions must be taken, especially if a traitor still loiters somewhere in the network.

Despite knowing that rescue is almost impossible, SOE continue to search for their lost agent. He is by no means the only one they are trying to track information on, but he is special in that he has a powerful reputation within the secret service community. Even a budding spy novelist working with the Admiralty is caught up with the mystery of Shelley's loss and discusses it over dinner with colleagues. His name is Ian Fleming and he follows Shelley's story with great interest.

SOE is rife with rumours about the missing agent. A telegram arrives with a strange jumble of information; the source is a member of a sub-unit of 72 Wing, engaged in wireless jamming operations. The source, in turn, heard his information from a liberated prisoner of war called Corporal Stevenson, who had been held in the Bad Homburg camp by the Germans. Stevenson had met a man going by the name Maurice Chouquet, who claimed he was actually SOE agent Wing-Commander Davies. Stevenson did not relate how he had earned Chouquet's trust enough to learn such dangerous information (it was unwise for an SOE man to confide in anyone who was not also a known agent), but the significance of the message is that this could have been Shelley going by two assumed names.

Shelley is in fact making great efforts to convince his superiors and loved ones that he is still very much alive. He slips out whatever messages he can in the vain hope that they will reach home, and amazingly quite a few do. One finds its way into the hands of Sister Eanswythe of St Mary's Mission. She comes by the information via her contact with Warrant Officer John Lander, a wireless navigator in the RAF who was shot down in early 1944. He had sent his son to the mission's school before the war and regularly confided his family problems to the nun. When he failed to receive any post from his family during his confinement he complained in a letter to the good sister and asked her to see what she could do. In a short postscript he asked that she write to Mrs Thomas (Shelley's wife) to let her know that he had met her husband and that he was alright. He failed to elaborate any further and SOE are disappointed that the nun is a dead end.

There are other letters, and SOE acquires them as soon as they can in order to analyse them. Agents are taught secret codes that can be innocently dropped into letters to family should they be caught, and Shelley's letters are scrutinised for any clues. There is a feeling that SOE is clutching at very thin straws and their strained desperation even seeps into their analysis reports.

> We are sorry, but [the letter to Mrs Thomas] does not contain a message according to the innocent letter conventions arranged here with [Shelley].

> [However] it would seem that an investigation of the names and addresses [mentioned in the letter], and possibly replies, containing hidden messages on [Shelley's] conventions might achieve good results.[1]

SOE is beginning to piece together a timeline of Shelley's whereabouts during his absence. He has left clues wherever he can to let them know that he is still alive – scratched missives on walls, short messages, even contact with other British prisoners – but while they can pursue his route, SOE can do nothing to bring him home: that is up to the man himself.

But why is Shelley so important to SOE that they are pursuing him so diligently? Other agents vanish from official papers when captured, only being vaguely mentioned in a report about a more favoured agent. The files on Shelley are a bumper crop of information on one very special agent, but what made him so important? Who was he and why was his role so significant to SOE?

....

Note
1. Extract from interrogation report from Forest Frederick Edward Yeo-Thomas' SOE personnel file.

2

The Secrets of a Tailor

SHELLEY'S REAL NAME WAS Forest Frederick Edward Yeo-Thomas, something of a mouthful, but a name that incorporated his French and British origins. Born on 17 June 1907 at a nursing home in Holborn, London, Yeo-Thomas was a child of two nationalities. Though British citizens, his parents, John and Daisy, spent the majority of their time in Dieppe, a tradition that went back to Forest's grandfather, John Yeo, who had abandoned South Wales in the 1850s to travel to Dieppe and marry his sweetheart, Miss Thomas. The move had been spurred on by disapproving parents and to spite them further John incorporated his new wife's surname into his own – the Yeo-Thomases were born.

The first Mr and Mrs Yeo-Thomas settled into Dieppe life, with John selling high-grade Welsh coal to the railways and securing his fortune; by 1895 they were so accepted within the community that grandfather Yeo-Thomas was able to form and become honorary president of the Dieppe Football Club, as well as becoming vice-president of the Dieppe Golf Club. Both his son and grandson were known as good amateur football players and in the 1960s players in the Dieppe area were still competing for a Yeo-Thomas Cup.

Despite being well integrated into the local French community Forest's family still had strong British roots: they were ex-pats with firm loyalty to their king and country. A large photograph of Edward VII presided over mealtimes, inspiring obedience from Forest, who learned to sing 'God Save the King' as soon as he was able. When the king died his effigy in France was draped with black and the household remained in a state of mourning, talking only in whispers, for several weeks.

The influence of France could not be ignored, however. Forest spoke to his father in French, and it was natural that a child born into a foreign culture would tend to pick up its habits and quirks.

Forest's parents chose to correct this by giving their son an education in England so Forest was sent to Westcliff School in Sussex, a typical boarding school and terribly English in its attitudes and methods. John hoped that this would instil some Britishness into his young son, but Forest was not the doting patriot that his father was, and Westcliff seemed totally alien to him. Switching cultures, despite the stern gaze of Edward VII looking over him since birth, was impossible for the young boy. He refused his school porridge in disgust and snuck out of his dormitory at night to sit on a nearby railway embankment to watch the trains. No doubt he was punished for his excursions, but Forest already had the stubborn streak that had taken his grandfather from Wales to France, and no beating could take that away from him. Fortunately his parents saw sense (or realised that it was hopeless) after a year, and he happily returned to France.

However, Forest's French life was changing too. In 1908 a brother, Jack, was born and quickly became John's favourite, pushing Forest further and further away. Forest attended the College de Dieppe in 1910, enjoying its naval links, before going to the Lycée Condorcet and the University of Paris. Forest was already favouring his French side and in Paris he studied history, eventually taking his *Bachelier ès Lettres*. His loyalties were now truly divided, with France's influence being the strongest. The gulf between him and his father only increased his independence and made him favour French interests over British.

Forest may have felt awkward with his strange dual life, in essence living in two countries, but that would change with the First World War. The first advance of the Germans served to draw France and Britain together to stand against a common foe and suddenly being Anglo-French was a boon, rather than a disadvantage.

Naturally John Yeo-Thomas joined the British Army as soon as he could and quickly became a staff officer due to his fluency in French. Daisy also volunteered for the British Army as a nurse. While Forest felt proud of his family's contribution, he could not have been unaware of the strain the war work put on his parents' already fragile marriage. In fact Daisy and John were becoming virtual strangers to each other, a situation that only worsened when Jack contracted meningitis and died in 1917. John, devastated by the loss of his adored son, blamed Daisy for being too occupied with her war duties to properly care for the boy. In the bleak atmosphere that penetrated the family home, Forest saw one way out – joining the army.

His father was not oblivious to this desire and, understandably desperate to protect his remaining son, contacted both the French and British recruiting offices in Paris to make it clear that if a young Forest Yeo-Thomas were to arrive he was to be turned away for being underage. Forest was only thwarted for a short time, however.

The entrance of the Americans into the war gave Forest the opportunity he needed. The American troops were under-manned and under-equipped. Desperate for troops, their recruiting examinations were minimal, to say the least, and in late 1917 Forest joined up under the name of Pierre Nord, declaring he was 19, despite barely looking his real age of 16. He was accepted, and so Forest enjoyed his first success at subterfuge, which would become such an important part of his life later on.

Anyone who has even a passing knowledge of the First World War will realise the horrors that Yeo-Thomas was marching into – he could hardly have been unaware himself – but Forest was eager and determined. He was also lucky, which was a trait that would carry him through a second war. By 1917 the war was coming to its conclusion, not that the ordinary soldiers realised this, and life in and out of the trenches, the fears of no-man's-land and the horrific death tolls seemed just as great that year as any year before. But Germany was weakening, and in another year they would be defeated and signing an armistice that would become the basis for grievances that would spur more conflict.

What Forest did in that intervening year is rather hazy. On the MI9 questionnaire that he filled in when being assessed to be an SOE agent, he stated that he was in the US Army from 1917–22 and during that time visited Germany, Austria, Poland, Russia, the Balkans, Turkey and the USA. After the First World War it is thought that he joined an American Legion set up to assist the Polish in their fight against the Russians.[1]

Whether that is the case or not, Forest did end up at the battle for the city of Zhitomir and was captured by the Russians. As a foreign national he was automatically sentenced to death, but made his first impressive escape by strangling his guard and fleeing through the Balkans and into Turkey. He finally arrived in the USA to spend two more years in the army before leaving, as he stated on the M19 form, 'to go into business'.

There is no doubt that this was a fabrication on Forest's part and whatever his real reasons for leaving the army were, he kept them close to his chest. In reality, Forest returned to a France crippled by war, where many ex-servicemen found themselves unemployed and in desperate circumstances. Forest was no different: his parents had separated and John was involved with his former secretary (there was never a greater cliché) and was struggling to make ends meet. Some of his business investments had been tied up with Russia and after the Bolshevik revolution these had simply disappeared. There was little he could offer his son, and Forest drifted, at one point ending up selling bootlaces and matches in London. For the history graduate and war veteran it was demeaning.

Forest's fortunes seemed to turn when his father managed to get him an apprenticeship with Rolls-Royce in 1922, but the economic climate saw even the mighty car manufacturer struggle, and Forest was let go.

Forest made another complete change of direction and went into accountancy. This seemed to suit him and for a time he was successful in the banking industry, serving as a senior cashier before moving on to be a business manager.

He needed the money his new job brought because in about 1924–25 he met Lillian Margaret Walker, a British/Danish national raised in France. He fell madly in love with her and they were married on 12 September 1925, and it wasn't long before Forest's first daughter, Evelyn Daisy Erica, was born in 1927. In 1930, a year after his parents had divorced and John Yeo-Thomas had finally married his secretary, a second daughter, Lillian May Alice, was born. In later records Forest's daughters and wife would fade from memory and were virtually eradicated from military record, but in those hazy post-war days Forest seemed to have found some form of contentment.

Then, rather remarkably, he changed direction yet again. Giving up his banking career, he moved first to become an assistant general manager at Compagnie Industrielle des Pètroles, then made an even more radical change by joining the fashion house of British-born designer Edward Molyneux. It can only be imagined what pressures caused the change. France's cracking political façade and the exhausted economy probably made a move into a thriving business seem sensible, but it is still interesting to wonder what Forest, a man who could strangle a Russian guard and partially build a Rolls-Royce, could have had to offer a fashion designer.

Molyneux must have liked his new general manager however, as Forest remained with the company until the outbreak of the next war. In the meantime he kept up his interests in sports by boxing, competing as a flyweight or bantamweight, and writing for the British magazine *Boxing* under the anglicised name Eddie Thomas. He was successful enough to hold a part share in a gymnasium and for the time being Forest looked set to follow a contented and successful career in the fashion world.

But all was not so rosy in the world of Yeo-Thomas. France was in turmoil as successive ineffectual governments crippled its economy, and Europe's desperate fear of another war was leading to political appeasement towards the belligerent Germany, which was turning into a frightening power under the auspices of a hitherto unknown leader called Adolf Hitler.

While his business life was stable, Forest's marriage was disintegrating. In a strange echo of his parents' disastrous union, Forest and Lillian found themselves increasingly incompatible, and this little domestic war resulted in separation in 1936. Forest moved back to his father's house, now run by his new stepmother.

Forest regularly met with Lillian to arrange money for his daughters. Divorce seemed the inevitable course for them, but even on this they could not agree. Forest was fearful he would be cast in the role of scapegoat and would lose access to his two young daughters, so when Lillian pushed for it he held back. Ironically when their roles were reversed and Forest sought divorce, Lillian was the one to oppose it, and as war loomed in 1939 they were still at an impasse. To add to his burdens, on 17 July 1939 Daisy passed away and Forest had to deal with arranging her funeral. His only consolation was that his mother would not see France crumble into war again.

The relative happiness Forest had experienced in the 1920s and early '30s was now truly vanishing. The invasion of Poland thrust France and Britain back into conflict with Germany yet again, and for the fiery-natured Forest sitting on the sidelines was not an option. As war was declared he was preparing to sign up with whoever would take him but, just like in the First World War, it wasn't so simple to find a unit that wanted him.

Note

1. Report by B Group to RF, dated 27 February 1945, the National Archives.

3

A Heart for Conflict

WAR BROKE OUT IN a Europe optimistically unprepared for conflict. Being forced to face reality also meant being forced to take stock of what they had and what they didn't. One major service that had been neglected after the war was the intelligence division, but that was just the tip of a very large iceberg. Faith in appeasement had left Britain in a state of unreadiness and now it was necessary to pool what resources the country had and recall men who had experience from the previous conflict.

In France the situation was similar: disbelief at the dramatic turn of events seemed to be staying military hands, much to the frustration of Forest, who expected to be snapped up as a keen First World War veteran and volunteer. His aim was to join the British Army, but his first attempts via the British Embassy in the rue du Faubourg St Honoré ended in failure as no volunteers were being accepted. Annoyed, but not thwarted, he tried the French Foreign Legion, but they would not take on a British citizen, even if he did consider himself French.

It seemed that no one wanted Forest's help, but he was not discouraged and returned to the British Embassy and made himself a nuisance to the air attaché until he finally accepted him as a volunteer driver under the condition that he supply his own car and petrol. Forest hovered uncomfortably between civilian and military status; he was neither one nor the other and his frustration was boiling over yet again.

All this would change on 26 September when he was finally accepted into the RAF as Aircraftman 2nd Class 504896, but his excitement quickly returned to disappointment when he was bluntly told that he would be serving as an interpreter as he was too old to fly. The irony that in a few short years he would be parachuting into rural France would probably not have impressed the RAF recruiting board. Forest, who had kept up his boxing and regularly sparred four to eight rounds with younger men, was angered by the implication, but the truth was that no one was particularly desperate for men as the war looked likely to be over before it had begun.

Perhaps the biggest problem was the desire not to fight that many felt and which acted as a psychological barrier to aggressive action. Britain and France, barely recovered from the First World War, did not want to enter into another conflict and there was a distinct impression of heels being dragged even as British forces crossed to France to support the defensive Maginot Line. Allied instinct felt that a quick, forceful assault, coupled with a blockade of German shipping, would result in sending the old Huns running back to where they came from. Unfortunately these weren't the old Huns anymore, and strategies that might have worked a generation ago were now woefully out-dated. A hint might have come from the Germans' easy defeat of Poland, but those in charge chose to be dangerously optimistic and the war effort crawled along rather than speeding to meet the threat. This period would become known as the Phoney War, the opening rounds when Britain and France both failed to realise the German might they faced and the risks ahead.

Forest was in the midst of this apathetic war. His role within the RAF seemed little better than when he was a volunteer driver and escorting VIPs and diplomats around and did nothing for his need to get into the action. But there was no real action. Even when Forest managed to get onto the Advanced Air Striking Force at Reims, which was supposed to be targeting Germany, he was disappointed to discover that they were not allowed to do anything unless the Germans hit first.

Forest had drifted into a hazy world of harmonious inactivity. The Reims authorities were as confused about the situation as their counterparts in Paris were, and the Phoney War had cast a fog over their bureaucratic preparations. Forest was posted to the interpreters' pool, but when he arrived no one could tell him where he was supposed to go, so he found himself a hotel room and hoped to be able to locate his office in the morning. He was in luck, for the next day he bumped into an old friend, Sergeant Albertella, who was able to direct him to the Château Polignac where the interpreters were being housed. When he reached it he was in for a further surprise as he had been unexpectedly promoted to acting sergeant. This triumph was unfortunately tainted, as Forest was still acting as an ununiformed interpreter to senior staff officers. This made his position among the other officers untenable at times and Forest's dislike for incompetent authority quickly became apparent. To one squadron leader who asked him to summon a pilot officer with the phrase 'send that sod out there in', he replied that he would be happy to oblige when the request was 'properly expressed', to which he got the response: 'Of course, you're not an officer and you can't expect the same respect as I can.' On another occasion, when this same man learned that Forest had been employed in the fashion industry, he announced: 'My God, what is the RAF coming to!'[1]

Worse was that the air attaché's original conditions that Forest pay all his own expenses still held true. Forest's pockets were soon empty as he tried to keep up with his superiors. In an effort to recoup something, he collected receipts and sent them to the RAF for payment. Conveniently for the paymasters, they were lost in the invasion of France before they could be paid and they refused to listen to any further requests on the subject from Forest without seeing duplicate receipts. Even in war bureaucracy gives no quarter.

Forest was far from being alone in feeling that no one was really taking the war seriously, as this was the overriding feeling of many ordinary soldiers and airmen. It seemed that the authorities had blinkered themselves to the danger and were spinning out time until they had to do something decisive. Part of the problem was a need to hastily rearm, and both Britain and France had gone into a buying frenzy with the US to stock up on much-needed weapons and equipment. Meanwhile the RAF ran pointless sorties to Germany, dropping not bombs, but propaganda leaflets. Aside from a few odd skirmishes, the troops on the Maginot Line were enjoying a quiet stalemate. The real action was happening out at sea with the opening stages of the Battle of the Atlantic.

It was with nervous optimism that Forest joined the Forward Air Ammunition Park (FAAP) near Reims in the hope of carrying out duties more to his liking. He was at last given a uniform and it was with some relief that he realised he could be truly useful at the posting, using his bilingual abilities to create links between the military and the local population. Though he did not know it at the time, it would prove good practice for when he had to liaise between resistance groups and London.

Forest was perfect for the role, his natural charm and charisma as well as his confidence led people to instinctively trust and listen to him. He also slipped into the role of a leader easily and people automatically looked up to him. He might not have had the traditional good looks of a future secret agent – one author called him 'terrier-like' in appearance – but he radiated honesty and sincerity, which meant far more.

His time at FAAP was cut short when he was sent to attend an anti-gas course in England on 23 November. Forest had not been 'home' in seventeen years and, right at that moment with Germans on his doorstep, he was hardly in the mood for a sojourn abroad. He stepped into an England about to experience the harshest winter it had seen in forty-five years, with temperatures plummeting while Forest and four fellow NCOs sat through lectures at a camp on Salisbury Plain. At least the RAF lecturers impressed Forest, and there were some opportunities for fun and games. This included a car trip into Salisbury with a civilian employee on the camp. Forest and four of his companions agreed to the arrangement but were stunned when their charitable friend demanded 10s each for giving them a lift. Too keen to get out of the camp and into city life to argue, they paid up, though on their return Forest tried his hand at 'wartime' sabotage and put half a pound of sugar into the petrol tank of the man's car. Salisbury had proved a pleasant break from the stalemate in France, but it was only to last a fortnight and Forest was soon back at FAAP.

It seemed that the military could still not quite decide what to do with him, and he was not the only one. Trying to keep men who wanted to be fighting occupied was not easy. Just before Christmas another training course was arranged, this time at Fighter Command at Stanmore, Middlesex. Forest had barely unpacked when he was ordered back to Britain in the bleak midwinter. It was not to be the nicest of trips as Forest found himself stuck aboard a transport ship in the middle of the Channel on Christmas Day, his mind returning to past Christmases with his family. He was still in touch with Lillian, though their relationship was now as cold as the ocean surrounding him, and Forest found himself suffering in his loneliness for the first time. Not a person prone to worrying about being by themselves or requiring someone to lean upon, he now found that his isolation was becoming uncomfortable.

Matters were not improved by his arrival at Fighter Command on Boxing Day, when he was abruptly sent away for another 48 hours of unwanted leave.

Stuck in London with nothing to do and with the December weather biting at his heels, he would later remark: 'I don't think I have ever hated any place more than I did London that night.'[2]

When he returned to the RAF they yet again seemed to consider him surplus to requirements and, increasingly frustrated, he was sent off for another week's leave. Forest now sunk into one his lowest ebbs; it was not until he found himself interned in a German concentration camp that he felt so miserable and alone again. He withdrew money from the bank, slept in several luxury West End hotels and went on a week-long bender.

It was while Forest was extinguishing his misery in various bottles of alcohol that another wartime volunteer, who would change Forest's life, was also finding the Phoney War an inconvenience. This was Barbara Dean, born in Kent in 1915, partially orphaned when her mother died shortly afterwards and unloved by a father who blamed her for his wife's death. Stubbornly independent and with plenty of opinions and a rankling dislike for authority, Barbara was almost Forest's female counterpart. She was not a conventional beauty, but pretty and with a sense of flare about her appearance that summed up her personality. She was described by one contemporary as 'one of the few exceedingly pretty women I have known who are also sweet and humble and charitable.'

While Forest was battling with temporary depression, Barbara was struggling to fit in with the WAAF. Spurred on by a desire to protect and defend her country, she had willingly volunteered for the service only four months before, but quickly discovered that military life was too uncompromising to suit her. Unlike Forest, who not only responded to the discipline of uniformed life but encouraged it in his later dealings with resistance members, Barbara could not stick being told what to do. For her it was all petty bureaucracy – pointless, stupid and infuriating – and she finally had enough when she argued with an officer about her hat being crooked and was put on a charge. Barbara 'volunteered' her way out and was waiting impatiently for the paperwork to be finished at the same time as Forest was kicking his heels in London.

There was always something that felt like the hand of fate, or perhaps lady luck, in Forest's life, and his first meeting with Barbara has precisely that feeling. They could easily have missed each other by a few days and they weren't even based at the same station, but on Forest's return to Stanmore Forest, he discovered that he was being sent to the Bomber Liaison Section, where he would meet the woman who would sustain him through the war and beyond.

At Bomber Liaison, Forest was sent to the Filter Room, the secret control centre where all radar reports on hostile intruders were sent. The RAF had several of these Filter Rooms operating during the war, manned almost exclusively by WAAF members such as Barbara. There were strict rules for choosing operatives: 'Must be under twenty-one years of age, with quick reactions, good at figures and female' stated one criterion.[3] Though these were obviously not always followed, as Barbara was 24. Still it was a decidedly young, female environment and a hub of activity.

The purpose of the Filter Room was what its name suggests – it filtered information from the various radar stations across the country. Raw data was sent in and was then checked and sometimes recalculated to compensate for human error. This information was then arranged on a giant table map – so familiar from old war movies where WAAF girls pushed blocks representing German planes around with long pointers – before being passed on to the Operations Room.

In a gallery above the WAAF workers, senior officers monitored the maps and acted according to the information present, whether that meant instructing air raid warnings to be sounded, scrambling fighter squadrons, alerting anti-aircraft defences or monitoring damaged homecoming planes that might be in need of assistance. It would be from this eyrie that Forest would operate and from where he could have a good bird's-eye view of Barbara as she hurried back and forth.

Forest was surprisingly cautious in his attempts to attract Barbara's attention; the disaster of his marriage and the fact he was not yet divorced probably damaged his confidence in approaching her, but he was still determined. On long watches in the Filter Room he would talk with Elizabeth Trouncer, a friend of Barbara's, and try to surreptitiously draw out ideas on how to woo the elusive woman of his dreams. He prolonged these interrogations by taking Elizabeth out to dinner, but she was no fool and knew he was using her as a means to an end. Offended at being so obviously misled, she told him bluntly that he had no chance with Barbara; Forest shrugged this off and even wagered £5 with her that he could win the feisty Miss Dean over.

Elizabeth now found herself in the unenviable role of go-between, and Forest regularly sent her with messages for Barbara. One of the first, with typical Forest abruptness, was to inform her that he was married. Less than impressed, she sent back via Elizabeth: 'well tell him to spend his weekend with his wife.'[4] Fortunately Forest's stubborn streak was not about to let him back down and he sent further notes explaining that he had been separated from his wife for four years and had every intention of getting a divorce as soon as the war was over.

It was not until Barbara's final day in the WAAF that she finally relented and agreed to meet Forest at the Windmill pub, situated just outside headquarters. Having promised herself never to date an airman, she consoled herself at this change of heart by thinking of it as purely for practical reasons as Forest could carry her suitcases to the train station.

The meeting did not go smoothly. Barbara was under the impression that they were meeting outside, following the protocol that it was improper for a lady to enter a pub unescorted. Forest had missed this British social convention and was happily ensconced inside by the warm fire, while his date lingered outside in the freezing January weather. It was only when Barbara's impatience got the better of her that she finally entered the pub and spotted Forest waiting for her. She then found that Forest only had an hour left before he had to go back on duty and therefore could not escort her to the station. Despite all these problems however, there was enough spark between them to arrange to meet again in Leicester Square, London, in two days' time.

Their second meeting went as smoothly as the first; Barbara was violently sick just before leaving the house to meet Forest and, with no means of getting a message to him, she had to pass two fraught hours wondering what he would think of her before she felt well enough to leave home. It seemed pointless to hope that Forest would still be waiting, but Barbara went anyway (which suggests the depths of her feelings already). To her amazement he was still in Leicester Square, perhaps having formed the opinion that his date was prone to being remarkably late. This went a long way to improving him in her estimation, even if he did give her legs a long, appreciative look when the wind gusted up her skirt slightly. Her illness behind her, the pair carried on to a French restaurant to enjoy an intimate meal.

By now it was obvious that both were quite besotted with each other. Forest had set his sights on Barbara and despite any objections she had stood no chance against his determination. Forest was perhaps not the obvious ladies' man, but his confident manner and forceful personality seemed to attract them to him nonetheless. To fuel his affair with Barbara, Forest spent his inheritance from his late mother like there was no tomorrow, determined that his estranged wife would have no part of it. When it finally ran out their romance was already well advanced and could withstand becoming more frugal.

Barbara had freed herself from the restrictions of the WAAF and took a job running a Harridges dress shop in Surrey, where she rented a cottage for weekend rendezvous with Forest when he was able to get forty-eight hours' leave. Like so many couples at that time, with true war a close prospect, they wanted to cement their relationship with marriage, but Lillian would not consent to a divorce from her estranged husband. They finally agreed on 9 February 1940 to simply become 'married'. There was no church service or anything official, but from then on Barbara was Mrs Yeo-Thomas (more often shortened to just Mrs Thomas). It was not an easy arrangement and led to criticism from outsiders who learned that the couple 'lived in sin'. Forest would have undoubtedly loved to have married Barbara properly, but with Lillian being so obstinate his hands were tied. Still, it was not a legal arrangement and even when filling in his MI9 papers later on, Forest felt it necessary to list his next of kin as Lillian Yeo-Thomas and his two daughters. Barbara fell down an official loophole.

Their 'marriage', however, was significant for other reasons, it was a promise of loyalty to Barbara even as Forest determined to return to France to fight the war he was certain was looming. He was afraid that it would only be a matter of weeks or even days before the Germans made a conclusive move. He felt torn in his loyalties and needed Barbara to know how much he loved her even as he prepared himself to face Hitler and the possibility of his own death. So, on 6 April 1940, after a farewell meal with Barbara, Forest headed for an airfield just outside Paris run by Bomber Liaison Section, little knowing that France's future now rested in German hands.

Notes

1. Marshal, B., *The White Rabbit*.
2. Seaman, M., *Bravest of the Brave*.
3. 'Memories of Eileen Younghusband', The Wartime Memories Project.
4. Seaman, M., *Op cit*.

The Ruination of France

IN EARLY MAY A German force was seen amassing in front of the French Maginot Line. For the defenders of this epic fortification spanning the length of the French/German border, it seemed a laughable effort from the enemy.

The Maginot Line had been constructed following the principles of First World War trench warfare, which dictated that it was necessary to defend static positions. Veterans of that war remembered the fraught battles for small patches of land well, along with the hasty construction of earthen fortifications to protect newly won territory. With this in mind, when Germany started to become a threat yet again, the majority opinion was to build significant defences along the border to protect against assault or a surprise attack.

Support for the plan came from national hero and Marshal of France Henri Pétain, whose valour in the First World War gave weight to his opinions. He was an elderly man as war loomed yet again, and pre-empting an invasion seemed a sound solution. But his opinions were not unanimously held: an upstart French general named Charles de Gaulle, another First World War veteran, was adamantly against the plan, wanting investment to go into armour and aircraft, rather than an expensive series of forts. But Pétain's views won the day and the Maginot Line (named after French minister of war, André Maginot) grew up along the border like some modern-day Hadrian's Wall.

It was not a simple undertaking. There were systems of heavy turrets, anti-tank defences, sophisticated barracks for the defending force, border guard posts, communication centres, machine-gun posts and supply depots. At some points the line was 20–25km deep (12–16 miles). This was no small investment and Pétain hoped that it would buy France valuable time to amass their own army and strengthen their military.

Connected by a series of underground passages, the line was a hive of activity, with British and French forces manning the various posts. Popular opinion was that it was impregnable and would save France from invasion. Initial construction had stopped at the Belgian border, but the line had been extended after Belgium announced its neutrality in 1936. Despite this, it was still thought unlikely that Belgium would be invaded and even if it was, Pétain felt confident that his troops could push them out. Aside from a gap at the Ardennes forest, which French advisors pointed out was virtually impregnable anyway, the line was an unbroken barrier between the hostile Germans and France.

On 10 May the amassing Germans made a sortie against the line and were easily driven back. No one realised that this was a diversion and a second German army was marching through that impenetrable Ardennes forest, and, worse still, that German forces had invaded neutral Belgium and the Netherlands. The line defences along the Belgian border, always less substantial than the rest of the line due to the high water table, which risked flooding, now fell under the German assault.

The large forts were simply overrun. On 19 May all 107 members of one French crew were killed defending their post when the German 16th Army pummelled them with heavy artillery. Within days of the initial assault Germany was pushing into France and the Maginot Line had become pointless. By 24 May the British Expeditionary Force had been separated from the French Army and had fallen back to the port of Dunkirk with the Germans breathing down their necks. No place evokes a greater sense of tragedy and heroism. The British were sitting ducks at Dunkirk and it was only due to the Germans holding back that they were able to evacuate.

The French were in similar disarray. Many soldiers began to openly desert and even those that continued fighting soon found themselves being forced to withdraw. Among them was Forest, who was stunned to find that the embassy staff had already left Paris, including the air attaché who he had hoped to get orders from. He saw that there was no choice but to follow his superiors in a retreat to the coast.

Forest watched his beloved France collapsing around him. At Bomber Liaison some of the French aircraftmen had already fallen into defeatism and watched refugees streaming down the roads with a mixture of pity and inevitability. The aerodrome had been bombed on 3 June, but much to Forest's frustration there was no call to return the action, and on 11 June communications were finally cut. It was in this state of chaos that the embassy staff had simply vanished and Forest was left with no choice but to evacuate also.

It was a bad time in Paris. Forest had been sleeping at his father's flat, which was conveniently located at the Passy Métro station – four years later Yeo-Thomas senior could witness his son's arrest from his own window – and returned there to collect his belongings. The skies were black, with thick clouds spewed from the burning remains of oil factories at Port Jerome, which the Nazis had bombed in yet another effort to cripple the French defences. A black layer of heavy dust would fall on the city like mourning clothes and for months everything would be cast in tones of black and grey. Even the birds were leaving and for the next year Paris would become eerily quiet without their song.

Few people were out in the streets, but those that were cast unfriendly glances at Forest in his RAF uniform. One snapped at him: 'Hold, an Englishman, I thought they had all buggered off long ago.' Although Forest personally resented the insult, he recognised the feelings behind it. Allied politicians had underestimated the German threat and had sat on their hands when action was called for. The end result was Paris under occupation.

It was with a heavy heart that Forest walked the streets of his beloved city, not knowing when he would see it again. 'The Champs Élysées [was] deserted, invisible almost in the fog of rolling smoke. He walked slowly along the avenue Kleber, took a last look at the Trocadero and the Eiffel Tower, and dropped into a small café at the corner of the rue Franklin for a drink. He was the only customer.'[1]

Paris was emptying ahead of the Nazi advance. Every vehicle still functioning was on the roads and packed with people, those without petrol rode bicycles and those without even that simple transport walked. The refugees formed a shocking procession, which Forest had to drive through on his way to Tours. Among them he caught glimpses of soldiers and even officers fleeing for their lives. From time to time a German plane would fly over and take pot shots at them or attempt to bomb them, and everyone would scatter for the nearest ditch.

Forest and his comrades eventually made it to Tours where they carried on with their normal duties for a few more days until the German advance forced them to decamp and retreat to Limoges. It was here that they heard of Pétain's request for an armistice, a move that would leave Vichy France unoccupied but would make their government and police as much of an enemy as the Nazis in Paris. The situation seemed to be rapidly becoming hopeless and again the RAF retreated, this time to Bordeaux.

For the despondent Forest it seemed that his government had betrayed France and were colluding with the Germans. Pétain had taken defeat too graciously and was still eager for appeasement despite it already being proved pointless. He would buy southern France a brief respite from occupation, but it would not be a lasting or complete freedom. As the British retreated, Forest caught a brief glimpse of General Gouraud, former Military Governor of Paris, still wearing his French uniform with pride and determined not to collapse under the weight of invasion. Famous for his heroism in the First World War and for leading the French Fourth Army, he was something of an icon of the old honour of France for Forest. Standing with his many decorations, including the Légion d'honneur and Croix de Guerre, he carried himself with dignity despite the chaos around him. He was a lasting memory of the France that Forest would fight for even as the British abandoned Bordeaux and drove with all haste to Pointe de Grave, where two cargo boats were waiting to take them to England.

Forest and his companion Flight-Lieutenant James almost didn't reach the boats – they stayed behind in Bordeaux to try and locate two of their men who had been separated from the main party in the night-time rush to get away from Tours. When their hunt proved in vain they alerted the local military authorities to be on the lookout for two men in British uniform and then made their own dash to Pointe de Grave, only to run out of petrol en route. Yet again luck played out for Forest when a petrol tanker happened to be travelling along the same road, but even so the driver was not happy to help them out and had to be threatened before he would give them a couple of gallons. This was not Forest's finest moment, but in that instant getting out of France to fight another day was more important than the hurt feelings of one Frenchman.

At the Pointe de Grave troops trying to get aboard the cargo boats had created a bottleneck and Forest could afford some time to wander the Pointe and visit the local war monument that commemorated the arrival of US troops in 1917. As he stood there he penned a postcard for a dear old friend, Mademoiselle Jose Dupuis, remarking: 'I know how you're feeling at present, but don't get discouraged. We will return and liberate France.' Despite the occupation this quickly written note managed to reach its recipient.

As Forest stood by the war monument at Pointe and stared at a blue sky that seemed out of place with the terrible events unfolding around him, he could only see a snippet of the future and for him it was all about patriotism and anger at a conquering nation. His overriding emotion was a burning desire to free France once and for all, and he would achieve that any way he could. For a moment that desire almost had him desert from the RAF and head into France to prepare his people for the re-entry of British forces which he was certain would happen, but he recognised that that would only serve as a short-term means, perhaps with no definable results. So he said a last goodbye to France and boarded the cargo boats with everyone else, ready to offer his services to free France as soon as he set foot on English shores.

It was a three-day voyage to Britain and the port of Milford Haven. Awaiting the despondent ranks of British evacuees was a well-dressed RAF warrant officer who took one look at the returning men and yelled: 'Make it slippy, you f***ing lot of slovenly bastards.'[2] Forest knew he was home.

Paris was now effectively under the full control of the Germans, while southern France was nominally under the governorship of General Pétain and the Vichy authorities; in reality every move they made was with one eye on Hitler and his Nazis. Paris was now a German city; enemy soldiers marched proudly in the streets and German reconnaissance planes landed in the Place de la Concorde. Famous hotels and buildings were draped with swastika banners: a giant one was draped on the Arc de Triomphe, to the great distress of watching Parisians.

There were odd, sporadic bursts of rebellion. One remaining French soldier opened fire on a group of Germans, killing one and wounding another before being gunned down in a spray of machine-gun bullets, but on the whole Paris fell quietly.

Businesses briefly closed and then reopened to serve their new clientele, some café owners offered free drinks to the invaders and the brothels merely closed their shutters for a short spell of mourning before welcoming the Germans with open arms. The first attacks on Jews began soon after; shops displayed 'no Jews' signs and the Theatre des Ambassadeurs announced that it was under new management, having been stolen from its Jewish owner, Henry Bernstein. As despair kicked in the suicides began: Thierry de Martel, a descendent of Mirabeau and a famous surgeon, injected himself with strychnine, leaving a note for his assistant that there would be no point trying to resuscitate him. At least fifteen other Parisians chose death over watching their city be trampled by the Germans, and there were probably more that have gone unrecorded.

Britain watched on in horror and wondered if it was to be next.

Yet again Forest felt at a loss. His first desire was to see Barbara and assure her that he was well, but at the back of his mind was the throbbing need to do something for France. After a brief reunion with his lover, he was posted to Uxbridge to serve in the Personnel Dispatch Centre. It was a desk job yet again, aside from frequent excursions to conduct groups of airmen to the Burroughs Wellcome Institute at Euston station for yellow fever vaccinations.

It would have been easy for Forest to grow despondent again, but he managed to find ways to brighten his days. His greatest triumph was getting hold of OHMS (On His Majesty's Service) envelopes, which he addressed to various officials including the medical officer at Burroughs Wellcome Institute and the commanding officer at Uxbridge. Filling the envelopes with blank paper to make them appear full, he was able to present them to the guard on the camp gate and thus leave the Dispatch Centre any time he wanted to.

After a short time his skills as an interpreter were needed once again and he was transferred to Odiham in Hampshire where the Free French Air Force officers and men were being trained. The Free French movement was the brainwave of General de Gaulle, who was now in England trying to form an organisation that would rescue France. De Gaulle was adamant that the French people should resist wherever they could and announced this on a BBC radio broadcast to Paris. It was a complete contrast to the announcement Pétain had made on 17 June: 'I tell you today that you must cease fighting.'[3] That same day de Gaulle left for London and put out his own, contradictory, broadcast on 18 June.

It was not enough, and de Gaulle knew it would not be. On 22 June the armistice between the Germans and the French was signed and for the time being Paris was lost. De Gaulle formed the Provisional French National Committee on 27 June, but the idea of a political committee was quickly quashed in favour of a military party and on 28 June the British government announced that it: 'recognised General De Gaulle as Leader of all Free

Frenchmen, wherever they may be, who rally to him in support of the Allied cause.'[4] Effectively de Gaulle had become the British symbol of the French nation and its resistance to oppression. The Free French movement soon had its name set in stone and it would become both an ally and a nemesis for Forest in the future. But for now he knew of it only as a fledgling organisation seeking to break the Nazi stranglehold on France.

In October Forest was selected for a recommendation for a commission. He was disappointed, when he arrived for his interview, at the quality of his fellow candidates, who he later described rather caustically as: 'wingless wonders determined, if chosen, to do all they could to save the Administration Branch.'[5]

Forest remembered his own interview with bitterness: he entered the room as smartly as he could, determined to give a good impression, and faced a row of critical inquisitors who seemed equally determined to disapprove of him. The questioning was superficial and became bogged down with Forest's French roots, which clearly did not appeal to his inspectors. When one asked about his education and was told that Forest had attended the College Dieppe and the Lycée Condorcet, he remarked volatilely: 'College de Dieppe? Never heard of it. What sort of college was it?' He was even less impressed with the Lycée Condorcet and wanted Forest to explain what they were equivalent to in Britain. Feeling a tad annoyed, Forest announced that he imagined they would be approximately the same as Oxford or Cambridge. There was no room for modesty during this ordeal.

Despite this humiliation, Forest received his commission and was even passed by the medical board as A1-4B. His superiors still thought him too old to fly and Forest was unwillingly marshalled into the ranks of the 'wingless wonders' he had so criticised, and reported to Babington, near Coventry, to become an intelligence officer for the 308 Polish Fighter Squadron.

This was his first taste of another side of warfare: the gathering of information from the enemy and determining its accuracy. But he so desperately wanted to do more than sit at a desk and analyse other people's information – he needed to be hands-on.

He liked the men in the 308, but that only made matters worse. The young Polish pilots were training up for combat readiness in the winter months of 1940–41, something that should have at least put off the perils of war for a short time, but this was not to be. Air crashes during training in Hurricanes caused several fatalities. For Forest, who had become the unofficial father figure of the regiment and was fondly called 'Papa' (being the oldest officer in the squadron), these deaths hit hard. The situation only became worse when the squadron moved to Northolt, near London, in June 1941 and the young pilots saw real action for the first time. The death toll began to rise and 'Papa' Yeo-Thomas felt helpless and frustrated as he watched young men fly off and impatiently awaited their return.

Forest now tried to move himself into MI9 – the division responsible for escape lines within France – and had even been interviewed, but it was a chance meeting with a member of the newest secret organisation, SOE, that sealed his fate for the rest of the war. It was while visiting friends among the French forces at their offices at St James's Square that he was introduced to Captain Eric Piquet-Wicks. It can be imagined that this meeting was contrived by his French contacts who knew of Forest's frustration at being so 'out' of the fight. But whatever the case, this short conversation with Piquet-Wicks made such an impression on the captain that the course of Forest's war changed forever.

....

Notes

1. Marshal, B., *The White Rabbit*.
2. *Ibid.*
3. Perrault, G., *Paris Under the Occupation*.
4. MacKenzie, W., *The Secret History of SOE*.
5. In Marshal, *Op cit.*

An Ungentlemanly
Type of War

THERE WAS ALWAYS A notion among certain layers of the British military that war had conventions. There were rules to be followed that governed what was and was not allowed; to break them was considered not only ungentlemanly but simply not British. To a modern mind some of these restrictions seem incomprehensible and it is frightening to think that many significant decisions of the Second World War were based on the principles of warfare from the past – principles that no longer made sense in the first modern conflict.

One of the difficulties that British authorities struggled with was the idea of 'subversion'. Spies and the intelligence service as an organised body was a relatively new concept, as was the notion that they were official, recognised by the government and had their own legitimate department. Gathering information from the enemy and occupied countries was one thing, and perfectly acceptable as a logical consequence of war, but sneaking in fellows undercover to stir up trouble among the locals stuck in the throat of many upper-level staff.

The only secret services prior to the war were MI5 and MI6. They were officially inaugurated in 1909 by a Cabinet decision and spent the interwar years watching over the tangled politics of Europe and, closer to home, those of Northern Ireland.

The 'Fifth Column' scare began to change everything in 1938 when governments started to look at their own people with suspicion. The idea that large numbers of citizens could be working undercover for the enemy was frightening simply in its intangible nature. Today we know that the Fifth Column scare was just that, a scare hyped out of all proportion, but step back to 1938 and it seemed very different. Anything seemed possible as the Nazi machine rumbled into action.

When conflict became inevitable in 1939 it was necessary to arrange for special divisions to deal with the new problems that open war would cause. Among these newly formed departments was the inappropriately titled Government Code and Cipher School (they deciphered intercepted messages but did no teaching), the Radio Security Service and MI9, which was set up at Christmas to organise escape routes for Allied airmen and refugees from enemy countries. There was also a deception service covered by the meaningless title of London Controlling Section.

All this was legitimate intelligence activity; intercepting and deciphering communications and rescuing individuals from enemy hands was a perfectly acceptable aspect of warfare and one that did not trouble any ministers when they went to bed at night. Indeed they could feel pleased that the sophistication of these departments was outwitting Jerry time and time again.

The real problem came from those at the forefront of intelligence work who realised that defensive security was not enough in this new, ever-changing wartime climate. As early as a year before Hitler invaded Poland, some sections of Whitehall were quietly investigating the possibilities of propaganda, subversion and sabotage, and their potential effects on the enemy. The War Office, Foreign Office and MI6 all had secret departments, unacknowledged and unofficial, working on these topics. The idea of this secretive, yet aggressive, warfare was anathema to politicians and government officials that it was kept hidden even from them.

Those at the heart of the intelligence services knew that the old rules of warfare were long lost and that if they didn't take advantage of undercover agents, rebel movements and stirring up popular dissent, then the Germans certainly would. Spies and double agents were a constant threat to Britain; it was only because the Abwehr (the German counter-intelligence force) were as much novices at the game as the British that they never posed a real threat.

In 1940 it was decided that a separate organisation was needed to deal with the three unpopular intelligence sub-divisions (propaganda, subversion, sabotage). The fledgling groups would eventually form into SOE (Special Operations

Executive), but to begin with they were a mixed bag of departments. Section D, which became a part of it, was stolen from MI6, much to the displeasure of the head of that department who was not informed of the change for three weeks. There were also problems with overlaps: MI6 felt that SOE were stepping on their toes when it came to intelligence gathering and MI9 wondered if their role as an escape routes department was about to be subverted.

Everything was a bit rushed and nobody was entirely clear on what they were supposed to be doing. The departments shaped up with time and eventually divided into F Section (sabotage in France usually by non-French agents), DF Section (escape routes), EU/P Section (worked exclusively among Polish speakers), AMF Section (operated in Algiers for only twenty months between 1943 and 1944), Jedburgh Section (only uniformed operatives sent in during Operation Overlord to reinforce the Maquis in France and hold up the German forces), and lastly RF Section (a subversive movement that worked to reinforce French opinions against the Germans and Vichy government, and assisted the resistance).[1]

A splinter group, PWE (Political Warfare Executive) to which fell tasks of 'black' propaganda and rumour mongering, broke away from SOE. There was always rivalry between the two branches and they never co-existed well.

While all of this was going on, Parliament was kept in the dark. The new secret service was so controversial that it was not possible to admit its existence to Parliament and certainly not to the press.[2] However, the organisation did capture the imagination and attention of the new prime minister, Winston Churchill. He had always been a progressive thinker when it came to the war and was not averse to playing a little dirty. He liked the concept of SOE, as did the Civil Service's principal strategic expert, Lord Hankey. Churchill ensured that a document officially creating SOE was drawn up by his predecessor Neville Chamberlain just before Chamberlain's death.

SOE had a simple agenda: to develop an underground resistance movement among the local population that would disrupt Nazi influence and control. This could be done by simply spreading information and keeping up morale or by taking risky acts of sabotage to hamper the Germans. There was a greater risk to the general population by the latter action, as the Nazis would initiate fierce reprisals for any act of destruction. While this was not a matter to be taken lightly, reprisals almost universally had the effect of stirring up more resistance and strengthening that which already existed.

While their objective was simple, putting it into effect was much more complex. For a start the resistance movements that had already formed in France were divided by their political ideas as much as by their operating methods. The biggest factor in this was General de Gaulle, who on the one hand was useful for stirring up people to fight back, but on the other often divided potential comrades.

It would be a mistake to believe that de Gaulle was universally popular among the French, as nothing in politics is ever that easy. France has always been a hotbed for political debate and contention and the war only interrupted that for a matter of months until it resurfaced within the underground. While the majority of resisters despised Pétain for 'kissing up' to the Nazis, there was just as many who despised de Gaulle and did not want to fight off the Germans just to get him into power; they also found it difficult to fight alongside 'Gaullists' who were now part of the Free French Independents (FFI). Add to that de Gaulle's own personal dislike for various resistance elements and his refusal to aid them in any way, and the situation soon became unmanageable. Also in the mix were the French Communists, with connections to Russia. It was feared that they were working to see the Soviets take control of France. And let's not forget the Maquis, the men who had fled to various mountainous and forested regions to escape being sent to Germany as forced labour. They lived permanently outdoors and in hiding, but built stocks of weapons and practiced guerrilla warfare.

Somehow SOE had to bring together these differing groups to form a unified resistance. They didn't have to like each other, but they must not conflict or hamper each other's efforts. This would prove the full-time job of RF Section, and would cause a great deal of argument among the politicians back home, not least the Foreign Office, which was trying to keep on reasonable terms with Pétain.

In warfare, nothing is as simple as it seems.

Meanwhile, Forest was trying to find his way back into France via the intelligence services. He had been interviewed for employment within MI9 in December 1941 and then shortly after by Captain Strong of MI5. After his chance meeting with Piquet-Wicks he was sent to Boodle's Club for another interview, this time by Major David Keswick. It was remarked that he gave 'a favourable impression.'[3] The resulting papers from the interview reveal revelations about Forest's personal life and affairs.

They record that Forest's wife and two children were still in France and being looked after by his former employer Molyneux;[4] Barbara was unmentioned. Forest listed Lillian's address as rue de la Pointe and stated that she was the person named in his will. He also gave his religion as Calvinist (a branch of Christianity named after French reformer John Calvin), though later writings and records suggest that he was more inclined towards atheism. Intriguingly he claimed he had no political views, which seems oddly neutral for a man normally so full of opinions, but was perhaps a tactic for ensuring that he wasn't disqualified from service by favouring the wrong party line.

Barbara finally received a mention under section 23 – 'First Person to be informed if you become a casualty' – where her original surname, Dean, was tactfully written in. Under his personal particulars Forest gave his description as thickset, blue-eyed and fair-haired; he could almost be imagined as having German ancestry. He also mentioned that the third finger on his left hand was 'defective' but this did not prevent him from being able to shoot, mountaineer, swim or box, all things that the SOE interview asked if he could do.

When it came to promoting his usefulness to SOE, Forest was not a shrinking violet and when asked which areas of France he was familiar with he bluntly responded 'all'. He also made it clear that he had many contacts within France, both personal and professional, which he could use in his secret work. How much of this was accurate and how much was a ploy to ensure that he was employed by SOE is only known to Forest; he was indeed widely travelled and knowledgeable about France, but whether his fashion industry contacts could have been any use to the resistance is debatable. Forest was not afraid to promote his own self-interests if it meant getting into the service.

He told his new potential employers that he had been approached by MI9 (rather than him approaching them) but had come to the conclusion that he could do more for SOE. This was actually quite true as he was exactly the type of individual the fledgling SOE needed for their work with the resistance. He was therefore already being interviewed with a mind to being placed in the RF Section of the organisation.

SOE liked the determined and dogmatic Forest, and after a final check into his background run by MI5 they were keen to offer him a place. But as usual in Forest's life nothing was ever that simple. The Air Ministry kicked up a fuss about losing one of their own. The RAF and SOE never had an easy relationship: SOE was reliant on RAF aircraft to transfer their agents in and out of various countries, but the missions were not only time away from bombing raids for the pilots and planes involved, but were also high risk.

With unhappy relations between the two organisations it was unsurprising that the RAF made a fuss about Forest's transfer; it was not so much that Forest was indispensable to them, but that they were disinclined to respond favourably to any SOE request.

Forest was furious. After so long trying to achieve his goal he had been thwarted by petty bureaucracy and internal politics. It had been a long time coming, but Forest finally exploded. He demanded to be released from the RAF, threatening to go to the national press and tell his story if he was not allowed his transfer. SOE, meanwhile, tried to stay in the background, not wanting to sour relations further between themselves and the RAF. Forest was therefore alone in his battle, but that had never bothered him and he kept pestering the Air Ministry until finally they relented and on 3 February 1942, Forest joined SOE.

Barbara discovered Forest's new role late in the day. She was aware that he had had a number of interviews about transferring from the air service, but had not realised he was trying to get into a secret operation. When she did find out she was understandably worried and cross. There was no getting away from the fact that Forest was trying to get into a division fraught with risk and danger. While SOE's work was top secret and the public knew nothing about it, Barbara was aware of the terrible risks any agent had to take to achieve his goal. It is unclear how much Forest revealed to Barbara in those early days about his new role. SOE agents were meant to keep a lid on their work even with loved ones, but it was difficult not to say something to a person you might never see again. It seems likely that Barbara had a better knowledge than most families of what Forest was going to be up to, but that hardly alleviated her concerns. Her only hope had been the Air Ministry dragging its heels and refusing a transfer, and she tried to persuade Forest not to make a fuss and push too hard, but Forest was far too stubborn to listen.

Forest stepped into a world of very complicated politics. SOE's operations in France had been split into two independent sections (though in practice complete independence was impossible): F Section and RF Section. F Section was the British arm of the organisation, recruiting its own agents (either French or French-speaking British) and remaining, as much as it could, neutral among the various resistance movements. RF Section worked closely with de Gaulle's Bureau Central de Renseignements et d'Action (BCRA), the Free French Intelligence movement. As such there was a natural antipathy towards it from the Independent French movements and the communists. There was also a constant niggling conflict between F and RF, whether it was over supplies or missions overlapping. F Section was a source of perpetual upset among the exiled French leaders in London and Forest often wrote unsympathetically about his co-division.[5]

RF Section had its problems as well. Formed in May 1941 and originally comprising of Captain Eric Piquet-Wicks and his secretary, it had flourished into an operation supplying the resistance with arms and equipment as well as helping to transport Free French agents in and out of the country.

Forest entered RF Section when it was at No. 1 Dorset Square (critics of the division rather enjoyed the irony of RF taking over premises recently vacated by the Bertram Mills Circus). His main responsibilities at the start were sorting through the reams of information that came in from the field, learning to recognise the pointless from the important, and to coordinate the equipping of supplies to whatever section project was running at the time. By this point he had been promoted to flight-lieutenant, but was no nearer being airborne.

Forest quickly came into contact with the significant figures within the section and became familiar with names that regularly reoccur in histories of SOE and the resistance. Commandant (later Colonel) Passy, the head of BCRA, whose real name was André Dewavrin, impressed Forest, who considered him cool and efficient. Passy was not afraid to join his colleagues in the field when the need arose and parachuted into France in 1943 with Pierre Brossolette, another man who became a close friend to Forest. Via Passy, Forest came into contact with a number of young agents who he would later work with in the field.

At the other end of the spectrum there was Piquet-Wicks, the man who had inspired Forest to join the section, but who Forest now developed a distinct dislike for. He described him as having a 'brilliant mind [but his caustic wit] made one feel like giving him a hefty kick in the pants.'[6]

The sentiment was mutual and Piquet-Wicks felt that Forest carried a permanent and rather hefty chip on his shoulder. He probably had a point, but that did not make their working relationship any easier.

RF spent the majority of 1942 building up their organisation within France. Arms dumps and secret stashes would be essential when the section went into full operation and Forest was integrally involved in sorting these issues out. While RF was supposed to be a purely non-combative team (they were organisers, not saboteurs) they still trained agents in the art of destruction, as well as radio operators and specialists detailed to find landing grounds for planes and parachutes.

By the autumn of 1942 the unit was considered important enough to be issued with a senior officer commander to replace Piquet-Wicks. This was Lieutenant-Colonel J.R.H. Hutchison, who quickly became nicknamed 'Hutch'. He was enthusiastic and courageous, insisted that everyone at Dorset Square speak French exclusively, and in 1944 parachuted into France with a Jedburgh team when he was well into his fifties. Hutch rapidly became a driving force at RF and he was just the sort of man who would not restrict another's entrance into the field due to age. This was great news for Forest who was beginning to suffer the same dismal feelings he had endured at 308 Squadron while watching young pilots going into action while he was left behind. His requests to be sent into the field had been turned down, but his persistence was always his strongest point and after making himself a nuisance it was agreed that should a mission requiring his talents come up he would be assigned to it.

Forest set about finding himself just such a mission and his first thought was to get assistance from his old friend Molyneux. The navy was short of small craft for coastal operations and Forest recalled that his friend had a motor yacht moored in Monte Carlo harbour. Thinking this could be his ticket in, he suggested that he be given the mission of seizing the yacht and taking her on a mad dash to Gibraltar. The idea was approved, Molyneux gave his consent and an agent named Charvet was assigned to provide a crew of three. A felucca[7] would provide supplies in the form of 450 gallons of petrol, 50 gallons of oil, two light machine guns and food. Forest would either travel on the felucca or be parachuted to the location. His excitement was mounting, as it seemed he was finally going to get his chance; he even had his first operation name, the rather obvious 'Seahorse'.

But typically, just as everything seemed to be going swimmingly, something happened, and on this occasion it was the changing wartime situation and someone realising that the risk being undertaken for one small yacht was ridiculous. The mission sounds utterly absurd in the cold light of peacetime and proves how desperate Forest was to get involved in anything. The project was unconditionally shelved. Fortunately for Forest this did not translate into relegating him back to his desk duties and he was allowed to keep himself in readiness for another mission and to attend parachute training. There was hope yet that he would finally get himself into action.

....

Notes

1. Foot, M.R.D., *SOE in France*.
2. MacKenzie, W., *Op cit*.
3. Yeo-Thomas SOE personnel file, the National Archives.
4. Molyneux was listed as a captain in the MI9 records, having served with the Duke of Wellington Regiment in the First World War. Having lost an eye in that conflict and being 48 at the time of the next he was not involved in the fighting, but carried on work in his fashion house, temporarily moving it to London during the Second World War. It is not clear how he was looking after Mrs Yeo-Thomas, but it was possibly financially.
5. F Section is best known for the many heroic agents, such as Odette Sansom, who operated under its auspices. It was keen on encouraging sabotage and much of the SOE material already published deals with the people working in this division.
6. Seaman, *Op cit*.
7. Small motor-powered craft.

The Man with the White
Streak in his Hair

THE PARACHUTE WAS STILL in its infancy in terms of military use when Forest travelled to Cheshire in November 1942 to undertake his training. Initially introduced in the First World War as a means of escaping from air balloons or damaged planes, it had been suggested that they could be used as a means of dropping troops en masse as early as 1917 by an American general.[1] However Britain remained unconvinced by parachuting, and held off forming a parachute regiment until 1941.

The military authorities could hardly be blamed for their scepticism. Parachutes were a dangerous business, as SOE agents would learn. The usual means for deploying a parachute involved a static line attached to the transport aircraft. When the paratrooper or agent jumped from the plane the static line became taut and automatically caused the parachute to open. This was the easiest way to release inexperienced jumpers, but it had its problems and there is at least one reported incident of a man plummeting to his death because his parachute was not attached to the static line.

Even if a parachute was deployed safely, the landing still had to be endured. Harry Peulevé, who met Forest in 1944, parachuted into France as an SOE agent only to break his leg on landing. As most agents had to be dropped in 'blind' (at night and only with a rudimentary idea of the exact location they were being launched over) the risks of hitting something or landing badly were all too high, and the number of SOE agents whose stories begin (or end) with them being knocked unconscious or fracturing something upon arrival is rather dismaying.

But if Forest wanted to get into France the parachute was his only real option. SOE had its own training field for parachutists at Ringfield, near Manchester, and Forest arrived there in the early hours of a cold Sunday morning. He had only a brief moment of respite before he had to be up and doing physical training for an hour and a half. The experience was gruelling after being stuck behind a desk for so long.

Forest then got to try some dummy jumps. A pretend plane fuselage had been built with an exit hatch of the correct size in order to teach the men how to launch themselves from the aircraft, and once this had been practiced for a while Forest moved on to swinging in a practice harness to get a feel for parachuting.

The next day Forest experienced his first real descent and the jump terrified him despite his grim determination. He later recorded his thoughts at the moment of having to jump as: 'You damned fool, why ever did you undertake such a silly job – in a few minutes you'll have to jump through that hole and it doesn't appeal to you a bit, you are scared stiff and you'll have to force yourself to do it. Twerp!'[2] He was not alone in being unnerved by the prospect of the fall and it was some comfort to know that his fellow jumpers were equally scared. He summoned his courage and made his first descent without a hitch; he landed so elated that he was instantly ready to try again. Over the next few days he had plenty of opportunities. The training school had their pupils jumping from planes and balloons day and night. His only real disaster happened during a water jump, when he was dropped over a lake at Tatton Park into freezing water. His waterproof suit quickly began to leak and the inflatable dinghy he had been provided with turned out to have a tear in the bottom. He was supposed to inflate it using a CO_2 gas canister, but this proved to be almost empty and he had to resort to using a hand pump that, in the freezing conditions, would not connect properly to the valve on the dinghy. After a fraught 15 minutes the dinghy had enough air inside it to be usable, but when Forest climbed in his added weight caused the tear to worsen and water flooded in. By desperately bailing out the dinghy he was just able to reach the shore before it sunk completely.

Despite these accidents Forest enjoyed his training and returned to Barbara in high spirits and full of hope that soon he would be descending into action.

The resistance groups within France were not operating as well as de Gaulle and SOE had originally hoped. They were constantly harassed by the Gestapo, the Vichy Police, the Group Mobile and Darnand's Milice[3] and were still trying to operate independently of each other. SOE knew the only way to make the resistance efficient was somehow to unite them under one organisational body, preferably something operated by the British. In particular the paramilitary divisions of the movements needed to be brought together under a single commander if they were to be any use when the Allies invaded France. In the background there were also the communists, who out of all the groups proved most adept at keeping their activities secret and even SOE wasn't certain of the extent of their work or what combat units they had created.

To try and resolve the situation it was decided that the BCRA would send in two representatives to assess the problem and work to combat it. One of these men would be Colonel Passy and the other was Commandant Pierre Brossolette.

Brossolette was to become a name synonymous with French resistance. A history student and left-wing journalist, before the war he had evolved from being a pacifist to an ardent denouncer of fascism and communism. At the outbreak of war Brossolette had joined the army as a lieutenant and reached the rank of captain before France fell. He was awarded medals for the orderly manner in which he evacuated his troops from the area. After the armistice Brossolette hoped to teach but was banned by the Vichy government who knew his past lectures on Hitler's regime in the 1930s had caused a good deal of controversy and didn't want to displease their new occupiers. Instead Brossolette opened a bookshop with his wife, Gilberte, which rapidly became the hub for Parisian resistance movements, and plans for potential sabotage targets were exchanged on the premises.

Inevitably these activities drew negative attention and Brossolette's efforts to develop one of the first French resistance movements brought him dangerously close to capture. He narrowly escaped the dismantlement of his network and headed to London in 1942 to meet de Gaulle. The meeting went so well that he was hired by the general to help bring credibility to the Free French movement among the various resistance groups and to discredit de Gaulle's main political rival, Henri Giraud. Brossolette created a civilian intelligence arm for the BCRA and closely liaised with RF Section and in particular, Forest Yeo-Thomas.

Brossolette was not quite 40 when he met Forest. Small and thin, always immaculately dressed, and with a distinctive white forelock in his otherwise black hair, he was an easily recognisable face to the French. On missions he would dye his white streak of hair to avoid being identified by the Germans. Colonel Passy would later describe him as: 'without doubt, the man who, amongst all those I have met in my life, made the greatest impression on me.'[4] Forest would equally come to respect his new colleague and would consider him one of his greatest wartime friends.

However, on Forest's return from Ringfield he only knew of Brossolette as another Frenchman fighting the Nazis. SOE headquarters, having concluded the Seahorse mission was a non-starter, were now disinclined to send Forest anywhere. Hutch had tried to get him involved in a mission to have a 'general look round' in France, but this was turned down with the slightly snide comment that as Forest was credited as being such a talented officer, his skills would be wasted on such a mundane mission. Hutch was not defeated however. He recognised the same desire to get into action in Forest that he felt in himself and he continued to push to secure his man a mission. It was the mission to send Passy and Brossolette back into France that tipped the scale. Judiciously, it was suggested to HQ that an unbiased representative should go with the two BCRA men to report on the matter for the British, and there was just such a man, with a superb knowledge of France, stationed at No. 1 Dorset Square.

HQ agreed and finally Forest had his chance to get into action. There were still matters to be resolved, however. Forest was sent for more training, this time in the art of sending encoded messages, while London's forgery department was working overtime on his false papers. Forest's new identity was that of Francois Thierry, a bachelor born at Arras on 17 June 1901. Before the war he had worked as a clerk and lived in Paris at 41 rue St Ferdinand; he had also spent time serving in the 34th Battalion de l'Air and was demobbed at Marignane on 27 August 1940. Since then he had returned to his employment as a clerk and now lived at 9 rue Richepanse, Paris. Forest had to memorise this entire story, which was backed up by an array of false documents including a French identity card, demob certificate, driving licence and ration cards. Armed with all this it was hoped that he could infiltrate France without attracting any attention.

As one last quirk it was decided to retain the codename Forest had been assigned for his abortive first mission – Operation Seahorse was ready to go.

Agents were typically dropped during a moon period (between the times when the moon was in its first quarter and last quarter phase) ideally when the moon was at its fullest to provide the parachutists with the best possible light. Forest eagerly calculated the most likely time for his drop as between 17 and 28 February. As the first date rapidly approached he was surprised that he was not frightened at the prospect, and his mind instead turned to Mademoiselle Jose Dupuis, who he had penned a postcard to on that sad day at Pointe de Grave when he fled France. Now he couldn't contain his excitement to be heading back and arranged for a message to be broadcast on BBC radio: 'From Tommy to Jose. We'll soon drink again good Chignin wine.' Tommy was another nickname Forest had used when writing for a British boxing magazine and he was certain the mention of Chignin would remind Mademoiselle Dupuis of the holidays during which they had drunk that wine in a village near Chambery.

The BBC ran a busy trade in these types of message, one of the few ways to communicate freely with France. Some were simple messages of hope to loved ones, others were meaningless phrases added in to confuse German operatives listening, and others were secret communications between agents in France or the resistance. This was the first time Forest had used the service, but it would not be the last and from that point on his messages would not be so innocuous.

On 24 February 1943 Forest was informed that his mission would commence that night. Brossolette had gone on ahead, so he would travel alone with Passy. Forest started to wrap up his world, for at the back of his mind there was always the whispered idea that he might not come back. He had a farewell dinner with Barbara, who was now working on a civilian basis with the BCRA, and at 3 p.m. picked up Passy and drove through thick fog to Tempsford in the Midlands, from where they were to take off.

Fortified by a strong cup of tea, they changed from their uniforms into the civilian French clothes they would wear on the mission. There was one last examination of all their belongings for any giveaway clue of their English origin. SOE had learned from hard experience that the German Gestapo would be amazingly thorough with any suspect they arrested and the smallest mistake could blow an agent's cover. Clothing labels were examined and pockets turned out to make sure they didn't contain a forgotten bus ticket or British receipt. Satisfied with the check the agents were given their last essential – a cyanide tablet. The suicide pill was in case of extreme emergency and needed to be carefully concealed. Forest hid his in a waistcoat pocket, while Passy had a Bond-like gadget of a signet ring with a swivel top where the pill could be concealed.

The base CO treated them to a last decent meal and topped them up with a decent bottle of Burgundy. Then it was on with their harnesses, rubber helmets and spine pads. Special outer pockets had room for a revolver, compasses and knives, and then it was on with the heavy parachute. Feeling like beasts of burden, the two men were driven to a waiting Halifax bomber, half hidden in the swirling mist, and clambered awkwardly aboard.

Inside the Halifax were several carefully wrapped packages containing the men's suitcases, arms, wireless set and explosives, the latter of which it was doubtful there would be any opportunity to use. Each package, secured in rubber and canvas, had its own parachute and would be dropped with the agents and with a healthy dose of luck would land somewhere near them.

As the Halifax opened its engines and taxied down the runway, Forest could do little but sit and contemplate his own thoughts. It was too noisy to talk to Passy and there was no window to look out of, so he thought of France and wondered how it had changed since he had last been there. What would it be like to walk the streets of Paris under German occupation? What would it be like to be constantly on guard and hiding your true motives from a hostile invader? It was a long journey to examine these dark thoughts in detail.

It took the Halifax half an hour to reach the French coast and the first challenge of its journey. Anti-aircraft guns opened fire and the pilot jinked, dived and swerved to avoid the arcing spray of bullets. For an awful moment silence overcame the plane and it veered sideways in a wild motion. Forest was convinced that they had been hit and would have to bail out, his mission to France curtailed before it had even begun. Then, miraculously it seemed, the engines kicked in again and the plane righted itself.

The flak guns faded into the background and within a short time the pilot began to circle, and Forest guessed that he was trying to pinpoint their chosen landing spot, which should have been illuminated by a reception committee waiting for them. But the plane circled and circled with no sign of anyone and finally the despatcher had to make his way to Forest and Passy and give them the bad news that low cloud cover meant it was impossible to find the drop site. They would have to turn back.

Forest must have felt that France didn't want him back the way he kept coming so close only to be disappointed. Passy sitting beside him was just as furious. They turned back, the Halifax having to run the gauntlet of search-lights and anti-aircraft guns yet again as they returned from another aborted mission. They arrived at 4.30 a.m., disgruntled and fed up. Nervous exhaustion had taken its toll and they retired to bed immediately before heading back to London the next day.

It wasn't long before Forest was summoned for another attempt on 26 February. Conditions in Britain looked good, the moon was waning but was still bright enough to guide them and there was little cloud. Shortly after midnight, once again attired in their heavy gear, Forest and Passy sat in the Halifax as it took off. The journey was far quieter than the last one, there was less trouble with flak over the coast and by 3 a.m. the despatcher had come to tell them that they were over the landing site.

The hatch of the plane was opened and Forest could see down to the twinkling lights of the welcoming committee. Armed with only hand torches the resistance were eagerly marking the spot where the jumpers hoped to land. Passy was to jump first and positioned himself over the hole with his back to the engine and an eye to the despatcher who would signal when he should jump. Sitting behind him Forest saw his companion tense in preparation and eased himself closer. He was surprised by the strange calm that had overtaken him; the moment seemed too surreal to warrant fear. As the red jump light switched to green and the despatcher raised his arm, he saw Passy launch himself through the hole and a second later the static line went taut, jerked, and then it was Forest's turn.

There was no time to think much about what was to happen. He swung his legs over the hatch, his vision filled now with those twinkling stars on the ground, then he pushed himself off. The cold night air rushed past him as he fell, then there was the sensation of being pulled back and temporarily halted, before his parachute blossomed and Forest began his steady descent.

Forest could now catch his first real glimpse of occupied France. A little below him Passy's parachute seemed enormous in the dark night sky, such an easy target if any Germans happened to see it. Further below the figures of the welcoming committee gradually came into sight. Chosen from the resistance, they did not cut an awesome figure, just ordinary people hoping as much for the agents' arrivals as for the supply packages that even now were being pushed from the plane. For the first time Forest could see the people who he hoped he could help to free France.

Both jumpers landed safely. Forest remembered his training and rolled as he touched the ground, taking in a shaky breath as he stood and surveyed the scene. He had done it, he had returned to France.

A man ran up to him, grabbing his hand and shaking it excitedly. 'It's you, Shelley?' he asked in French.

Forest had never heard the name before. He smiled at the man and answered 'Yes', deciding that it was wiser to 'play along' at that moment than to cause further confusion. He discovered later that Shelley was the second codename he had been given for operations in France, though no one had bothered to mention it to him. Within a year that name would be infamous among the German intelligence services, but for the newly arrived Forest it was just another nom de plume to remember.

The packages that had accompanied the jumpers were now also arriving. There was no way to tell as they bumped to the ground if their cargo had survived the descent, but the important thing was to get it hidden before any inquisitive German eyes spotted it. In a wood a few hundred yards away a pit had been dug to hide the supplies and Forest and Passy helped carry the loads into the trees.

The rag-tag resistance committee shivered as they worked to bury the precious gifts, frozen to the core after their long wait in the wintry night. Forest and Passy handed around a flask of rum, feeling more sorry for these poor individuals who had spent several hours awaiting what might have been another abortive mission, than they did for themselves after their dangerous journey and descent.

As they stood sipping rum the leader of the committee approached the two agents. 'Go, my children, to work!' he said. This was Jacot, one of the original members of the Confrérie de Notre Dame, an early resistance movement. His vast experience gave him a natural leadership over the others and now he would see to it that Passy and Forest made it out of the woods safely.

A guide and bicycles had been arranged and while the reception committee picked up ice-cold shovels and began the arduous job of burying the crates, the two agents were escorted to a safe house 15km away. Their guide was a stickler for security and secrecy, which, in itself, was not all that common among the resistance. A curfew had been put in place by the Germans and if stopped the cyclists could be in serious trouble for being out so late. The guide had therefore concocted a suitable cover story: 'We must say we are returning from a wedding party. We stayed too long because we were a little drunk, but must get home tonight as we have work in Rouen in the morning.'

Passy and Forest were asked to hand over their pistols as they would be far too hard to explain away should the Germans spot them.

'Bring only your suitcases,' the guide instructed.

The agents rummaged through one of the packing cases for their suitcases; they could hardly see in the dark, but finally found them.

'On no account must you make any noise,' the guide continued as he gave them their bicycles. 'If I make a sign you are to dive into the nearest ditch or bush.'

Forest took his bike despondently, it had obviously been made for a much taller man and at 5ft 8in, he would struggle to ride it. At least it had a carrier for his bag, with an extendable piece of elastic to hold it in place. He secured the suitcase and then spent several moments trying to find a small mound or pile of stones that he could use to assist him onto the bike.

Their guide was not particularly patient or sympathetic to his plight. He put a finger to his lips to indicate utter silence and then he rode off. Passy followed and Forest brought up the rear. They had hardly gone 100yds when there was a dreadful crash from Forest's bicycle. The guide turned around in panic, motioning frantically that they must be quiet, while Forest, grumbling, descended from his cycle to retrieve the suitcase that had fallen off so dramatically.

The elastic strap of the carrier had perished and there was no point even attempting to try and use it again. Somehow Forest managed to mount his bicycle (having found a suitable lump of stones) and precariously balanced the suitcase with one end against his chest and the other propped on the handlebars. It was not a happy compromise. Having trouble reaching the pedals of the too-tall bike and with the suitcase threatening to tumble off again every time he hit a rut in the road it was unsurprising that when the bike hit a big bump that the suitcase would lurch and set off the bell on the handlebars.

Once again the guide scowled and motioned for silence. Even grumpier than before, Forest descended again and spent precious moments wrapping a handkerchief around the bell to silence it. Next he had to try and find a suitable mounting block, all the while his companions tutted impatiently, anxious to get off the road. No sooner was he back on the bicycle then the guide signalled trouble and both agents flung themselves into the nearest ditch. This was but the first of many false alarms that would have Forest diving for cover, and each time he re-emerged more frustrated and cross, and had to try and find something to stand on so he might mount his bicycle again.

It was a long and infuriating ride to the outskirts of Lyons-la-Forêt with the suitcase banging into Forest's chest and crushing his fingers. They paused in the shadow of a wall. The guide told them to wait and went on ahead to check the coast was clear. Forest stretched his aching legs; his return to France was not at all what he had expected.

The guide returned quickly and they rode off yet again, but this time their journey was thankfully short and within moments they were outside a small door, which opened immediately as though someone had been waiting for them. Pushing the bicycles inside, Passy and Forest were led into a brightly lit room with a table laden with food. Their hostess was the pretty wife of a local chemist, who had himself been part of the reception committee. Madame and Monsieur Vinet had spent their savings on the lavish display of food they now set before Forest. Bayonne ham was served with galantine and truffles, rounded off with a sweet cider and a glass of old calvados.

Forest was stunned by the meal. The Vinets, though usually living as sparingly as their neighbours, had used the black market to splash out on the banquet. They wanted to welcome their English helpers in grand French style, which made Forest feel a touch guilty knowing that his mission was unlikely to be the battle cry for the resistance and the death blow for the Germans his hosts hoped for. He was made even more emotional when the reception committee members turned up and handed back the agents' pistols. They had risked their lives to bring them and Forest was close to tears as they drank a toast to French victory.

Upstairs in the room they had been offered for the night, Passy opened his suitcase and gasped. In the confusion of the dark reception grounds he had not, as he had believed, pulled his own suitcase from the crate, but one containing a wireless transmitter, hand grenades and explosives. Unwittingly the agents had been carrying equipment that would have marked them out instantly as spies to any curious German patrol and left them open to torture and death. Passy could not apologise enough, but the matter was over and Forest could only reflect on the Yeo-Thomas luck that had brought him safely to Lyons-la-Forêt.

The next morning they were on a bus for Rouen with Jacot. The vehicle had been converted to run on the fumes of burning green wood, as petrol was impossible to get hold of in France unless you were a Nazi or a collaborator. Forest looked around at the other passengers, grim-faced, thin and smelling of stale wine. They clutched parcels of food and produce, some carried whole suitcases ready to sell on the black market. The German ration books they also carried were pointless as their quantities were hopelessly inadequate and only enough to enable people to starve to death slowly. So the black market had become a vital resource, the only thing keeping some people alive, and farmers who sold their produce on it could make a good profit. Despite thoughts of the money they might make that day, the peasants on the run-down, groaning bus looked unanimously sullen and bleak. No one spoke. Forest wondered if they suspected he was a German spy. If only he could explain that the opposite was true.

On that uncomfortable journey Forest saw his beloved France in a new light. It had been three years since he had fled its shores and now he was returning to an almost alien world. Throughout those long years of exile he had found consolation by associating with other French refugees, particularly his comrades at the BCRA. They had sustained his hope, but also his despair. When they gathered together and drank to France, they also inevitably came to discussing its fall and Britain's seeming heavy-handedness in their resistance work. General de Gaulle did not like feeling he had to cooperate with, or worse, ask permission of his British hosts and at times tensions were high. During spells of drinking Forest would sometimes resort to joining his BCRA colleagues' abuse of Britain. This did not sit well with Barbara and not long before Operation Seahorse came into being she had kicked Forest and his BCRA guests out of her flat for being unpatriotic.

Now he looked at France under the Nazi boot and trembled with outrage. Those cosy dinner parties and half jovial rants at the British now seemed pathetic. They had been naïve in their abuse and now Forest rankled at having been away from his country for so long. How could he have sat and drank when SS men marched on *his* roads? Trampled *his* people? What was Pétain thinking of letting these men dominate one of the greatest empires in Europe?

'Look out Shelley. If they see you looking at them like that you'll be arrested.' Jacot's whispered words brought Forest out of his dark thoughts and he realised he had been glaring at the grey-suited Nazis walking outside. It would hardly do to fail in his mission so early by allowing his hatred to govern him.

They were due to meet Pierre Brossolette in Paris. The bus dropped them in Rouen where they would have to wait 2 hours before they could board a train for the capital. Jacot decided to use the opportunity to give them a crash course in 'France under occupation' etiquette. First he took them to a typical café, the patrons looking dowdy and cold, and ordered them 'ersatz' drinks. Ersatz was a German word meaning an inferior substitute, which became popular in the First World War, especially to describe POW food. As the Germans dominated the French streets, ersatz became a byword for a way of life. Ersatz coffee was the best-known example, made from chicory or acorns and hardly deserving of the name coffee. It only made drinkers crave the real thing. Forest tried ersatz alcoholic drinks, which did nothing to improve his mood.

Jacot worked his way through occupation protocol with his apprentices: there was no milk anymore, to ask for a *café crème* would bring instant suspicion on a person for being unfamiliar with French shortages. There were meatless days and days when even the disgusting ersatz alcoholic drinks were not served, except in black market restaurants. All this had to be remembered to avoid making a fatal blunder. Then he took the men's ration books and tobacco cards and explained how they were used.

The train to Paris was another depressing affair. Forest spotted the first-class carriage with its 'reserved for Wehrmacht' sign and the various grey and black uniformed individuals who were boarding it, while the remaining passengers willingly hopped into the third-class carriages: who would want to sit with the Nazis anyway? Forest was shown to one of the few first-class carriages not restricted to the Nazis and once again was surrounded by bleak-faced French citizens, now numbed by the misery of life under Hitler's thumb.

Forest was becoming familiar with the menacing presence of the German troops all around them. Semi-dozing in the train compartment he watched them march through stations, carelessly pushing aside civilians who got in their way. When he first saw this he felt a renewal of his outrage, but as the sight was repeated again and again he started to feel immune to it like the men and women around him. It became expected and therefore was no longer so threatening or insulting. As his first sense of shock subsided, Forest took the time to watch the Nazi troops more closely and begrudgingly acknowledged to himself that their discipline, even in the train carriages, was impressive. Every officer was saluted as he boarded the train and there was no relaxing of their manner as might be expected of other troops travelling. As impressive as it was, it was also chilling. Where was the humanity in this race of super-troopers?

Pierre Brossolette, his white streak dyed black to match the rest of his hair, was awaiting them in the rue de la Faisanderie. The friends shook hands and greeted each other warmly. Brossolette had organised a temporary safe house in the flat of a schoolteacher named Madame Claire Davinroy. He considered it a particularly amusing choice, as the rest of the apartments in the building were all rented by the Gestapo, who would hardly expect the resistance to be so brazen as to house their people among them. As Forest entered the building he couldn't help feeling a twitch of anxiety at his friend's audacious scheme: was it genius to lodge enemy spies under the Nazi noses or just over-confidence? Madame Davinroy was warmly welcoming but Forest was relieved when after dinner it was suggested that they split up and establish other safe houses around the capital in case they had to make a hasty move.

Forest left Passy and Brossolette behind to be escorted to another flat, this time the once-luxurious home of the son of the ex-vice-president of the senate, Roland Farjon. The Farjons had been hit by the restrictions of the German occupation like everyone else and their home had taken on a tomb-like quality, a memorial to better times. There was no heating, since there was very little fuel and the meagre breakfast they could offer Forest consisted of ersatz coffee, approximate jam and grey bread. It was a depressing meal, though the family swallowed it down with relish. It crossed Forest's mind that if this was the breakfast of the rich under occupation, what were the poor living on?

By 8.30 a.m. Forest was outside taking his first good look at occupied Paris. It was a grim sight, and the grey sky above seemed to mirror his dismal mood. Around him swastikas appeared in windows or were scrawled on walls alongside posters listing the latest restrictions or announcing the execution of hostages in retaliation for the death of a Nazi officer. Notices in shop windows announcing that they did not serve Jews, sat above a paltry window display of fake goods, most of which could not be found in the shop and were a memory of pre-war conditions. Women wrapped in frayed coats formed lines or argued over a scrap of bread. Some rummaged behind displays in the hope of forgotten treasure, a cabbage maybe, or a carrot. When bare arms or legs were briefly exposed beneath the winter clothing they were stick thin and ghoulish grey. Forest struggled with the scene, trying to process such a medieval sight of famine in his beloved and once-decadent city.

For a time the utter silence of the roads baffled him, then he realised the shortage of cars. The only petrol-fuelled motor vehicles were the polished black German staff cars that whizzed quickly through the streets. Troop transports rumbled along, while the odd French car that had been converted to producer gas bubbled its way down the road with its huge gas container either strapped to its fender or roof. Bicycles had become a necessity of Parisian life and everyone now had one. A new crime wave of stolen cycles was on the rise and Parisians carried their precious two-wheelers into their homes as tenderly as if they were newborn infants. The industrious taxi men had invented the vélo-taxis, a cart pulled by the driver on a sturdy bicycle. They became a distinctive Paris sight and Forest saw many of these strange contraptions as he wandered around.

Forest remembered Jacot's words however, and tried not to look like a gawping tourist. Already as he was walking the pavements he was formulating the first of the 'Yeo-Thomas Rules':

1. Get used to operating while surrounded by the enemy.
2. Study the habits of the police.
3. Watch out for new regulations and merge with the population – you must *not* stand out!

At the same time Forest had to learn to be a secret agent 'on the job'. No amount of cipher training and parachuting could prepare him for stepping into occupied Paris and being faced with an inquisitive, suspicious and deadly enemy.

It was not long before Forest faced his first real challenge as a spy. A whim of nostalgia and familial conscience had led him to his father's apartment over the Passy Métro station (it was never an auspicious place for Forest to visit) where a combined German and French police blockade had been set up. From either side of the road a line of policemen barred the way and inspected anybody trying to pass. There was no knowing what they were after, or, more precisely, whom It might have been a routine spot check near a Métro station, or they may have been rounding up Jews or even looking for suspected resistance members. Forest hesitated, his instinct being to turn on his heel and flee, but his common sense overruled him – that would make him an obvious target for the police.

Instead he approached as calmly as he could. The police were working in pairs: a German and a French collaborator. Bitterly, Forest pulled out his forged identity cards and handed them over, trying not to glare at his countryman so ably helping the enemy. The checking of his papers seemed to take forever, and Forest knew now that he was entirely at the mercy of the skill of the SOE forgers. One slip – an incorrect stamp, an out-of-date signature – could lead him straight to the Gestapo. Trembling inside, he didn't realise that even those with genuine papers felt the same way when faced with the German spot checks. After what seemed like an eternity the German policeman handed back his papers and waved him on. Forest walked through the line resisting the temptation to run as fast as he could and feeling a surge of elation that his SOE papers had proved their worth.

His delight quickly died when he saw that he was approaching a second police line. It was obvious now that this was not a routine spot check. The Gestapo were after someone and the fact that a Black Maria[5] was parked nearby and three or four men were being pushed into it only confirmed his fears. Despite this he kept his cool and passed through the second line as easily as the first. He left as rapidly as he dared trying not to think of the poor souls being forced into the car and into the eager hands of the Gestapo.

....

Notes

1. General William Lendrum 'Billy' Mitchell (1879–1936) was considered a founding father of the US Air Force and was the only individual to have a type of American military aircraft named after them: the B-25 Mitchell.
2. As quoted in Seaman, *Op cit.*
3. French militia created by the Vichy government to hunt down the French resistance, often more feared than the Gestapo due to their more intimate knowledge of the country and its people.
4. Marshal, *Op cit.*
5. A slang term for a police car or van, usually painted a distinctive black. It was the standard euphemism for Gestapo vehicles during the Second World War.

7

Good Agents Always
Arrive Punctually

THIN, TALL BROSSOLETTE STOOD at the Port Maillot with Passy as the clock struck eleven and Forest arrived with precision timing. Neither man noticed that Forest seemed a little flustered by his run-ins with the police; both had their minds on other matters.

With little talk Brossolette escorted his two comrades to the apartment of his cousin Hélène Peyronnet[1] at 102 avenue des Ternes. Hélène was already an active member within the resistance and quickly organised separate safe houses for Passy and Forest. Passy's flat was on the ground floor of a complex at Neuilly near the busy rue Demours and with a courtyard leading to another building, therefore offering good escape routes should the worst happen. Hélène had arranged for Forest to stay in a luxury apartment owned by the French film star Jeanne Helbling, which also overlooked a courtyard and offered easy escape, despite being on the first floor. Brossolette was to remain in the rue de la Faisanderie. After assigning these quarters the group also organised several secondary locations that they could retreat to if their cover was blown.

Finally they could begin the daunting task of assessing the resistance effort in France and what the British could do to unite it and assist it. Passy set to work on collating intelligence from various sources, while Forest and Brossolette started sending out feelers to existing agents in France, especially those involved in organising weapons stores and parachute landings. Some of these men, such as Michel Pichard, Jean Aryal, and Jean-Pierre Deshayes, Forest had already met in England, while others were new to him. Brossolette worked keenly to establish contacts with the various resistance networks, but this was easier said than done. Away from the action in London, many of the networks and smaller groups were unknown to him, while other names that he had believed were clandestine organisations were something else entirely. It had been assumed that Voix du Nord, Le Cerle, and La Ligue were all names of resistance groups. These had filtered into the SOE offices through various sources and, at a distance, seemed likely candidates. On location Brossolette and Forest discovered that Voix du Nord was actually the title of a clandestine publication produced by rather under-active resisters as a platform for their opinions. The other two were groups either purely political (and therefore not interested in the form of resistance SOE would propose) or associated with the Freemasons, a group that was regularly attacked by the Vichy forces and the Nazis, but that did not throw up active resisters.

After a few false starts Brossolette and Forest were able to start assessing the various resistance movements they came across. Some were too embryonic to be worth their time or could be absorbed into bigger groups, while others did not have the manpower or the leaders to maintain them. Eventually five important resistance groups presented themselves:

Organisation Civile et Militaire (OCM)
Ceux de la Libération
Ceux de la Resistance
Liberation
Front National (FN)

By 2 March a meeting had been arranged with the representative of OCM, Colonel Alfred Touny.[2] Tall and imposing, Touny was now in his fifties and a strong figure in the resistance, and was accompanied by Roland Farjon, Forest's former host; both would eventually be shot by the Germans, just two of the 4,000 members of OCM who perished fighting for their cause.

OCM would become one of the greatest resistance networks of the war, and even at the meeting with Touny it was clear that it was one of the most secure and complete organisations operating in France. In 1941 the organisation could only boast a few hundred members but by 1943 it was stated that they had around 45,000 members, many of whom were keen for military-style action.

At the meeting in March 1943 it was clear that the OCM was going to be a significant asset to the British plans for the re-invasion of France. SOE's priority was to rally national resistance in France in order to harass the Germans and seriously hamper their forces when Britain landed its troops on D-Day. The resistance would never be able to retake France alone, they simply did not have the military might or political support, but by eating away at the Germans, pecking at their morale and their feelings of safety within Paris, delaying them and preventing troops from moving efficiently they were a vital tool to the Allies who knew the landings in France would be bloody and costly. Resistance helped pave the way for the advance of the British and Americans, as well as for the return of the exiled French troops, and also kept the country alive in those dark days and prevented it from slipping into a morass of despair and apathy.

Not all encounters were as successful as the one with Touny. Forest and Brossolette met with Colonel Henri Manhes, who while undoubtedly brave and keen for action, had come up with several completely unfeasible ideas for resistance work and seemed very reluctant to coordinate plans with London. His choice of assistant was also deemed questionable. Pierre Meunier failed to inspire confidence despite later becoming a significant figure in the resistance. The situation resolved itself quite quickly when Manhes was arrested.

Uniting the resistance movements was going to be a difficult task. Brossolette struggled to keep his temper and sarcasm under control in meetings and offended leaders and representatives. Among the resistance there was a feeling that the new arrivals were undermining the work of ex-prefect Jean Moulin, who was pursuing similar lines to coordinate the resistance. Moulin was a dashing, charismatic figure with a film-star presence and innocent charm, but he was a formidable personality who very rapidly crossed swords with Brossolette. Forest could only watch as the two passionate Frenchmen argued continuously in Madame Claire Davinroy's apartment and wondered how long it would be before the lady's Gestapo neighbours came to investigate. Despite their opposing politics the men managed to maintain a united front when in public, but it was a tense arrangement. Brossolette felt that Moulin was completely unequipped to deal with the resistance problem in occupied France when his previous experience had been with organisations in the unoccupied zone.[3] His dominating personality and attempts to unite the military power of the resistance single-handedly under his own control also created tensions.

Forest, though not deeply political, had his own strong opinions and views on life and none of these gave much room to the concept of communism. So the meeting with the clever and youthful Georges Beaufils, codename Joseph, was something he dreaded, knowing that the courageous young man was a representative of the intelligence branch (FANA) of the Front National, a communist resistance cell.

There was an uneasy relationship between the other resisters and the communists, largely because their politics were linked more with the fortunes and whims of Russia and the Soviet principles that they treasured rather than with patriotism towards their own country. When the Soviets had agreed to a pact of neutrality with Germany, this left ardent communists with a difficult choice. On the one hand their country was under threat, but on the other they were supposed to place their loyalty to the Soviets over loyalty to their own nation. The internal politics of the Communist party at that period were so complicated that even at the time few knew exactly where they stood. Some communists saw it their duty to collaborate, others distrusted the Germans and chose a quiet path of passive resistance. It wasn't until Hitler attacked Russia that minds were made up and the communists came wholeheartedly into the fray.

Still, there was always the worry that should Russia's politics change, so too might the views of the communist resistance, and they were powerful adversaries. Then there was always the niggling concern that they actually might be planning to let Russia take Paris.

With all these doubts in mind Forest met with Joseph. He found the young communist eager but sensible and the security precautions already imposed within the communist cells impressed him: communists were such a hated faction that even before the war they had learned the invaluable nature of secrecy.

All was not well, however. Forest suggested the arranging of wireless telegraphy between FANA and London to speed cooperation. Joseph declined, arguing that the groups' communication lines were already overwhelmed with transmissions. As there was no communication between London and FANA, this could only mean that they were in close communication with Russia, a situation that came uncomfortably close to their fear that the Soviets still had their eyes on France. Joseph was not against getting what he could from the

British however, and he complained that his people were not receiving weapons from London. Forest agreed that this should be resolved, but first Joseph should send some key men to Britain to be trained in the use of these weapons, a reasonable enough request to which Joseph quickly agreed. But the men he promised never appeared.

Forest was even more convinced that the communists still had their loyalties firmly tied to Russia and that their Soviet masters did not want them linking too closely with another nation whose ideas and political outlook was so opposed to their own. Despite this, he also recognised that Joseph's organisation would be vital to the resistance work: they understood the need for security, were prepared to take risks and, bluntly, did not flinch at the thought that their actions would impact on innocent civilians who would suffer in German reprisals.

If Joseph was a complicated and disputed contact, Lecompte-Boynet of the Ceux de la Resistance could only be deemed an asset. Lecompte-Boynet was the chief of the party and had amassed around 1,000 supporters for the group, which was largely paramilitary. Unlike many resisters the party maintained quite neutral politics, looking only to restore France to liberty. MI6 had already made contact with the group and used them for gathering intelligence and Lecompte-Boynet proved a willing co-operator. His party members were ready for action and he estimated that by D-Day he would have between 25,000 and 30,000 troops at his disposal to fight the Nazis.

Forest found an even more significant contact in the Ceux de la Libération (CDLL) leader Roger Coquoin.[4] Coquoin was the same age as Forest and Brossolette when they met in early 1943; the son of a chemist and the former head of the chemistry laboratory at the Academy of Medicine, he had only been leader of the group for a short time having taken over from Maurice Ripoche after his arrest. Coquoin was keen to work with the British and his group was well established and neutral in its politics – always an asset. They also boasted links with Transports Routiers, the French organisation that controlled all road transport through the country. The managing director of the company was a member of CDLL and was quite willing to disrupt German traffic whenever he was needed to. He also regularly fed the group intelligence on the movement of German troops. Most exciting to Forest, the director knew the locations where the Germans had begun stockpiling vehicles in case of invasion and the CDLL was ready to sabotage these sites when the time came.

Coquoin could also list trustworthy comrades in the police, fire brigade and Garde Mobile, a rare and valuable resource for the Allies. (The Garde Mobile was created during the Franco–Prussian war as an auxiliary to the French army and expected to guard home territory. They were briefly revived during the Second World War to counteract the 1940 armistice which had reduced the official French army to 95,000 men.) Coquoin estimated his manpower at 35,000 and was keen to work with the British, but sadly he was not destined to see the fruition of his plans, as like his former leader he was arrested and shot in June 1943.

It was now becoming obvious to Forest how dangerous working with the resistance really was. One minute he was holding a meeting with an eager comrade and the next that same comrade had vanished into the clutches of the Gestapo. It was a desperate situation. The Germans were working hard to decapitate the resistance groups as fast as they could and leaders evaporated as quickly as they were assigned, either via betrayal, carelessness or bad luck.

The dangers Forest now faced were all too prevalent in his mind as he met with Joseph to be introduced to Pierre Ginzburger, the elusive head of Front National. The communists took their security seriously and Forest, Brossolette and Passy were told to await a contact at a park bench in the Luxembourg Gardens. Sitting opposite an empty bandstand that had once been filled with French musicians serenading passers-by, Forest spotted a cautious looking bearded man. It was the clichéd spy meeting: the furtive stranger approached the three men and asked them to follow him. He led them on a deliber-ately circuitous course, doubling-back several times to ensure that no one was following until, eventually, he brought them to the Luxembourg station and joined them as they caught a train to Sceaux.

On arrival, their secretive guide led them on another intricate dance around the roads to detect a tail, before escorting them to a smart villa. Forest expected to meet the great Ginzburger privately and quietly, but to his astonishment when they entered the villa was alive with people, and not just communists. Catholic priests shook hands with men intrinsically opposed to their views and principles. The meeting was clearly going to be a far cry from the quiet interview Forest had expected.

The communists would later become an integral part of Forest's work, but as he sat quietly and listened to Ginzburger testifying to the strength and might of his organisation, he knew that it would not be an easy alliance. Ginzburger was a typical Front National, believing firmly that all resistance should be coordinated under a communist banner. He sang the praises of the Franc-Tireurs et Partisans (FTP), the paramilitary arm of the Communist party, who were already producing significant results against the Germans. They had killed several officers in audacious shootings and had no intention of stopping. That in itself was not something the British or Forest objected to, it was necessary to pick away at the Germans, but it was the sinister subtleties underlying Ginzburger's words that worried him. The communists had deliberately chosen the name 'Front National' (FN) for their group to avoid obvious links with their communist politics. Communism was an unpopular political view and the party was well remembered for their troublemaking and recent disloyalty. By creating the Front National they enticed people to join the group who would otherwise have turned their backs on them.

Forest was not fooled. While Ginzburger talked of the necessity of unity, of bringing the various small groups together under FN to form a significant force, which in itself was a logical and sensible approach, Forest could only think of the communist powers that stood behind him. Once he had control Ginzburger would bring all the resistance under the communist regime and there was no telling where that would lead.

Ginzburger talked in figures, proudly claiming that the FTP committed 250 attacks and killed between 500 and 600 Germans per month. The penalty for such success however was heavy reprisals from the Germans, largely aimed at any communist prisoners they had in custody. Posters across Paris extolled the terrible death toll for each single act of rebellion, but it did not stop the FTP, and for every man or woman they lost, others joined their ranks. However, Forest recognised a flaw in Ginzburger's logic: his newest recruits, drawn in due to the German reprisals, did not necessarily ascribe to communist politics. They had merely joined to fight back at the Germans and because the FN was the only party they knew of.

The new recruits hastily drawn in had weakened FN's security. Gossip leaked out and the Gestapo were hot on the heels of the party. To try and counteract this, the party had been divided into individual cells, each working separately and with little knowledge of the others. The result might have been more security, but it was at the cost of ease of communication. The existence of many leaders meant that distributing orders was time-consuming and labour intensive, but despite this by D-Day the FTP would be able to call on 100,000 troops.

As Ginzburger wrapped up his lecture on the FN, Passy and Brossolette asked him one simple question: would the FN cooperate with London on the same terms as the other resistance groups. In the typical words of every communist leader they had met, Ginsburger promised to give them an answer at a later date. Forest later summed up the problem of the FN in a report to SOE:

> From my contacts with them I imagine that the rank and file are really patriots
> and only interested in a free France, whereas the heads have other ideas in mind
> and are planning well ahead, in fact, so far ahead as the period which will follow
> the 'Gouvernement Provisoire' [after Vichy].[5]

Meanwhile SOE had heard of round-ups orchestrated by the combined French and German police to detain and ship men to Germany as forced labour. Hitler had overstretched himself: while his troops marched on, industry in their homeland was stuttering and something needed to be done to forestall the rot. It only seemed logical to look to newly conquered countries for slave labour. It was not called that of course, it was the Compulsory Labour Service, and every Frenchman between the age of 19 and 32 was automatically signed up for it. Some men had managed to avoid registering for the service, but that only gave the Germans another excuse for police round-ups. All over France, town and countryside were being searched for deserters from the labour force. If captured the men were sent to German factories to work on the armaments or machines that were fuelling their enemy's war effort. Some unfortunate souls even found themselves stepping into the frozen wastes of the Russian Front.

It was still not enough. Even with POW labour and work parties from concentration camps the Germans were still short and the rumours were spreading that soon they would be upping the age limit to 42 or even 55.

For Forest, Brossolette and Passy this was disastrous for their plans. A secret army was of no use if most of its number had been shipped to Germany as forced labour. Every week it was said that 20,000 Frenchmen were taken from Paris, and there was no way a secret army could be sustained unless something was done.

Forest reported to London on 14 March making it clear that if the situation continued there was no hope for a resistance army. The forced labour details were even more detrimental than the Gestapo culls, which tended to only catch a few members at a time and often resulted in more resisters enlisting with the cause. The same could not be said when 20,000 men were simply lost into Germany. As much as Forest was appalled by the treatment he was also practical, and advised SOE that propaganda should go out encouraging men to evade the conscription in any way they could; this would be either by leaving the country or living in hiding.

The first solution was hardly ideal for most people, but the second option could not be achieved without help from London. Conscript escapees would need money and forged ration cards so that they could live without being detected. Forest also pointed out that financial aid would need to be generous, as there was no point sending pocket money if the men were expected to live in secret and be ready for D-Day. Thus Forest was paving the way for the Maquis, the resistance organisation of outlaws who often set up camps within the woodlands of France and lived in hiding for years until the Allied invasion, when they took up arms and guerrilla warfare tactics. Forest would never really get to know the men he helped in this way; though he always longed to make contacts within the Maquis, he had to just be satisfied that his efforts helped them to exist.

Meanwhile Forest had also been inspired to create his own *réseau*, a network of reliable agents exclusive to himself that would help him keep in contact with the various acquaintances he was making within the resistance. His first recruit was unexpected. He paid a visit to Jose Dupuis to whom he had sent the postcard and the enigmatic BBC message. Jose was astonished by his arrival on her doorstep and overcome with emotion she sobbed and laughed as she told him how she received both missives.

Dupuis was running a private girls' school, and her thirty pupils followed their teacher in being devoted patriots. But Dupuis was desperate to do more and as Forest sat in her apartment she begged him to let her become actively involved. For Forest his first recruit was probably his hardest. He trusted Jose Dupuis implicitly, which was the first prerequisite of picking a recruit, but he also cared about her as a friend and was keenly aware of the risk she would run.

Forest himself had come close to detection only a short time previously when he tried to help a compromised agent to leave France. Jean Aryal, a man Forest had first met in London, desperately needed to escape the city and RF had arranged to help him get out to the provinces. Forest agreed to meet

Aryal outside a church and to escort him to Brossolette and Passy to receive his final orders before fleeing Paris. Armed with a .32 colt, a risk in itself if discovered, and a cyanide tablet in case of capture, Forest waited for his comrade, his mind flicking over possible problems and escape routes. Aryal arrived on time, but looked worried and flustered. He confessed to Forest he was sure he was being followed.

Tails were a constant danger to SOE agents and Forest knew a trick or two to draw out the culprit. Gestapo informers or even Abwehr agents were not the best at furtively pursuing a suspect and it only took a few sharp turns and doubling-backs before Forest was certain Aryal was right. Aryal was in dreadful danger and there was simply no way he could be taken anywhere near Brossolette with a man following him. Forest knew he only had one option, to lure the pursuer into following him instead.

'Pretend to pass me a note' he told Aryal.

The agent complied and Forest made a deliberate hand motion to suggest that he was trying to pocket something without being seen. Of course, he ensured that the tail could have a good view of the deed. The colleagues walked on again for a few paces then parted company, and to his relief the tail chose to pursue Forest. Now all he had to do was shake him.

Forest took his tail on a comprehensive tour of St Philippe du Roule before finally losing him in some of the back streets. After taking a few more precautionary turns, he was satisfied that he was safe and carried on.

Now sitting with Jose Dupuis, he explained the risks of such a situation, told her about tails, informers and the ultimate result of capture by the Gestapo. Dupuis was unmoved, and firmly she assured him that she wanted to be a part of the resistance. Forest made up his mind and recruited her into his private network, and before long she was his second-in-command. Forest couldn't help wondering how the forceful teacher would be able to keep herself secret, bearing in mind that she was 5ft 10in in height and not exactly difficult to recognise, but even so, he was glad to have her aboard.

Forest was now rapidly learning the necessary subterfuges to stay alive and free as a secret agent. Just sending messages back to London was risky enough. The only safe communication was via a wireless telegraphy set. When SOE sent teams in they were usually in pairs with one designated as the W/T operator and responsible for his set. W/T operators were in constant danger of detection when they were transmitting.

Messages were encoded before being sent, though accidents did occur: Jean Moulin's death was in part caused by a message being written in plain script, which was then obtained by the Germans. *Agents de Liaison* were used to delivering messages to W/T operators, and they were usually on thin slips of paper that could be hidden in a packet of cigarettes or a matchbox and destroyed easily if necessary. W/T operators were supposed to switch location regularly to elude the Gestapo (though some did not, usually to their detriment) and this meant lugging a heavy suitcase with the W/T set in it around Paris. There was no hope for them if they were stopped and the suitcase was inspected.

Forest quite enjoyed the challenge of outwitting the German teams who were sent to shadow suspects. He started by observing them and learned that they worked in groups with members passing on descriptions of a suspect and working in relays. To make their lives harder Forest purchased a range of hats of different type and style, as well as a number of scarves in different patterns. Throughout the day he would change his accessories numerous times to fool pursuers. At some point he had picked up the nugget of information that a sleuth was trained to recognise a suspect by his gait. This had his mind working overtime on ingenious solutions and soon he had shoes with steel tips and some without that would alter his walk, and for a dramatic alteration he would put a wedge of cardboard under the heel of one foot. In this way he was a man of many simple, yet effective, disguises.

Even his cleverness and disguises could not completely safeguard him from the vagaries of chance, however. On one occasion Forest was sent with another agent to inspect the Civile et Militaire at Nevers and had to board a train. Train travel was always dangerous as the Germans liked to perform regular check-ups on the passengers. In one notorious incident a resister boarded a train with a suitcase full of names and addresses of members of his resistance party. He fell asleep and when he awoke discovered that the suitcase had been stolen by a particularly astute Gestapo agent. The resulting arrests and deaths that arose from this failure were atrocious.

Forest always travelled first class, just as he always wore good clothes and new hats, to give the impression that he was a well-to-do Parisian, and the only way to be a well-to-do Parisian in 1943 was to be an active collaborator with the Nazis. It usually worked and he was often overlooked by German officials, but on that particular train ride it was not a German he had to be concerned about.

Just as the train was pulling out of the station another passenger entered the carriage. Forest glanced up automatically and to his horror recognised a man he had known before the war, and even worse he remembered that the man's political views were very much pro-German and anti-British. A number of options whizzed through Forest's mind, the immediate temptation was to retreat to the corridor and stand out there for the rest of the journey, but that was likely to attract more suspicion on him than braving it out in the carriage would. Forest resorted to his second option, burying his head in his paper and trying to ignore the man opposite him.

It all went well at first, but there was only so long that Forest could convincingly read the rather brief newspapers that were now in circulation without appearing either an incredibly slow reader or deliberately hiding from view. He hoped the man might get off before he had to put the paper aside, but this time his luck was out. As calmly as he could he put aside the paper and turned to look out the window. As he did, he caught sight of the man's face and knew he had been recognised.

He could feel the man staring at him. He turned his head back, briefly caught the man's eyes and then turned to his fellow agent to talk about innocuous topics. A moment passed in which he could feel the man's eyes still on him and then the passenger leaned forward and tapped his knee.

'Haven't I met you before the war?' he asked.

Forest looked him full in the face and, with no hint of uncertainty, answered 'Perhaps I look like somebody you know or maybe you've seen me somewhere else, but I'm sure I've never seen you before.'

The Frenchman hesitated, then smiled and agreed that he must be mistaken, even though the resemblance was startling. He wanted to spend the rest of the journey discussing the peculiarity of 'doubles' and doppelgangers and it was with some relief that Forest saw them entering the final station on their journey and could escape. Yet again his Yeo-Thomas luck had enabled him to escape detection.

The risk of the train was well worth it, however. Nevers proved to be a hotbed of resistance activity. The local resistance leader was Courvoisier, rather dramatically codenamed Napoleon. Napoleon was a thickset ex-regular NCO with the dynamic personality all resistance leaders needed to inspire men to follow them. He had built up his small group to number 2,000 with impressive branches in intelligence work, supplies and operational activities.

Most significantly he had enlisted the entire gendarme force in the area, numbering 350 uniformed individuals, and their commander. This was their greatest asset as the gendarmes protected the reception committees and could transport messages about the area without attracting attention. They could even spy on the Germans and report their movements.

Napoleon enthusiastically introduced Forest to his men as 'le Capitaine Shelley de la Royal Air Force' and requested that he give a lecture to raise the men's morale. Forest hesitated; talking before the men would expose his identity to a large group of unknown individuals, was it worth the risk?

In the back of his mind were the continuing arguments among the resistance over whom to follow: de Gaulle or Giraud? For the British, de Gaulle was the only option for a unified France, but the escape of First World War veteran General Giraud from German hands in 1942 had muddied the waters. Giraud and de Gaulle were political opponents prior to the war: Giraud had staunchly stood against de Gaulle's views that France needed to put money into troops and weapons rather than the false hope of the Maginot Line. After his escape he returned to the Vichy government, who he supported, though he insisted they should resist the Germans. The situation then became complicated, as Himmler wanted Giraud assassinated, correctly realising that he could be a rallying point for the French people, and some of the Vichy politicians tried to persuade Giraud to return to imprisonment in Germany.

For de Gaulle it was apparent that Giraud wanted to be in on the action and when he began secret negotiations with the British, completely cutting out the Free French movement from the discussion, it was clear that things were not going to be amicable between them. Giraud and de Gaulle did work together, but the presence of two leaders of opposing views divided the resistance in a way that could cause serious problems when a unified paramilitary team was needed on D-Day.

Forest had firm opinions on the matter: he was a staunch Gaullist and when he realised Napoleon's request gave him an opportunity to sway the Nevers resisters to side with de Gaulle he knew he had to take the risk and speak to them, as he later said:

> I had weighed the dangers carefully and considered that I was justified, as the moral effect would be considerable, particularly because a British officer who spoke of de Gaulle as the only leader of the French, would exert more influence,

and help to combat the deplorable consequences of the 'Giraud affair' which very nearly wrecked French Resistance. The talk was a great success, and my right hand ached for days afterwards from the vigorous handshakes I got.[6]

Forest developed a strong comradeship with the rural resisters, not least because of their overwhelming generosity. In the Pouilly area Forest and his co-agent were invited to taste local wines and without too much difficulty persuaded themselves that it would be a good act of public relations. It was only after accepting the offer that they were dumbfounded to discover that their host had twenty-one wines ready for them to sample. They rallied through the task valiantly, only to discover that two more local resisters also wanted them to visit and sample their well-stocked cellars. Fortunately Forest had a stomach for wine and felt he had conducted himself adequately as he sat in the van that was to take them back to Nevers and stuck his head out of the window to let the rushing fresh air sober him up.

His hosts in Nevers were keen to see him back as they had arranged a surprise: the family had been busy cooking a feast in honour of the two SOE agents. Forest felt his stomach churn looking at the array of dishes. The head of the household, a spry man of 65 disappeared to the cellars, as well stocked as any in Pouilly, and returned with a basket of cobwebbed wine bottles. Excitedly he showed Forest a bottle of pre-war Pernod and poured him a generous glass.

There was no option for the agents but to steady themselves and work their way through the rich and lavish meal, washed down with brimming glasses of white and red wine, and champagne, finished with coffee and liqueurs.

By now feeling bloated and ill, the agents hoped to excuse themselves and stagger to their beds, but the ordeal was not over yet. It was almost as though some mischievous sprite was enjoying tormenting them, for just then an Alsatian forestry officer arrived and insisted on taking the agents to his home where his assistants were eagerly waiting to meet them. Somehow Forest managed to maintain his composure through the introductions and hand shaking, then their new host brought out a selection of Alsatian wines, which he insisted the agents must taste. It was almost another 2 hours before Forest could extract himself, and feeling so sick that he could hardly concentrate on where his footsteps were falling he stumbled to his bed. He was only able to catch a few brief hours respite before he was up again to catch the 5 a.m. train.

He returned to Paris bilious with terrible indigestion and his head pounding. 'We were almost killed by hospitality' he later remarked.

Forest returned to Paris to join the two men who had become his comrades and friends. The bond between Passy, Brossolette and Forest had been strengthened by their shared danger and ambitions. The fight for France had united three men who otherwise would never have met. Forest was intensely loyal to both BCRA men and protective too in his usual bulldog manner; anyone who threatened Brossolette or Passy threatened him and he was quick to react. In many ways he was very happy, the close bond they all shared in their work was something he had never really felt before and it stuck in his memory throughout his life. After the war he wrote:

> When I look back on those days, I can picture the daily talks we had. They always took place in the evenings, in the flat occupied by Passy and Brossolette in rue Marcel Renaud, in a small back room where there was a wood-burning Mirius stove. Colonel Passy would sit in an old armchair on one side of the stove, I would sit in another armchair on the opposite side, while Brossolette would sprawl full-length on the floor between us, as close as he could to the stove, as he was very fond of warmth and suffered much from the cold. We would discuss everything for hours. When we had gone over all the problems we had to deal with, we would either fall silent and think our own thoughts, or we would talk about our loved-ones, our plans for the future if we survived, the shape of things to come. Sometimes, Brossolette, who was a historian, would hold forth and we would listen enthralled. We got on famously together, in spite of the abysmal fundamental differences in our upbringings. We had a common ideal, and each of us relied upon the two others … brothers could not have been closer than we were. There grew between us a bond that nothing short of death could break.[7]

Unfortunately it would be death that broke the brotherhood into pieces.

Notes

1. Hélène became an integral member of the resistance, along with her 16-year-old daughter Poucette, who acted as a courier. Her apartment soon became a regular meeting place for the resistance until it was compromised.
2. Colonel Alfred Touny (1886–1944) eventually became the president of OCM, but was arrested on 25 February and shot at the end of April 1944.

3. When the Germans first took France they occupied only the northern part of the country, leaving the southern part controlled by Vichy. These areas then became known as the Occupied and Unoccupied zones.
4. Roger Coquoin (1897–1943).
5. Marshal, *Op cit.*
6. Seaman, *Op cit.*
7. *Ibid.*

8

The American

BUNDLING ONTO A TRAIN as the first signs of springtime in Paris were dotting the streets, Forest had much to contemplate. They were heading back to Lyons-la-Forêt to meet a Lysander plane sent by London to pick them up. Forest glanced at the familiar streets as the train pulled out of the station, knowing he would soon be back and fighting to get the Nazis out of his capital.

It had been an emotionally draining visit. The resistance was alive but fractured and attempts to pull it into cohesion still seemed in their infancy. Before leaving Jean Moulin and General Delestraint had entered the discussions. The charismatic Moulin had dominated the proceedings, much to Brossolette's annoyance, but there was no denying that he carried an audience and inspired men. But he also had plans: Moulin agreed with the SOE agents that a good secret army should be about quality not quantity. Training was essential and not just in the art of killing cleanly and efficiently, he firmly believed the men needed to be disciplined, to know how to march and to salute an officer. If they wanted a worthwhile army, Moulin extolled, they had to look to the formalities of obedience as well as to killing.

His words had not sat well with the FTP, naturally. A heady battle of wills began. Moulin was adamant, but so was the FTP. Communist resistance was not about saluting officers (weren't they all equals anyway?) or marching in an orderly fashion, it was about action, it was about killing Germans and sabotaging their military network. The FTP was already uncomfortable, having finally

agreed to put some of their number nominally under the governance of de
Gaulle and fight for his cause on D-Day. Even Moulin's charm could not sway
the FTP who were irate that any 'training' for their men, which they deemed
unnecessary anyway, would take them away from their mission to attack the
Nazis as often as they could. There was no way to easily resolve the matter and
as Forest turned his thoughts to home he knew that there was still no resolu-
tion between Moulin and the communists.

Aside from that worry, there was Delestraint. The retired general was a fear-
less and bold character, with much to say about the nature of warfare, despite
having spent most of the First World War in a prison camp. He had befriended
de Gaulle, which spoke volumes to the British authorities, and he was a well-
decorated officer. His courage was not in doubt, but Forest doubted that he was
a good recruit for clandestine work – he didn't have the necessary guile or skill
for deceit. Forest would be proved right, much to his disappointment, a couple
of months after Operation Seahorse when Delestraint was confronted by the
Gestapo and pulled out two sets of different identity papers from his pocket.
The blunder made it impossible to deny his participation in the resistance.

Forest was at once inspired and terrified by the eclectic creation the resistance
had become. Was it the vital resource the British believed it to be? Or was it a
liability to security? Forest hoped for the former, but worried about the latter.

Then there was the matter of his father. Jose Dupuis had carefully revealed
to Forest that his father had fallen into the hands of the Gestapo, who were
trying to discover Forest's whereabouts. What suspicions the Gestapo had
at that time were unclear: perhaps they were merely trying to track down a
French citizen who was known to serve the British as a precaution. Whatever
the case, John Yeo-Thomas had proved as stubborn as usual and the angered
Gestapo had thrown him into Fresnes prison. The old man had similar luck
to his son, however. Someone in the prison authorities had been sympathetic
enough to release him on grounds of his age and poor health. He returned
home to find his apartment looted and in disarray.

Just before he left Paris Forest paid a visit to his father, following the precaution that Jose Dupuis had warned him about and ringing the bell five
times. The Gestapo visit had shaken the old man more than he would care
to admit and when he opened the door he made no obvious sign that he
recognised the man on his doorstep. Father and son stared at each other, then
John calmly said:

'Entrez monsieur.'

With the pretence of welcoming a stranger, he ushered in his son and closed the door. Motioning for silence he listened to ensure there was no one nearby, then he turned on Forest.

'What the bloody hell have you been doing for the last two years?' He snapped, 'You ought to have been here long ago.'

Forest could only apologise, especially as he could not do more than hint at his current work with the resistance. He wanted to ask about his father's time in Fresnes but the old man refused to comment on the matter.

'I've been doing a little resistance work,' he admitted, but would not elaborate.

The whole conversation proved stilted, with neither man prepared to push the other on the details of their work. Both were as stubborn as ever and Forest could at least console himself with the fact that Fresnes did not seem to have done any lasting damage to the old man. After giving his father tea, coffee, sugar, cigarettes and a little money he left with as little commotion as he had arrived, wondering when he would see his father again.

Sitting next to Forest on the train leaving for Lyons-la-Forêt was a well-built young man nursing an injury to his shoulder and apparently deeply engaged in a recent French newspaper. Forest paid as little attention to him as he could and certainly avoided conversation, not that it would have mattered if he had tried to start one, as the man next to him was completely ignorant of French.

Captain John Ryan was a downed American pilot trying to get home. Struggling with a fractured shoulder and all too easily identifiable by his broad American accent, he had managed to make contact with the CND and they had arranged to get him out of France. A professor[1] among their number set his arm and the group had organised that Ryan would be evacuated out of France with the three returning SOE agents.

Ryan was not an easy travelling companion. Ignorant of French, he had been strictly informed to remain silent and to answer any questions presented to him with a prosaic '*oui*' or '*non*'. The silence was obviously difficult for Ryan who was a jovial and exuberant person, but stuffing him behind the thin sheets of a newspaper at least made him slightly more clandestine. Forest was all too aware that his guest, as friendly and affable as he was, was a terrible risk to them. Should he slip and speak, or should a German policeman get too interested in him then everyone could be exposed.

The tension this produced had an unsettling effect on the usually stoic Forest. Perhaps it was having someone speaking English near him again after so many weeks or just the constant anxiety he was under in case Ryan blundered that caused him to make a rare but serious mistake.

Their train pulled in at the Pont de l'Arche station outside Rouen without anything untoward happening and as much to celebrate their safe arrival as to help ease his worries, Forest hopped off the train to visit the station buffet and order a beer for himself and Ryan. The station was busy and crowded, Forest ordered his drinks and fumbled in his pocket for his wallet. To his alarm it wasn't there, fumbling in the other pocket he snapped out in English: 'Where the hell is my money?'

The second the words were out of his mouth, Forest knew he had blundered. It would have been so easy at that moment for someone to overhear and betray him, or for a German to be nearby and be startled by the burst of English. Cringing, Forest looked about him. Luckily it seemed the bustle of the station had been his saving grace, as no one appeared to have heard or have taken notice. Still, it served as a reminder of how easy it could be to slip up, and all because of something so foolish as a momentarily misplaced wallet.

He returned to Ryan a little shaken but none the worse for his mistake, and turning to the smiling American it occurred to him how torturous this must be for the young man, knowing that a single spoken word could be his downfall. Could he even say yes and no without revealing his accent? Thankfully their journey was nearing its end; a local train took them on the last leg to Fleury-sur-Andelle. There they were met by a party of bicycles, their last transport before the Lysander collected them. Forest grimaced at memories of his last trip on a bicycle and Ryan uncomfortably mounted his with his fractured shoulder. Balancing suitcases as best they could (this time, fortunately, Passy was carrying genuine luggage and not a concealed W/T set!) they rode along the country lanes to Lyons-la-Forêt.

They arrived after dark and the village was quiet except for a small reception group keeping an eye out for the returning men. The Vinets greeted Passy and Brossolette as warmly as before and took them directly to their home; a neighbouring farmer took in Forest and the young American. The next 24 hours would be a tense time. Lysanders only came at night to avoid German patrols and they were scheduled for the following evening. During the day Forest and Ryan had to keep out of sight as there was no knowing if anyone who saw them might betray them, accidentally or deliberately. For Forest it was a chance to rest. For Ryan it was yet more torture for his exuberant nature. Throughout the day he struggled not to speak and would occasionally burst out loudly with a comment in his strong accent. More than once the farmer's wife crossly ordered him to be silent.

At 10.30 p.m. Ryan and Forest were bundled into a van and hidden behind sacks of potatoes. It was an undignified journey along bumpy country roads and Ryan was uncomfortable with his shoulder, but he managed to hold his tongue, and luckily the subterfuge was not needed as no Germans stopped the van for inspection.

They were unloaded at the edge of a field. The moon was full and the grass in the field shimmered in the light. At the far side there was a copse of trees, which was to be Forest's hiding place for the next few hours. Scuttling across the field with Ryan like a giant startled rabbit, Forest prayed that the Lysander would be on time and would not be spotted by the enemy. It wasn't long before Passy and Brossolette joined them.

Forest lay on the damp floor of the copse and found his mind drifting from elation to be finally going to a safe place again, to anxiety that some last-minute catastrophe might prevent his return to England. His alert mind was all too good at conjuring up scenarios that could turn the evening into a disaster. The weather might not be so good in England and the Lysander may not have been able to take off, or it might have encountered heavy anti-aircraft fire and been damaged. It might have experienced a problem or become lost. Then there were the German patrols, which were numerous in the area. They may have been tipped off or heard the plane arriving. Surrounded by leaves and earth Forest could only let these thoughts circulate in his mind, unable to control the fears that overwhelmed him. It was one of the rare times he felt uncertain and nervous, and it was also one of the few times that he was not the one in full control. He was reliant on someone else and their skills and that was not something that sat easily with Forest.

Out of the darkness the hum of a plane engine sounded over the trees. It seemed inordinately loud after the silence of the copse, but no curious Germans appeared, so perhaps the landing party had chosen their location well. The three resistance members ran out of the trees and switched on a line of torches they had set up earlier in a large 'L' shape. It was a rudimentary landing strip for the Lysander but it was all they had and for much of the time it worked.

The Lysander banked then lined itself up with the long vertical arm of the 'L'. Steadily, it swooped down and landed on the grass, following the vertical stretch of torches before veering right at the foot of the 'L' where the torches created a horizontal strip of light. The landing had taken mere moments and now the plane stood at a standstill, the wind behind it, ready to return to the skies as soon as its passengers boarded. Forest had never seen a more welcome sight.

Forest, Ryan and Passy fled the copse and hurried to the gunner's cockpit of the Lysander. In some accounts Brossolette went with them, in others he flew home on a second Lysander that was waiting to land once its counterpart had taken off again. In any case, very soon the three SOE agents and their American guest were on a plane and taking off for home. As they left France behind, Forest felt he could relax completely for the first time in many weeks.

On 17 April the BBC broadcast a discreet message on its French service: '*Le petit lapin blanc est renter au clapier*' (the little white rabbit has returned to his hutch). The white rabbit was the code word used to identify Forest to his friends in the resistance. It was only used on the BBC broadcasts where the use of any of his other codenames (particularly Shelley) would have instantly alerted German interest. How he got the odd name is a slight mystery. Barbara claimed that one of her friends gave Forest the nickname, though exactly why she didn't explain. But it was unusual for SOE to take on a person's normal life nickname to use in operations. Perhaps some clue could come from Colonel Hutchinson, or 'Hutch' as he was affectionately known. Calling one of his agents the 'white rabbit' would have appealed to his sense of humour, and the dry wit that tended to run through all operation coding. Hutch seems to have had some affection for Forest, perhaps he saw himself in the younger man. Whatever the case the message was wholly appropriate – the rabbit had returned to his hutch.

It was not long before Forest was compiling reports and expressing his firm opinions about the resistance situation to his superiors. There was so much that he needed to get across to the SOE heads that at times he may have seemed like a broken record to those who did not understand the realities of trying to resist in an occupied country. He insisted over and over that the invasion of France could only be a success if a strong secret army was ready and waiting in the country, and he was probably right. In hindsight it is easy to forget the part played by the resistance, particularly the Maquis, on D-Day.

Forest recognised the significance of the resistance long before D-Day and found it frustrating that his views seemed to fall on deaf ears among his superiors. He bitterly informed them time and again that the resistance was vital and a secret army was essential, but it couldn't be built without weapons and supplies.

Forest ranted against the imposter Giraud who he saw as the enemy of organised resistance. Again and again he repeated that the French resistance must unite behind de Gaulle, and that Giraud was a nuisance who was muddying the waters. He talked about the French fear that the Allies would remove part of their colonial empire after the war (namely North Africa), so the British and Americans must announce publicly that they would not do this.

He spoke of the difficulties of operating clandestinely, and of the constant dangers and anxieties. He particularly emphasised the risks that W/T operators took. Was it not to be expected that W/T operators would struggle to send out messages that were error free? Yet time and time again the British complained about the muddled messages they were sent. Forest stated that they needed to be more sympathetic.

His strongest criticism, however, was reserved for Jean Moulin. Moulin had not made a friend in Forest, in part this was due to Forest's strong loyalty and belief in Brossolette, but it was also due to his concerns that such a character as strong as Moulin's could do more harm to the resistance than good.

Forest felt his concerns were not listened to by his superiors:

> It was impossible for people who had not lived the clandestine life of an agent, to realise how sensitive one became. They could not always appreciate that seemingly simple things were frequently very complicated and difficult to do.[2]

From his superiors' point of view, the reports, though rather dogmatic, were logical, and Churchill's advisor Sir Desmond Morton felt that Forest was a sensible and level-headed fellow, though dismissed him slightly as being pro de Gaulle.

At least there was one office in which Forest's belief in de Gaulle as the uniting force of France was not so easily dismissed. On 20 May 1943 Forest was summoned to a meeting with the illustrious general himself. Forest's name had been noted in Passy's report on the Seahorse mission for the BCRA and the general was keen to meet the 'White Rabbit' who had sparked such attention from his subordinate. Forest did not know what to expect arriving at de Gaulle's room; he was not a man easily intimidated by authority but his first impression of the general was of an immense man, with a gruff manner of talking. He later said he felt like a pygmy standing before the gigantic de Gaulle. It was as much the general's presence as his stature that impressed this feeling of grandiosity upon Forest.

De Gaulle wanted to know Forest's feelings on France and was somewhat surprised at the strength of 'Gaullism' in his country, but he was also impressed by the bravery and determination of the SOE agent. Before Forest left, de Gaulle awarded him the Croix de Guerre, a significant French medal awarded for heroism. It was a special privilege for Forest to be recognised by his home country, but it caused some problems, as British officers were not allowed to wear foreign medals. Eventually Hutch had to get involved to persuade the authorities to give Forest permission to wear it. Later Forest heard that he had been awarded the Military Cross (MC). He bought the purple and white ribbon, Barbara sewed it to his tunic and the BCRA threw him a celebratory meal, only for an Air Ministry official to inform him that there had been a mistake and he not actually been awarded the medal. The ribbon had to be removed from his tunic and it would be another year before he would be properly awarded the citation.

This bureaucratic error forced Forest into another diplomatic controversy. The French expected him to wear his MC and after the debacle with the Croix de Guerre, it would not look good to try and explain the error. Instead Forest returned to his habits of subterfuge and kept one tunic hidden at his office with the MC ribbon still stitched onto it. Every time he had a meeting with the French he wore this tunic, and during the rest of the time he wore an undecorated spare. If he accidentally bumped into one of his French colleagues when not wearing the decorated tunic, he explained it away as that he hadn't had the time to sort out all his different tunics with the decoration.

The return to desk work, which had at first seemed such a welcome break from the strain of undercover operations, now began to test Forest's patience. He had consoled Barbara before Operation Seahorse with promises that it would be his one and only clandestine mission. Now he realised he would have to break that promise or go insane running from office to office and arguing with an array of detached bureaucrats.

Forest could never be labelled as unambitious. If his scheme with Molyneux's yacht had been far-fetched, his next idea was positively mad. The British had learned that Grossadmiral Karl Doenitz, the Commander-in-Chief of the German Navy, was prone to making regular trips from Paris to outstations in Cherbourg and Angouleme with only a small escort for protection. Forest came up with a dramatic scheme to attack Doenitz's convoy on one of these visits, hold up the three escort cars and kidnap the Grossadmiral and bring him back to England. Forest suggested that he would work with Gilbert Vedy or the CDLL on the plan and submitted his 'quite feasible' proposal on 18 June. Unsurprisingly the audacious idea was turned down.

Meanwhile the resistance situation in France suddenly deteriorated. Delestraint, who Forest had deemed a liability to have so high up in the resistance, was arrested by the Gestapo on 9 June. Three days after Forest had submitted his failed proposal, Jean Moulin also fell into the clutches of the Gestapo.

Moulin's capture came about partly through bad luck and partly through betrayal. A fellow resistance member, Rene Hardy, was tried twice and acquitted for his supposed betrayal of Moulin. Someone gave away the location of a meeting of the top leaders of the resistance to the Germans on that fateful day. Ironically the Germans were 45 minutes late and should have missed the conspirators. But unfortunately Moulin had also been delayed by 45 minutes. Had he been earlier or later the Gestapo may have never captured him, but as it was, his luck had run out.

Moulin was interrogated by the notorious Klaus Barbie, known as the 'Butcher of Lyon'. The interrogation was brutally efficient – too efficient. Moulin never recovered from his initial torture and later interrogations only compounded his injuries. He died on 8 July while his captors were frantically trying to ship him to Germany.

It was a disaster for the resistance. Forest had been right, Moulin's presence in the formation of the secret army had been too overpowering, making him indispensable; without him things began to fall apart. The circuits the men had been involved with were compromised and there was no knowing what had been said by the captives (the resistance was realistic about the chances of any man staying silent under prolonged torture). The networks broke themselves apart as people began to panic.

Two men were left holding the resistance reins: Capitaine Claude Bouchinet-Serreulles and Jacques Bingen. Bouchinet-Serreulles was an inexperienced young French army officer who had previously served in London as one of de Gaulle's aides. He had been pressing for some time for a more active role and after rudimentary training in the clandestine life he was landed in France on the night of 15–16 June. By 19 June he was in Lyon and meeting with Moulin, and two days later he was effectively trying to fill Moulin's boots and failing. Two months later Bingen arrived in France, landed in by Lysander on 15–16 August. Bingen found the more active role he had been pressing for to be more dangerous than he had imagined. A former head of the Free French Merchant Navy and aide to de Gaulle, he had been originally delegated to look after the Unoccupied Zone. Now these two novices were desperately trying to hold together the fragmenting French resistance.

Bouchinet-Serrulles and Bingen sent optimistic reports of their work back to London, but other reports quickly indicated the opposite. The plans for a secret army among the resistance were stuttering and dying. While the reception committees for supply or agent drops were still operating efficiently, information on the paramilitary side of operations was worryingly minimal. Regional military officers were complaining that they were not being supported by the resistance and it seemed that if something wasn't done soon the whole organisation would crumble and have to be rebuilt from scratch.

Abruptly Forest found himself on a new mission with Brossolette. This time it was to save the resistance. Filled with excitement as well as trepidation, Forest took on his new codename of Tirelli, along with a new identity and false papers. As he memorised his brand-new persona and prepared for another parachute drop, he could only wonder what fate had in store for him on Operation Marie-Claire.

....

Notes

1. Professor Pasteur Valery-Roudet, a descendent of the famous chemist and microbiologist.
2. Seaman, *Op cit*.

9

Dinner with Sophie

ON 13 JULY 1943 discussions were underway to resolve the calamity in France. Passy was eager to get back to deal with the situation and hoped that Forest and Brossolette could be spared to assist him. The main matter they needed to deal with was contacting the various resisters, particularly FANA and Capitaine Bouchinet-Serreulles, who had come into some doubt over his glowing reports of the success of resistance. With the loss of Moulin it was vital to get someone inside quickly who could act as damage control.

Codenames were already being considered. Forest had been given the signal 'Marie-Claire'; Brossolette would be 'Marie-Claire II'. Bouchinet-Serreulles had been codenamed 'Sophie' and SOE was determined to catch up with the elusive figure who they disparagingly labelled 'Moulin's understudy'.

Meanwhile the BCRA had given them their own affectionate tags: 'Magino' and 'Briand'. Add to this the new Tirelli identity that Forest had to learn, as well as the a previous set of papers under the name Thierry, and it was a lot of lies to keep straight in his mind. Forest did not have long to reflect on all this new information, as on 18 September he had a call at 1 a.m. to confirm that the mission would go ahead that night.

In the early hours of that Saturday morning, as Forest contemplated his next adventure, Barbara was fraught with worry. There could be no illusions between them that there was a very high risk of him being captured. Forest tried to comfort himself with the knowledge that SOE had introduced a new system of codes that made message sending even more secure. The 'one-time pads' as they were known had codes printed on slips of silk, which were used once and then destroyed. As long as his code pad kept in line with SOE's control version then there was no problem.

He tried his hardest to convince Barbara that every feasible security precaution was being undertaken and that she mustn't worry for him, but both of them knew the dangers he faced. When morning finally came, Barbara was trembling with nerves and insisted that Forest go to a photographer in Baker Street to have his portrait taken as a keepsake for her. Both of them knew it was meant for if he never returned, but despite the morbidity of the project Forest agreed and by lunchtime Barbara knew that she at least would have a memento of her lover if the worst happened.

At 4.30 p.m. an SOE car appeared. Forest said his farewells to Barbara and she saw him off, praying his luck would hold out, before slumping back into her flat and noting 'feeling terrible' in her diary. For Forest, some of his gloom was alleviated by being back with his team. The car picked up Brossolette, who had dyed his hair salt-and-pepper shades to cover his white streak and had dispensed with his moustache, and then Hutch clambered into the car tinged with a little dose of envy, as he too would have liked to be in the thick of the action.

The weather looked unpromising as they arrived at Tangmere airfield, causing Forest to wonder if this flight would be as abortive as his first one to France. Flight-Lieutenant Peter Vaughan-Fowler was there to greet them. He was an old friend of Forest's as he had been the pilot who had picked him up in a Lysander at the conclusion of Operation Seahorse. Jovially he took them to dinner, with no one quite able to shake the feeling that the exercise had a ring of a condemned man's last supper to it.

The night was still thick with fog and cloud, but the urgency of the matter convinced the men that the flight should be undertaken. At 11.30 p.m. Forest and Brossolette bundled their luggage into the converted gunner's cockpit and wedged themselves in after it. Hutch stood on the runway to bid them farewell. Forest, crammed next to Brossolette, hoped the man travelled well, as he doubted this was going to be the easiest of flights.

Take-off was smooth enough, though the impenetrable fog threatened to force them to land immediately. Vaughan-Fowler was keen however, and had faith in his skills. Undaunted, he flew them over the fields and houses of

England and on to the Channel. What came next surprised them all. As they reached the French coast, feeling confident in their camouflage among the clouds, a sudden explosion went off near them.

Suddenly they were surrounded by explosions. The Germans had somehow noticed their presence in the fog, perhaps radar or sound locators had given them away, but whatever the cause the exploding shells lit up the clouds around them in vibrant pink hues. Vaughan-Fowler knew the enemy had to be firing blind – they were hoping that a lucky shell would hit, he was hoping it would not. He was sufficiently shaken by the explosions to start taking evasive action and Forest clung to his seat as they rocked, soared up, swept down, twisted and turned through the night sky until the anti-aircraft batteries had been left safely behind.

The cloud finally began to break and below them Vaughan-Fowler glimpsed Poitiers and was glad to tell his passengers that the end was in sight. As the time slowly ticked on to 1.25 a.m. Forest caught a glimpse of three lights on the ground set out by their reception committee. Elated, Vaughan-Fowler exchanged signals to ensure the site was genuine, and then came in for landing.

Forest noted in his mission diary: 'Arrival: 01.30hrs. 19th September 1943, at a ground in the region of Angouleme called Serin.'[1]

By now Forest was used to the fact that things never went smoothly. The first problem proved to be just getting their luggage out of the plane: it had become firmly trapped under the seats during the flight and it took some pushing and pulling to free it. The reception committee looked on anxiously during the proceedings, they had already taken note of the large consignment of cargo the plane had delivered: a consignment they had not been expecting. They would have to hide it somewhere quickly, a daunting task with so few of them.

The luggage finally gave up its hold on the plane and Brossolette and Forest turned to their hosts to learn of the new problem. The reception committee had only brought a single car for transporting everybody and with a second Lysander landing and two more agents and numerous packages tumbling out it was obvious that there was not going to be enough space for everyone. This might not have been a problem had the safe house not been 40 miles from the landing site. Hasty discussions took place with the only conclusion being that the cargo would be transported first in the car to a disused house about 15 miles away. Once safely stored the car would return for the agents.

Gloomily the SOE men resigned themselves to their fate: hiding behind a bush for over an hour in thick fog, their only protection two men with sten guns. Forest first watched the car drive off and then Vaughan-Fowler taking off in his Lysander and heading for home once more. Damp and cold, with fog rolling in and dawn a long way off, Brossolette and Forest huddled in the dark and hoped that this was not a sign of things to come.

The car eventually returned. Nine men, Forest and Brossolette included, and all their personal luggage were bundled into the vehicle. It was going to be a long drive and the old car had seen better days. As they were passing through a quiet village the rear tyre burst, forcing them to stop and change it. The noise aroused the locals, who peered anxiously outside to see what was happening. The men with the sten guns ordered them back indoors. Brossolette and Forest hid in the dense shadows of a barn door, opposite them their two fellow agents hunkered down in a similar doorway. There was no knowing if a German patrol was just around the corner and everyone was on edge. Suddenly Forest saw pale light coming from behind a nearby shutter. Gradually the light grew and an old man gingerly peered through. Hardly thinking, Forest leapt from the shadows brandishing his colt pistol at the witness. The old man hastily slammed his shutters shut and retreated inside. Heart pounding, Forest hoped the man was not a collaborator and, more importantly, that he didn't have a telephone indoors. The reception was hardly a secret operation anymore and who could know if any of the curious locals would report the night-time activity to the local police or Gestapo the next day.

The spare wheel proved to be in as good a condition as the rest of the car, and the group were not long back on the road before it became obvious that they had a slow puncture. There was no pump in the car and certainly no means of repairing the other tyre, so everyone had to just pray that the wheel would last out until they reached their destination. It was not a promising start for Forest's second mission.

Still, luck was on their side, and the tyre finally 'passed out' as Forest put it, just yards from the safe house. The exhausted men descended from the car and entered the house to find a lavish meal spread out for them. The house was long and low, a style of property known locally as a *mas*. The eleven-strong reception committee were elated at their triumph. As they talked excitedly, it turned out that this was their first Lysander operation and they were thrilled by their success. They talked with the agents eagerly, wanting to know why the

Americans seemed so keen for Giraud to take over rather than their chosen de Gaulle. They complained about a lack of supplies and interrogated the men on the lack of publicity being given to the British war effort. By the time it got to 4 p.m. and a young man, Lepointu, was assigned to escort them to Chateauneuf, the British agents felt they had been thoroughly grilled.

Only a few months later all but two of the eleven would be dead and young Lepointu would have suffered six bullets to his stomach and his arm being blown off.

They arrived at Chateauneuf at 4.30 p.m., but an early curfew was in place and yet again Forest found himself waiting in the cold with rain dripping through the leaking station roof. It was a long night huddled in coats and trying to block out the autumnal weather. At 1.30 a.m. the train left for Gare d'Austerlitz. There were no seats in the carriage and the passengers stood uncomfortably, some leaning against the walls to try and ease their legs. It was nearly 6 hours of discomfort to their destination and on their arrival all they had to cheer them up was a cup of ersatz coffee.

The first port of call was the home of Madame Peyronnet, and ensconced securely in the safe house they began making contact with the fractured resistance groups, in particular Sophie and Jacques Bingen. Direct contact was impossible and far too dangerous. SOE had trained their agents to use intermediaries as 'letterboxes' for the purpose of sending messages. Brossolette had set up a 'letterbox' between himself and Sophie before leaving France after their first mission, while Forest had organised one with a Madame Bosc, a restaurant owner in the rue Richepanse. There were still risks involved in establishing contact and messages had to be securely coded; if the agent was still feeling worried he might take security a step further by using an innocuous courier or 'cut out' to deliver the message to the letter box and remove himself from the action in event of discovery.

Sophie arranged a meeting for the following day at his own safe house. With time to spare, Brossolette and Forest set to work tracking down the various contacts they had made on their last mission and trying to forestall the damage caused by the arrests of Moulin and numerous others.

Forest turned to Jose Dupuis to help him, relying on her judgement to pick out two new *agents de liaison* and a further two safe houses for him. Dupuis was as efficient as she was patriotic. She swiftly arranged for Madame Peyronnet's daughter, Poucette, to act as a messenger. Despite being only 16, the girl was eager and reliable and could carry correspondence innocently on her bicycle. Poucette went on to recruit another girl, Suni Sandoe, whose name is well remembered by resistance scholars. Two women volunteered their services: Madame Denise Martin, the wife of a solicitor, and Nicole Bauer, who became Forest's secretary and was nicknamed Maud. Maud recruited Jacqueline Devaux as a messenger cyclist and the last member of the team was a Canadian, Diana Provost, who volunteered her flat as a meeting place. Forest had formed a secure little *réseau* with people who he not only trusted, but who were deeply loyal to him. Every one of them risked torture and death at the hands of the Gestapo should their work be exposed.

On 21 September Brossolette and Forest arrived for their first pre-arranged meeting with Sophie at the rue de la Pompe. From the first moments they were alarmed by the pathetic lack of security and Sophie's merry over-confidence: his secretariat was in the same building and it was obvious that he had given little thought to the risks of being watched or followed (it had been remarked during Sophie's training in Britain that: 'Outwardly he is the complete man of the world; nevertheless it is possible that he might not prove very practical when faced with a difficult situation.')[2] Appalled, the men arranged a second meeting for the following day when Jacques Bingen, referred to in official papers as Baudet, could be present as well. Between them they endeavoured to give the two SOE men a favourable picture of their work. Forest later reported:

> From them we got what appeared to be a very rosy picture of the situation, the gist of their story being 'everybody is happy, the movement relations with us are very cordial, there is no friction among them and everybody is very nice and pally'. In addition we were informed by them that we [Brossolette and Forest] had greatly exaggerated the dangers of clandestine work and that since they had been here there had been no signs of any possible trouble.[3]

Forest could hardly keep his temper with the two men. They had been lucky but nothing more, and when he probed them further they were so out of touch with the true resistance situation that it was no wonder they had failed to rouse German suspicion – they were not worth the effort!

Horrified, the two SOE men knew they had to act fast to repair the damage. Forest had heard that a third man, Paul Marchal, codenamed Massena, had arrived in France on 14 September to act as the head of the secret army and it was imperative that they get in touch with him. Sophie and Baudet were pressed to arrange the meeting and reluctantly they agreed. It was quite obvious that they resented the presence of the two agents from Britain who they felt were treading on their toes. They had, after all, been running the resistance quite successfully, in their opinion, since Moulin's arrest, and didn't need any assistance. Frustrated by their impassable arrogance the SOE men began laying down ground rules. Sophie or Baudet would contact Massena and arrange the meeting, then they would contact Brossolette at the Peyronnet safe house. Nothing was to be written down and they would send a reliable and security-conscious messenger who would arrive punctually at 5 p.m. on a daily basis.

Should the messenger fail to arrive and contact be lost, the SOE men would appear at the rue de Sèze at 10 a.m., entering from the rue Tronchet end, while Sophie would come in from the boulevard de la Madeleine. It was a back-up plan in case things went wrong, but Sophie seemed unimpressed. Brossolette and Forest left the meeting with a deep sense of foreboding. Forest turned to his companion and said: 'This quietness has lulled our friends to sleep, but I have a feeling that there is going to be a terrific storm any minute.'

Brossolette agreed miserably. As they crossed the street an agent working for Sophie and Baudet passed them. Nard was the last person they wanted to meet and it said little for Sophie's security that Nard was arriving at the same meeting place barely moments after the SOE men had left. Brossolette had already criticised the resistance leaders for retaining Nard when he should have been sent back to London long ago as it was known he was 'blown' to the Germans and hardly secure. Their concerns were scoffed at. Now Nard stopped to say hello. Angrily, Brossolette brushed him off: one of the primary rules of clandestine work was *not* to recognise any fellow agents out in the street. Comrades should be treated as strangers unless a specific meeting had been arranged. Forest was equally furious, Nard was a dangerous man, and with his identity known to the Germans any person he recognised could come under instant suspicion as being a resistance member. More than one innocent person had fallen into the hands of the Gestapo because they had recognised an old friend who was a 'blown' agent. The pair hurried home, their worst fears and those of London now confirmed.

There was mild anxiety in the Peyronnet household as 5 p.m. came and went with no sign of a messenger from Sophie. Forest settled into a chair, his mind working over the possibilities. The worst was that the courier had been caught en route, but as long as Sophie had followed the strict precautions Brossolette had insisted on, that shouldn't prove a problem for them, though it was a shame for the messenger who might be at that moment suffering at the hands of the Gestapo. Forest hoped the answer was far simpler. It had been made clear that should the courier be delayed he should postpone his arrival until the next day at 5 p.m. It was routine security and it seemed that this was the most likely option, but with Sophie and Baudet in charge nothing was simple.

At 10 p.m. there was a knock on the door of the building in which Peyronnet had her apartment. The doors were locked after 8 p.m. and the concierge went to answer the summons with apprehension. On the doorstep was a man who wanted to come in, and when the concierge asked who he was visiting he gave the name Mr Shelley. This puzzled the concierge who did not know of any resident of that name, her two newest arrivals were called Mr Thierry and Mr Boutet and were refugees from Nantes staying with Madame Peyronnet. But the man was insistent adding that he had been told Mr Shelley was staying in an apartment on the third floor.

Naturally suspicious, the concierge let him in, but insisted on accompanying him to the third floor. There, at Madame Peyronnet's door, she knocked and was greeted by a startled Forest. The *agent de liaison* handed over his note, satisfied that he had made contact with Mr Shelley as he had been told and apologising for being late. He had been delayed, but instead of following security precautions he had decided to press on.

Forest looked warily at the curious concierge as he took an envelope neatly inscribed for 'Mr Shelley' from the messenger. There was no use pretending that the woman could have failed to understand that Thierry was Shelley. Peyronnet was at the door now taking in the scene. Thankfully the concierge was deeply loyal to her third-floor tenants and promised not to pass on what she had heard. The little scene over, the messenger was sent away and the concierge returned to her station.

Forest showed the envelope angrily to Brossolette, it had crossed his mind that it had been mislabelled out of spite for the arrival of the two SOE men. Opening it he discovered a typewritten letter listing names and full addresses of meeting locations along with dates and times. Had it been intercepted the Germans would have hardly believed their luck. Not only would Forest and Brossolette have been arrested but several other people would have been exposed – the damage could have been enormous.

On 24 September Forest met with an old resistance friend, Michel Pichard, codenamed Oyster, with some relief. Oyster was reliable and secure, though the news he shared with Forest was bleak. He completely agreed with the damaging impression Forest had formed of the new resistance leaders and added his own disagreeable information on Sophie's office and network. Then he added a further blow. Paul Marchal, Massena, had missed several appointments the previous day and, to all intents and purposes, appeared to have disappeared from the face of the earth.

Forest was shaken. He knew Massena, having met him in England and formed the opinion before he was sent to the field that he was not a good choice for the role and would be lucky to survive ten days. Now it seemed he had been entirely right: Massena had only managed nine days. Still it was another shock and as Forest and Brossolette headed for another meeting with Sophie and Baudet they were uncomfortably aware of the storm blowing up around them.

Sophie and Baudet also reported that Massena had failed to appear for arranged meetings, but were not particularly disturbed by it. Considering their own security precautions, that was hardly surprising. Sophie shrugged and expected that Massena had been delayed. Brossolette furiously went over the incident of the late-night visit of the messenger with the written message and made it plain yet again that it was direly important that couriers should be on time and carry no papers. The two resistance leaders agreed but were far from moved by his fury.

Returning to the Peyronnets' apartment, the SOE men were faced with the very real possibility that everything they had worked for was falling apart. Brossolette complained about Moulin and his insistence on being so indispensable. Forest felt more inclined to criticise the choices made in London over his replacements.

Yet again 5 p.m. was an anxious hour and yet again there was no courier. Forest glanced at Brossolette and said: 'Do we stay here?'

Was this yet another innocent slip by the messenger despite the promises elicited from Sophie and Baudet about punctuality or had something happened this time?

'Let's hang on a little longer.' Brossolette said, concerned that they had not made full alternative safe house arrangements yet.

The hours ticked by unpleasantly slowly. 10 p.m. came and went with no sign of the messenger and now everyone feared the worst. Forest and Brossolette began packing their belongings. The Peyronnets watched with trepidation: if the two SOE men were so concerned then perhaps there was a real chance of their apartment becoming a Gestapo target. Saying their thanks and farewells, the two men left, Brossolette heading to stay with Claire in the rue de la Faisanderie and Forest moving into Jacqueline Devaux's flat. They passed a fretful night wondering what had become of their friends.

Early the next morning Maud paid a clandestine visit to the Peyronnets. The story they told her showed how dangerously close Forest had come to arrest. This time it had been no innocent delay that had prevented the courier arriving at 5 p.m. – he had been intercepted by the Gestapo and arrested. On his person was yet again another typed note, this time stating: 'Mme P, 3 étage, 102 avenue des Ternes.' The only relief was that there was no mention of Shelley nor were the extant addresses and details of so many comrades included this time.

The Gestapo took the messenger to their offices and interrogated him. Miraculously the man, despite his naïvety, proved more courageous than Forest could have imagined. Faced with the quick-fire questions and threats of torture, he still insisted that he was engaged in the black market rather than anything subversive. He had been sent to the avenue des Ternes, a place he had never had cause to visit before, to meet with a potential customer, Madame Peyronnet. Threats failed to shake his story, which had a suitable ring of truth to it anyway. His tactics had the advantage of stalling the Gestapo and the delay was Forest and Brossolette's saving grace.

At 6 a.m. the Peyronnets had been raided by the Gestapo. It was a terrifying ordeal: a gang of Germans swept through the apartment searching for any sign of the two SOE agents. The concierge clung bravely to her loyalty to the Peyronnets and gave them no assistance, while Madame Peyronnet was able to discern from her interrogators the black market lie the courier had given and played on it. It was a devastating few hours, but by the end the Gestapo were satisfied that Madame Peyronnet was just another black market customer and left her home. Maud reported all this to Forest and it became apparent that there was no returning to the apartment. The two SOE agents set out to find a third safe house to cover their tracks and by 25 September they were settling into yet another apartment.

But the drama was only just beginning. On 26 September Sophie told them that his offices had been raided by the Gestapo. Four months' worth of incoming and outgoing communications, courier notes and file-loads of details on significant agents and resistance members had all fallen into German hands. Sophie himself had briefly been in Gestapo custody but had been released. Seemingly even the Germans found it hard to believe that such an incompetent man could have been sent to replace Moulin.

Sophie's right-hand man, Alain, had narrowly escaped arrest, while Nard had fallen foul of the round up. Brossolette pressed for more details of the confiscated material and was shocked to learn that 'all courier papers in and out for the past four months, all telegrams in and out … and lists of names of prominent people connected with the resistance had been captured'.[4]

On these lists were the names of senators Jeanneney and Farjon, and it was imperative that they should be warned as soon as possible. Forest changed to his newest identity, Tirelli, and once again parted company with Brossolette to go to a different safe house while his friend went to stay with Suni Sandoe.

Just when it was most urgent to contact London and let them know what had happened, wireless communications were jeopardised. In late September Forest gave Oyster a message to transmit via one of his W/T operators known as the pianist, but he came under German suspicion before he could do so and had to disappear for a while. The pianist only transmitted his message on 14 October.

More bad news was just around the corner. As the Gestapo mounted a breathtaking operation to sweep up all the resistance members on the lists they had so fortuitously captured, intelligence came to Forest that Massena was dead. Apparently his disappearance had been due to arrest by the Germans and to avoid breaking under torture he had swallowed his cyanide pill. A zonal chief codenamed Niel told the SOE men that he had conclusively established that the Gestapo knew the names of all the resistance officers who came to France in September; this of course included them. Niel claimed there was a serious leak somewhere in the system and Forest had to agree. Miserably he reported to London in early October that the resistance network Groupe Rabelais had been completely destroyed, all members having been rounded up in the previous two weeks.

Meanwhile Forest had to keep his own safety at the forefront of his mind at all times. He and Brossolette were still in contact with Sophie and Baudet, but the pair were making life extremely dangerous for them. Often they failed to turn up to arranged rendezvous claiming they had too much work to do, so an *agent de liaison* was set up for them who would meet with the SOE men's *agent de liaison*. It did nothing to improve the system. Sophie and Baudet's lack of punctuality seemed infectious and soon their *agent de liaison* was proving just as unreliable, not helped by his being sent on 'all sorts of errands' to make it even harder for him to contact Forest or Brossolette.

By now it was apparent this was all a deliberate ploy by Sophie and Baudet to infuriate and spite SOE. They were so sure of their own abilities that they quickly became a liability to those loyal to them. Forest referred to their idiotic use of their *agent de liaison*, which resulted in him being arrested, and his own *agent de liaison* had a narrow escape due to trying to restore contact. The situation was becoming hopeless and dangerous.

A representative of CDLL reported that he had official information that 32,000 Gestapo men were in Paris to crack down on the resistance and that Forest's father's flat was under surveillance. This hardly surprised him and now he had conclusive proof that the Gestapo knew his name and that he was in the field. The hunt was on for Shelley.

Forest was now a wanted man. The Gestapo had set tails on a number of *agents de liaison* and it was apparent that Forest was also being watched. Life began to become more precarious. Forest arranged through a CDLL member to get an authentic birth certificate, identity card and ration card under one of his pseudonyms in case the worst happened. He and Brossolette organised ten safe houses and six letterboxes between them. They would need them – during their remaining time in Paris five of the safe houses would be blown and one of the letterboxes would be rendered unsafe by Sophie's actions.

Forest was as settled as he could be in a safe house in Neuilly. Sophie was still a dangerous nuisance to him, phoning the house on a regular basis to try and arrange appointments despite the dangers it posed to both of them. Any attempt Forest made to impress this upon him was disregarded.

On a dull morning Forest rose barely rested from his disturbed sleep. His mind was a muddle of mission objectives and fears as he walked to the window and pulled open the shutters. For a moment he hesitated. Was that someone peering from behind a partially pulled curtain in a house on the other side of the street? It was a fleeting incident, probably more coincidence than anything, but Forest could not shake the nagging doubt in his heart that something was amiss.

Forest stayed in Neuilly for another night, trying to block out the fear that his presence there was blown. The next morning he opened his shutters and noticed the curtain twitcher opposite him was back. He no longer felt it was just a coincidence. Forest cast his eyes down into the road as casually as he could. There were several people going about their business, hurrying back and forth, but one man was hovering by the corner of the building opposite, seemingly without purpose. He was wearing the quintessential spy raincoat and had his eyes fixed on Forest's apartment. There was no doubting it any longer – the safe house was blown.

Forest left as fast as he could, having to leave some of his property behind in his haste. Immediately he informed Sophie of the discovery and once again his warnings were ignored. Forty-eight hours later Sophie held a meeting in the same house at Neuilly. The Gestapo must have wondered where this godsend had come from!

The net was closing around them. Brossolette and Forest dined with Claire Davinroy one fateful night. Claire was a childhood friend of Brossolette's and with the Gestapo drawing closer he didn't want her to be put in danger because of his presence. After their meal the two agents left Claire, and Forest promised to see her the next day at a prearranged meeting.

The night was uneventful for them and the next evening Forest appeared for his meeting with Claire, but she didn't show. Forest was immediately anxious, as Claire was reliable and punctual, not someone who would be late if she could help it, and that she didn't show at all had his stomach churning. He retreated to a little café with a telephone where it wouldn't matter if his call was traced. Nervously he dialled Claire's number. A woman answered.

'*Bonsoir, chère amie,*' Forest said.

'*Bonsoir chéri,*' replied the woman. 'Come immediately, I am waiting for you.'

'*Oui,*' Forest answered and hung up.

It had not been Claire on the phone.

Brossolette was distraught when he heard the news. It was obvious that Claire had been arrested by the Gestapo and a trap had been set in her apartment to catch an unwary agent. He desperately tried to learn news of her via his resistance contacts. Slowly details came in. Another resistance agent, Gulliver, had been arrested, and the Gestapo had started circling around his friends and acquaintances. The concierge at the house in which he stayed had endured a frightening interview with the Germans in which she revealed that Gulliver's apartment had been leased for him by a woman named Claire Davinroy. The Gestapo were quick to raid Claire's flat at 6 a.m. the morning after Forest and Brossolette had left her. In the flat they found money left behind by Forest and incriminating documents on Claire's desk.

The only consolation for Brossolette was that it had not been his presence that had caused Claire's arrest; it was one of those quirks of circumstance and a lucky escape for the two SOE men. Word went out that Claire was in the hands of the Germans along with her little white dog, which the Gestapo were trying to use to find her other friends: the dog barked at strangers and made a fuss of acquaintances it knew. For a time a man in a raincoat walking a small dog was a familiar sight at the rue de la Faisanderie where Claire had lived.

Danger was everywhere and the Gestapo was working overtime in recruiting men to follow resistance suspects. At a meeting with Oyster, Forest realised that they were being followed. They quickly discussed their options and it was agreed that they should head to a Métro station and part company unexpectedly. Oyster would jump on a Métro train and Forest would head off on foot. The plan went as expected and the tail had to make instantly decide who to pursue. As Forest was on foot he set off after him, much to the SOE man's amusement. Forest was never one to let danger stop him having a little fun and he spent an enjoyable hour leading his tail on a merry goose chase. The pursuer was wrapped in a grey overcoat (the movie cliché of the stalker in a long overcoat is in part based on truth) and suffered as he tried to keep up with Forest's fast pace. Later Forest chuckled and suggested that the man must have lost weight in the course of that manic hour.

But finally even he got bored of the chase and darted into a department store. While his pursuer was disentangling himself from a crowd of shoppers, Forest headed for the basement and nipped out a side-passage reserved for employees. It was a textbook tactic, but it worked perfectly.

On another occasion Forest lost a pursuer by darting onto a Métro train, getting off casually at a station and then jumping back on just as the train was leaving again. But by far the biggest danger was still the recalcitrant Baudet and Sophie; the two of them were utterly oblivious to the hazards all around them.

Brossolette and Forest met Baudet one day at an appointed place. To their horror Baudet arrived being followed by no fewer than three men. Brossolette tried to impress on the man that he had been tailed but he refused to accept it.

Exasperated with him the two SOE men walked him quickly around a building and hid in an arched doorway. Within a short time all three of his pursuers hastily rounded the corner to keep up. Indignantly Baudet had to admit they were right and that he had led three German informers straight to the two agents.

Somehow they had to lose the men. The first rule of eluding a follower is not to let the follower realise you are on to him. So the men doubled-back on their route and kept a fast pace with a number of turns to occasionally put them out of sight of the tail. At one such turn Baudet was unceremoniously sent packing and told to hurry down the rue Laborde and to vanish before the 'sleuths' (as Forest liked to term them) caught up. Baudet obeyed, already shamefaced by his foolishness. That left Forest and Brossolette with the problem of three tails.

Both men walked briskly to the place St Augustin, discussing their options in hushed tones. There was no choice but to separate and try to lose the tails individually. All being well, they would meet an hour later.

As they reached place St Augustin they spotted two vélo-taxis (bicycle taxis) hovering near the path.

'Change of plan?' Forest glanced at Brossolette, and in an instant they were racing for the taxis and each jumped into one.

Forest directed his to the Champs Élysées and Brossolette headed to Pont Cardinet. Behind them the sleuths came to a grinding halt, unable to follow any further. Forest surreptitiously watched them disappear into the background and let out a sigh of relief. An hour later he was back with Brossolette.

At this time Forest heard that incriminating papers found by the Gestapo had fallen back into resistance hands. After Gulliver's arrest, which had sealed Claire's fate, his network was rapidly rounded up and his headquarters searched for important papers. The Gestapo found intelligence the resistance had been gathering, in particular a document on the secret V-1 weapon the Germans were working on. In a moment of fatal overconfidence, the documents were left on a desk at the office, the Gestapo holding to the firm belief that all of Gulliver's people were safely in their clutches and that the documents would be secure until the next day.

But as with all things, someone had slipped through the net. This was a woman named Berthe, who had the courage to sneak back into the headquarters, with the compliance of the concierge, and steal back the documents. She took them to a safe house, hid them and then contacted Forest.

By now word had spread about the arrests. One of Gulliver's assistants had just returned from London when he heard the news. His life was in grave danger as his description was known to the Gestapo, so he went into hiding, but not before telling Forest about the significance of the papers Berthe had saved. There was no choice but to retrieve them.

Forest paid a visit to the location of the safe house to assess its security. It was obvious that the Gestapo were all over it and would watch any visitors. It was entirely possible that they had planned to leave the papers behind just so that such a trap might be laid. Berthe was perhaps followed or the helpful concierge may have been collaborating with the Germans. Anything was possible, but for the time being what mattered was getting the papers.

Forest formed a plan worthy of any secret agent. He discovered that a doctor lived in the same building as the flat where Berthe had hidden the papers. He went to the address with two companions, intending to tell anyone they met that he was ill and seeking medical advice. As it was the Gestapo had grown tired of their vigil and there was no one watching when they arrived. The papers were removed, the unimportant ones were destroyed, and the rest were sent to another safe house to be passed on to London when possible.

Aside from dodging the Gestapo and acting like James Bond, Forest was still faced with the task of maintaining the crumbling foundations of the resistance movement. Something had to be salvaged from the wreckage, and, surprisingly, it came in the form of Joseph, the eager communist from FANA Forest had met on his last mission.

Joseph was incomparable to the nightmares that were Sophie and Baudet. Despite their differing politics Forest formed a hearty respect for him and even considered him a friend in those turbulent days. He wrote:

[Joseph's] security measures were remarkable and he was an outstanding example of how clandestine work should be done; nothing was left to chance and he introduced me to one very useful method of holding a conversation in comparative safety. We would arrange to meet at the intersection of two streets but not show any sign of recognition, he would then lead the way to a hospital, I would follow him 30 or 50 yards behind, he would walk into the hospital through the visitors' gate and go into the grounds where I joined him a minute or so later. We could then talk quite at our ease.[5]

Joseph also proved an unexpected supporter of the centralising of orders via London, an issue that was controversial among the resistance. Forest was hopeful that Joseph might go to England for further training and Joseph agreed to the idea, but doubted that his party would ever allow it. He was a breath of sanity and common sense among the communists, far too many of whom were driven by the idea that they were the prime victims of the Nazis and therefore should be the only heroic resistance around. Slow communications and a complicated hierarchy meant that it was difficult to coordinate parachute operations with them and they were never quite the asset they could have been.

With danger mounting there was a greater need than ever to ensure loyalty. Forest was feeling the pinch of clandestine work, when his newest *agent de liaison*, Horace, arrived late one evening.

Horace, real name André Lemonnier, had been recruited by Jose Dupuis when the pressing shortage of agents de liaison was beginning to hamper the work of Forest's small *réseau*. He had been recommended, along with his friend Edmond Vacher (Ernest), by a priest known to help men on the run from the Germans. The patriotic Abbe Leveque had been convinced by the young men's sincerity and put them in touch with Jose Dupuis through a resistance contact.

Horace became Forest's *agent de liaison*, while Baudet engaged Ernest as an assistant. The desperate shortage of men had rather thrust Horace upon Forest and it wasn't long before he felt uncomfortable with his choice. Horace seemed more interested in chasing Parisian women and spending the money he earned via Forest than serving the resistance. He quickly proved himself unreliable, always late for appointments and vague when asked for information. Ernest was proving equally disreputable, when entrusted with 500,000 francs by Baudet he split it with Horace and another man, then vanished hoping to escape to North Africa before being caught.

That left Forest even more concerned about Horace. Ten years younger than Ernest and still very much a boy at heart, was he just incompetent and irresponsible or a traitor?

One evening Horace arrived at Jose Dupuis' flat where Forest was waiting for him. He had been set a test, a test that would seal his fate. Forest had his Colt with him, loaded and sitting to hand. He was in a dark mood and if the boy failed him this time he would have no mercy, the Gestapo were getting too close for any unnecessary risks to be taken.

Horace had been told to take a message to a house Forest knew to be unoccupied. He had been given the address along with the telephone number and was expected to report back as soon as the work was done. He was late as usual, further inflaming Forest's anger. When he did arrive Forest could barely contain his temper as he asked him how the mission had gone. Horace was nonchalant, the house had been empty when he arrived, but he had made inquiries of the neighbours and had arranged to return the next day when someone was home. Forest felt his fingers closing on his Colt.

'Describe the house' he demanded of the boy.

Horace hesitated, which was enough for Forest to see through his lies.

'You didn't go there, did you?'

Horace glanced to Jose Dupuis for help, but she was not about to intercede – this was Forest's business. Slowly Horace admitted the truth: he had not been to the house, he had telephoned and received no answer so had decided not to bother doing anything further.

Forest was incensed. He grabbed the Colt and aimed it at Horace. The boy froze in the face of the gun.

'You are a traitor and shall not leave here alive!' Forest bellowed, his finger on the trigger.

Horace, trembling, begged for forgiveness. He was reckless, yes, and neglectful, but not a traitor and he didn't deserve to die. Forest was unmoved by the boy's denials and tearful apologies, he no longer had any patience for him. He was tired of the incompetence around him, tired of the constant fear and above all, tired of Horace and the worries he caused.

He was about to kill him when Jose could stand the tension no more and moved to Horace's aid. Perhaps it was his youth that played on Jose's mind, or the fact that she had recruited him and now feared her mistake, but she could not watch Forest kill the boy in cold blood. Quietly she slipped between them and with gentle words persuaded her old friend to let Horace go with a warning. Forest lowered the gun, still glaring at the boy.

'You are dismissed from my service,' he told the terrified Horace, 'but never forget if you betray us the organisation will have you shot!'

Greatly relieved, Horace ran for the door and left them. Forest must have had a pang of doubt over what he had done and he was right to do so. Later events would prove that both Horace and Ernest were working for the Germans long before they had met with the patriot Abbe Leveque. Like so many traitors the Nazis employed, Horace and Ernest had no deep feelings of Germanic loyalty, but were driven rather by the thought of easy money. Both were lazy wastrels who found holding down genuine work problematic. Horace was recruited by the local Gestapo branch in his hometown and sent to infiltrate Abbe Leveque's escape network. It was pure coincidence that he met with his old friend Ernest at the abbe's home and that the other man had also been independently recruited by the Germans. They instantly joined forces and together set about infiltrating the network.

There seems no doubt that the entire time Horace was working for Forest he was in touch with his German controllers. At one point he mysteriously vanished and reappeared claiming he had been in the clutches of the Gestapo – this was probably true, though rather than an interrogation it had probably been a prearranged debriefing!

Ironically it was Horace's feckless nature that made him as poor an asset for the Germans as he was to Forest. He aroused suspicion almost immediately and this prevented him from penetrating deeply into the resistance network, but it was also the case that his natural disinclination for work meant he was barely trying to infiltrate anything. He worked for the Germans for convenience, the worst type of agent, and as proved by Ernest, should an opportunity arise for easy money they would take it and flee both of their respective masters.

He may have been an incompetent traitor and he may have gotten away lightly with his betrayal, but he would be back to haunt Forest in the not too distant future.

Notes

1. Official diary of events: Marie-Claire Mission, SOE files, the National Archives.
2. Report to SOE about criticism of Brossolette by advocates of Sophie and Baudet, 2/12/1943.
3. Courier from Marie-Claire, 18/10/43, the National Archives.
4. Official diary of events: Marie-Claire Mission, SOE files, the National Archives.
5. *Ibid.*

10

A Good Agent has no Routine

FOREST BROKE HIS OWN rules when it suited him and the Marie-Claire mission, with its endless pointless meetings and tiresome quarrels, was wearing him down to a point where he took risks. He was very conscious of these lapses and kept them hushed from SOE, but they happened nonetheless.

Madame Bosc's restaurant, where he set up his letterbox on the Seahorse operation, proved a temptation beyond his resolve. Visiting the building eased his tension for a time, but it was a dangerous indulgence, because his frequent visits were noticed. Forest recorded in his memoirs, several years after the war, what occurred one night when he left the restaurant. It was an ordeal he only obliquely revealed to SOE.

At 10.30 p.m. one evening he left Madame Bosc's restaurant. Across the road from the restaurant a man was standing in the shadows of a doorway. Forest felt his natural suspicions rising. Deciding to test his concerns he took a different route to that which he would normally use to get home. It wasn't long before he was aware that the stranger in the shadows had followed him.

A burst of adrenaline temporarily shrugged the tiredness from him; there was something about the chase that despite being frightening was also exciting. Forest headed for the nearby Métro station. At that time of night trains were not frequent, so there was plenty of time to get a good look at the tail while Forest waited for a train. Sure enough Forest had not sat down on a bench for long when the shadowy stranger appeared on the platform. He was a tall man, clean-shaven, wearing a brown felt hat and the stereotypical brown overcoat. Forest observed him cautiously, aware that he would need to get back to his apartment soon to avoid being caught out by the midnight curfew. The last thing he needed was to be arrested due to such a paltry thing as being out late at night.

A train pulled in at last and Forest jumped into the first-class carriage, while his shadow settled into the second-class carriage behind. Further along the line Forest got off the train and hurried to the Pont de Neuilly line, which would take him close to home. Again there was no train so he sat down to wait. His pursuer had followed, but this time he did not sit and quietly wait, but paced the platform, even passing in front of Forest once or twice. Forest suddenly found he was doubting his own suspicions – would a pursuer make such a dangerous error as to walk past the man he was following and risk being seen so closely? Forest had to be sure and time was running out.

When the train pulled in he hopped into the first-class carriage and yet again the stranger jumped into second class. Forest was desperate to test his theory and so picked a stop two before the one he really wanted in order to hop off the train and appear to head for a different line. No sooner had he done so, he doubled back and returned to his original platform. Sure enough the stranger followed and now he had no doubts or that he was being tailed.

But what to do? Time was slipping away from him, and he had barely half an hour before the curfew would make him an easy target for any patrolling Germans. If he made a dash for it no doubt his pursuer would instantly call for assistance from any passing Germans and have him caught. He was certain that the pursuer was also aware that he had been spotted, as Forest's frantic doubling back would have been enough to give him away. He could not therefore be following to secretly pick up a rendezvous or safe house, but rather was intent on keeping Forest in sight no matter what and as soon as curfew came and Forest had to make a dash for a house, he would call his chiefs and have the building cordoned off and searched. There was nothing clandestine about the situation anymore and Forest knew the next few minutes would either condemn or save him.

Yet again a train came in and Forest hopped into the first-class carriage while his pursuer jumped into second class. Sitting in a corner of the carriage Forest surreptitiously felt in his jacket for his .32 Colt. How often had Brossolette warned him about carrying a weapon? It would be an instant giveaway should he be stopped and searched, just the shoulder holster it was sitting in was a danger. But right now Forest could only feel relief that he carried it night and day. He had made up his mind – there was no choice but to dispose of his shadow.

So where to kill him? It had to be somewhere secluded, somewhere the noise would not attract attention, and he would need to dispose of the body quickly. A flash of inspiration hit him. Jeanne Helbling's flat, where Brossolette sometimes stayed, was not far from the next stop and right next to a river. A ramp led down to the riverbank where a bridge spanned the water. There would be little light down there and under the bridge no one would see a thing. If he could entice the man into the darkness for a moment he would have the advantage as the stranger's eyes accustomed to the sudden gloom. That moment could be all he needed to shoot him at point-blank range and dump his body in the river.

Forest checked his watch: there were only 20 minutes until curfew. It would be risky to kill his tail, but what choice did he have? The man had his back against the wall.

Off the train again he quickened his pace, heading towards the river, his shadow close behind. Dodging down a side road Forest could hear a group of Germans laughing and singing marching songs nearby, what witnesses they would be if they should hear anything! Forest slipped the Colt from its holster – it was loaded and cocked. He held it discreetly in his overcoat pocket, ready to draw it the instant he was under the bridge, and then on he ran. Now he broke into a trot to keep his pursuer concentrating and eager. He scuttled down the ramp and under the bridge. In the darkness he drew his gun and pulled his hat forward so that his face was obscured, then he waited breathlessly.

Mere moments passed before he heard footsteps pattering down the ramp. His tail appeared at the base of the bridge, brilliantly silhouetted against the moonlit night – he had forgotten himself in the heat of the chase. What a fool, Forest thought, as the man stumbled forward in the darkness straight into his Colt. The barrel of the gun was against the stranger's chest and Forest didn't hesitate to pull the trigger.

The man grunted and began to sag. Leaving no room for error, Forest brought his pistol barrel down on the man's head as hard as he could. His victim crumpled to the ground. Now he just had to get him into the water and make his escape, but even that would not prove easy. The man was incredibly heavy and Forest's burst of nervous energy had his whole system shaking with the exertion. Somehow he heaved the man to the edge of the bank and with a final push sent him tumbling into the water. All he had to do now was get away unseen. There was no one about and with no time to lose, Forest fled the scene and arrived at his flat with 5 minutes to spare before curfew.

It was only then that the gravity of the situation hit him. He had killed a man, or at least he thought he had killed him. Perhaps he had not been quite dead when he hit the water and had slowly drowned. It was an unpleasant thought, and Forest tried to clear it from his mind. His life had been at risk and there had been no other option; if the man had not been such a fool, perhaps he would have lived. Anyway, Forest was still free, and that was what mattered. He went to bed and slept deeply, utterly exhausted by the ordeal. (In an official SOE interview after his escape from Buchenwald this event is briefly mentioned as occurring during the Asymptote mission rather than the Marie-Claire mission. In his personal memoirs Forest wrote of it occurring as described above. The confusion of dates could be blamed on a number of factors, but was probably a misinterpretation by the interviewer).

More and more Forest found himself having to live his life in dangerously close contact with unsuspecting Nazis. They were everywhere, and more often than not they seemed be drawn to Forest, much to his exasperation. At one of his apartments, a personal bolthole, Forest discovered he was neighbour to a Wehrmacht colonel who was personal assistant to General von Stulpnagel, military governor of France. Forest toyed with the idea of killing him, but as the man always had bodyguards around the opportunity never arose. He had to satisfy himself with the knowledge that the good colonel was regularly exchanging pleasantries with a British agent.

After a much-anticipated visit to the Maquis organisation, Forest found himself in the company of Germans once more. There had been several train delays due to damaged lines (it was a resistance speciality, but an irony when it delayed one of their own) when Forest was trying to get back to Paris after his visit. Finally a train came into the station but it was almost full aside from the carriage marked 'reserved for the Wehrmacht'. Forest was in one of his belligerent moods and, as he had a first-class ticket and only a German general and his staff officer were seated in the carriage, he decided he would take a chance and flout the rules. Clambering into an empty Wehrmacht compartment he promptly fell asleep.

A short time later he was awoken by a German railway police officer who asked him if he had permission to be in a Wehrmacht-only carriage. With typical Forest bravado he replied he did not, but had been so tired and the train so full except for the Wehrmacht carriage that he had decided to settle down in the unoccupied compartment. He went on to complain bitterly about the sabotage of the trains, how it delayed everyone and messed up French business, and why were the Germans not doing more about it? For the next 2 hours he discussed similar matters with the German, who eventually had a look around the train and found a second-class passenger in a first-class French carriage, whom he kicked out and replaced with Forest. Shaking Forest's hand as he went to leave, he looked grave.

'I am sorry you can't stay in my compartment but orders are orders.' He seemed rather apologetic and added, 'Of course I am not at all suspicious of you, on the contrary I have the utmost confidence.'

Then he went to carry on his duties while Forest settled back and smiled at yet another German fooled.

But at tea in the restaurant car his next encounter proved more unsettling. The restaurant car was full when Forest arrived, but he heavily tipped an attendant to find him a seat. The man worked his way down the carriage and finally signalled that he had found a free space. Forest headed towards him only to hesitate when he realised his teatime companion was a Gestapo chief. The man had been pointed out to him as being exceedingly dangerous. Worse, he had been told the chief had been informed about the elusive 'Shelley' and may even have seen a photograph of him. It was a stomach-knotting moment, but if Forest scurried away now he would attract even more attention, so he sat down, his appetite suddenly gone.

The Gestapo man observed him openly. Gold-rimmed glasses framed cruel blue eyes and accentuated the duelling scar that ran down one side of his hard, clean-shaven face. He had a sparkle of hostile amusement in his eyes that pierced Forest 'as though a gimlet were being screwed into his head.'[1]

At the time Forest was unaware that this was Klaus Barbie, the murderer of Jean Moulin. It would have done little to ease his mind had he known the utter barbarism and cruelty that sat before him.

The waiter brought bread, ersatz jam and tea and, relieved, Forest paid attention to his plate rather than his tablemate. However, the Gestapo man was proving rather interested in his new companion. In slow, careful French he asked: 'Are you going to Lyons?'

'I have come from Lyons, monsieur,' Forest answered equally carefully, wondering if his interrogator had already deduced who he was. His stomach was churning as he tried to spread the ersatz jam on his bread and to think of any way to distract the steely eyed Gestapo chief.

Abruptly the train passed by some overturned carriages and trucks, very clear to see from the window. Forest turned his head as if curious and said solemnly: 'Seems to have been a bit of trouble here.' Finding refuge in such a controversial topic was dangerous, but he needed something, anything, to channel the man's curiosity away from him.

'These unfortunate events are always happening,' Barbie replied quite coolly.

There was something about danger that tended to spur Forest on and now he cast caution to the wind and decided to turn the tables on Barbie. With feigned nonchalance he said: 'I am surprised, monsieur, that the German Army has not yet found an effective means of dealing with such acts.'

'Sabotage is like the black market,' Barbie said with a glint of amusement. 'It has so many heads that we cannot strike them all off at once. But rest assured that the German Army will master both these evils in the end.'

Forest was uncomfortably aware that the man could be making an insidious comment directly for Shelley's benefit. He somehow managed to force down his tea and continued talking innocuously about the despicable thing that was the black market.

When the waiter finally brought the bills, Forest resisted the urge to leave quickly, but allowed Barbie to pay and leave first. With a sharp '*Auf Wiedersehen*', his nemesis rose and left the table. Forest hurried to pay his own bill and follow him discreetly to ascertain which carriage he was riding in. Alarmingly, it was Forest's carriage.

There was no knowing if he had been recognised by the unreadable Barbie and he was mortally afraid that at any moment a group of Germans would come to arrest him. Forest spent the rest of his journey – 2 hours – standing in the corridor in case anyone came for him, determined to jump out of a door onto the line before the Germans could lay hands on him. The arresting party never came, but Forest made sure to avoid the gimlet-eyed Barbie when he went for dinner. Finally the train arrived at Paris and Forest hopped off on the wrong side and quickly found a vélo-taxi. He made it to one of his safe houses and counted his blessings that yet another narrow escape had been made.

By now his nerves were almost shot to pieces, before he had even left for Lyons there had been another close call when he went to a rendezvous at a blown safe house, though at the time he was oblivious to the fact. Fortunately he was early, and decided to do a quick security sweep of the locale. To his horror there was a black Citroën with German police marks parked in a side street a short distance from his appointed meeting place. That was clearly not a good sign.

Forest casually walked to the house he was supposed to be meeting in, opened the door and climbed the stairs to the appointed apartment. He listened carefully at the door and was despondent to hear utter silence from inside. It did not bode well. He left the house and dropped into the next-door café, from there he could watch all that was happening.

A short time before his appointment the Citroën swept out of the side road and pulled up before the house. Three men charged in. They hastily returned with the protesting house concierge who was bundled into the car. The Citroën left and the men returned to the building. Forest watched miserably, knowing that his contact was in the clutches of the Germans and that a trap had now been laid for him. Paying for his drink he set off to walk home, on the way passing the same Citroën, which was returning to its former spot in the side road.

The net was closing and Forest knew it was time to get out of Paris. It was with great relief that he heard on the BBC Radio French broadcast the coded message that he was going to be airlifted out shortly. Along with it there was an affectionate note from Barbara, 'from the Sparrow to the Rabbit'.

Despite the risks he was constantly facing there was an element of disappointment as he set off for Arras to meet his Lysander. Brossolette was to stay behind; the decision was made that at least one of the SOE pair should remain at all times to secure the French resistance networks. Forest said an emotional farewell to his friend. Brossolette was a cautious and clever agent, but at the back of his mind Forest couldn't help wondering about all those familiar faces and names that had recently been arrested – some of whom had been equally cautious and clever. He said goodbye and promised to be back soon to relieve him.

Carrying two suitcases, one of which contained the extremely dangerous papers rescued by Berthe on the secret Nazi V-1 weapon, he made an uneventful trip to Arras. His first port of call was to a corset shop, where he was to enquire about an oversized brassiere to indicate to the shopkeeper that he was an agent. Unfortunately there proved to be more than one corset shop in Arras and he went to the wrong one. The female owner of the shop was very keen to make a sale and it was with some difficulty that Forest managed to extract himself and find the correct shop.

Having, eventually, passed the first test he handed over half a 100F note to the corset shop owner who had the other half. Only then was she satisfied enough to send him on to a local perfumery where he had supper before spending the night at the house of a gentleman's outfitter. It seems the resistance of Arras firmly followed fashion.

Forest was just starting to think that the worst was over when he heard that the Lysander operation had been delayed due to bad weather in England. He was used to such problems by now, but then news reached him that a contact Brossolette was due to meet had been arrested. There was no way of knowing if Brossolette had been warned about this development – he could be walking straight into a Nazi trap. Forest's loyalty to his friend had him back on a train to Paris immediately and news that the landing site of the Lysander might be changed meant that he took his incriminating luggage with him.

A Frenchman travelling into Paris with two cases of luggage was not going to be missed by the German authorities. The Germans had instituted body and luggage searches for anyone heading into the capital. Forest could not afford to have his suitcase searched. Ever resourceful, he watched the passengers on the platform, trying to form a plan in his mind. Something subtle, something quick. Two Luftwaffe officers were walking with an orderly and a stack of twelve suitcases: there was no way all the luggage would fit in the already overloaded baggage compartment. As Forest watched, the orderly was forced to put the cases in the corridor of the train and mount a guard over them for the journey.

Forest hopped into the same carriage and set down his suitcases in the same corridor. Using one as a seat he settled down with a cigarette. For a moment he smoked without thinking, then, apparently remembering his manners, he offered a cigarette to the orderly.

'*Danke schön,*' said the orderly.

Forest held a light to the cigarette and the orderly took a deep draw.

'You are very kind,' he said in rudimentary French.

'It is always agreeable to share with someone pleasant,' Forest replied.

At that point in the war Germans had been vilified to the point of utter hatred, and examples such as Klaus Barbie certainly deserved that, but any soldier with sense knew that this was not the whole story. There were many anti-Nazi Germans, and many more whose politics ran no deeper than wanting to defend their country. Conscription had forced the pacifists among the torturers and anyone with an ounce of intelligence knew that there were good Germans as well as bad. Even the communists had qualms about random killings lest they murder a good man or an anti-Nazi. Forest knew this all too well and he recognised in the orderly a man who was doing something he didn't care for and would ideally like to be at home living a normal life. They were soon on friendly terms.

Pulling out a worn photograph from his pocket the gentle German showed Forest his simply dressed wife and fair-haired children with obvious pride and sadness at being so far away. It was yet another reminder that here was a human being, a father, a husband, a man, who missed his loved ones and was as baffled by the war, its politics and its potential outcomes, as most ordinary French and English souls. Forest stared at the picture.

'I've got children too,' he said.

'War is bad for children,' the orderly said sadly, returning the photograph to his pocket. 'For soldiers too, war is bad.'

'War is bad for everyone,' Forest agreed, moved by the man's misery.

'You are right,' sighed the orderly.

Forest found his flask. It was full, on that occasion, of Mirabelle.

'We must drink to the health of our families.' He feigned taking a large swig of the drink then passed it to his companion who took a good swallow.

Offering another cigarette to the German, Forest sat in companionable silence with him, smoking calmly and letting the effects of the alcohol slowly work into his new comrade. After a time he pretended to think of something and, very deliberately, opened the suitcase containing his dangerous documents and removed a chocolate bar, which he presented to the orderly.

'For your children,' he said in stilted German.

The orderly looked on in amazement. Chocolate was scarce in Germany, even for soldiers, and certainly difficult for a minor orderly to obtain. The man was so deeply touched that he put his arms around Forest and thanked him, tears even sparkling in his eyes. It was not just French souls on that train who were driven to despair by the war.

'I think you are a good man,' the orderly said.

'On the contrary,' returned Forest, 'I am a bad man. Listen, I am in trouble.'

'Good men as well as bad man can be in trouble,' the German assured him, and the innocence in his tone made Forest feel a rare pang of guilt.

He was about to fool and potentially endanger this kind German who had caused him no harm and had, indeed, proved to him that it was not the German people who were the enemy, but a government turned foul on itself. But there was no time for regrets – danger was too close.

'You see, it is difficult for a Frenchman to make a living these days,' Forest continued in a world-weary tone. 'To provide for my wife and children, I am forced to do things which I do not like: black market in other words. In this suitcase here I have cigarettes and chocolates, which I am taking to sell in Paris. I don't like doing this sort of thing, but, as I say, I've got responsibilities. And if the police and the customs search my case the goods will be confiscated. And what's even worse I'll be arrested and my family will starve.'

Forest handed over the flask again. The German listened sympathetically, the question of why Forest had not thought of these things sooner, not apparently troubling his mind.

'You do see that I am in difficulties, don't you?' Forest emphasised, passing him another cigarette and then the whole packet.

The German gave a wan smile to his new friend and motioned to the cases stacked behind him. Then he took the suitcase Forest had very carefully taken the chocolate from and slipped it under a couple of valises belonging to the Luftwaffe officers.

'Now I do not think that the police will say much to you.'

The orderly was absolutely right. It was not long before the police and customs officials entered the carriage and began searching people's belongings. Forest offered them his second, perfectly ordinary, suitcase, containing his clothes and nothing incriminating. He had to go through the ordeal of having his pockets searched and his papers inspected, but nothing harmful was found. As the orderly had predicted, the police made no attempt to search the overflow of Nazi luggage.

For the rest of the journey Forest enjoyed talking with the helpful German, his guilt assuaged by the knowledge that he was travelling to rescue Brossolette from arrest. At the Gare du Nord in Paris, Forest helped the orderly offload all of the luggage and was discreetly returned his own. Knowing the Gestapo would be watching, he walked with the orderly to the exit and then, with effusive farewells, they parted. The German orderly never knew he had helped a man who was undermining his country's military force.

Forest's dangerous and rapid race to Paris had not been in vain; Brossolette was surprised at his unexpected return, but even more so by the news of his agent's arrest. He had not known and would have attended the meeting as planned and stepped straight into a Gestapo trap.

Of course, as usual, SOE life was never easy and when Forest listened to the BBC that evening he learned from a cryptic message that his rendezvous had been returned to Arras – he could have left his luggage after all and spared himself a nerve-wracking train journey!

At 1 p.m. he was back on the train, having left Jose Dupuis with instructions to help another circuit in his absence and having temporarily loaned Maud to Brossolette as a reliable *agent de liaison*. There was no Gestapo chief or kindly orderly to talk to this time, so instead Forest stared out his window at the carnage being inflicted on the German transport network by *his* people. Along the track the scattered remains of four derailed ammunitions trains created a morbid tableau of French patriotism. Overturned guns, damaged light tanks and ruined lorries littered the ground, while scavenging parties of German soldiers and French civilians sifted through the rubble for anything that could be salvaged. Was Forest proud? Undoubtedly. This was what he was here for, to see humble men and women rise to fight the Nazi monster. If he allowed himself a slight smile at the carnage it was only in secret; in public he would be an arch-critic of such grim and unfriendly action.

Back in Arras he spent his last few hours gathering lists of supplies from the resistance leaders. Their wish list included automatics, silenced pistols, daggers, rifles, grenades and lots more ammunition. As an adjunct to this horrific Christmas list, they also needed Benzedrine tablets, woollens, wind jackets, better torches, batteries, food and money.

The Arras resistance had arranged a landing site for the operation in an area dense with German patrols. It was not ideal, but few landing sites were truly secure now that the Nazis had upped their vigilance and expanded their net of collaboration. Fortunately the good shopkeepers of Arras had come up with a solution and, like a scene from a farce, Forest was to journey to meet the Lysander in a hearse. Pretending to be a corpse to evade the Germans had a certain irony to it and Forest could only hope that it was not an omen of things to come as he clambered into the motor hearse under the watchful gaze of local undertaker Monsieur Bisiaux. It was the first time any of his clients had helped themselves into the vehicle!

Seated with him in this novel mode of transport were two women, Marcelle Virolle and Mademoiselle Pichard, also destined for return to England. They huddled in the cramped, dark quarters of the hearse, unable to see outside or know what was happening. Forest had his Colt in his shoulder holster and a sten gun near to hand. The sten might not be the most accurate of weapons but it was fast and a burst of bullets would cause damage to any curious German inspecting the hearse. The vehicle rolled off at a leisurely speed. Bisiaux was ready with the cover story that he was driving a corpse to a church for a funeral the next day; this was a regular occurrence to spare local sensibilities the sight of mortality.

The hearse rolled unpleasantly. Suspension was not a prime concern for the occupant of a coffin, and besides they were usually secured, unlike the very alive passengers that Bisiaux was carrying that night. Forest and the two girls bumped about and flew from side to side on sharp turns. The sten cracked into Forest's thigh and left him bruised, while the women started to shiver from the cold. He offered them his ever-present flask of alcohol.

Forest couldn't tell how long he had been trapped in the cocoon of the hearse when the vehicle ominously slowed and the sound of heavy boots could be heard approaching. Everyone froze. Outside, the guttural tone of a German could be heard asking a series of questions to which Bisiaux answered quickly and concisely, it was not possible to know exactly what was being said through the muffling walls of the hearse and Forest quietly cocked the sten gun in case the worst happened. Silence suddenly fell. Forest aimed his sten at the dark shadows where the back door of the hearse was, quite prepared to spray bullets if the German should open the door. There was not a sound.

Then suddenly the heavy boots could be heard striding away and within a moment Bisiaux had started up the hearse and they were rumbling on again. Forest let his breath out through clenched teeth. That was yet one more narrow escape to add to his list.

Shortly after this encounter, the hearse slowed again, but this time it was to enable a contingent of resistance men to form a guard around it. From then on any interested German would have to get past twenty armed men if they wanted to inspect the vehicle.

There was a further stop at a farmhouse where Forest would wait out the last few hours before boarding his plane. A hot meal was a welcome sight as they arrived and even more reassuring was the resistance leader's confirmation that his men were guarding the farm and would follow them to the landing site.

'The only way the Germans will get you,' he promised, 'is if they have killed me and every one of my helpers.'

Forest hoped that it wouldn't come to that. At midnight he headed for the chosen landing site, and at regular intervals guards emerged from the bushes to confirm their identity, which further reassured him that at least security was being taken seriously in Arras. The plane was also on schedule and although there was a slight concern about the space available for take-off, everything went smoothly enough. One of the women discovered that she was indisposed to air travel and while perched on Forest's knee (there was not room for everyone to sit down) she had to endure a bilious journey to England.

London was a stark change from the constant drama of Paris. Suddenly Forest was back in a world of stiff upper lips and pompous military hierarchy. An Air Ministry officer reprimanded him for not updating his uniform according to the latest orders. As the orders had only been issued a month before, Forest had the perfect excuse: he had been risking his life undercover in France. This failed to impress the officer, however. Even more depressing was the crisp white envelope he found at his house, pushed through the letterbox by some 'kindly' neighbour. Inside was a white feather and a note with the word 'COWARD' emblazoned on it. Apparently someone was under the impression that Forest was sitting out the war in an administrative role. He could hardly contradict them, though for his pride it was a bitter pill to swallow.

....

Note

1. Marshal, *Op cit.*

11

Farewell, Dear Brossolette

THE FOURTH YEAR OF the war was slowly drawing to a close with Forest sitting back behind a desk glowering at the future. Men who excel at wartime adventures rarely find peace in less hazardous work. Forest was frustrated. Brossolette was still deep in France and the snippets of news filtering into London suggested that his continued presence was becoming more and more risky.

Meanwhile the usual politics had Forest almost tearing his hair out. He had composed a damning report of Sophie and Baudet after his experiences in France, but there were supporters of the pair in London who refused to believe the allegations. Instead they set out to blacken Brossolette's name and, by extension, Forest's. Even the officials Forest was reporting to were torn by the remarks. Forest knew all this but could do nothing about it. Instead he was put in an office interviewing prospective candidates for the Jedburgh teams SOE was forming.[1]

He was also increasingly troubled about Brossolette's safety in France. There was no doubting now that the Germans were actively searching for him and he needed to be rescued as soon as possible.

He was not the only one who was concerned. In December 1943 the Free French decided that it was time to bring back Brossolette and another agent, Emile Bollaert. Forest was given the task of organising the rescue operation and relished the chance to finally be doing something that could directly benefit his friend. He arranged for two Lysanders carrying four agents to France to pick up Brossolette and Bollaert before returning home.

On 10 December he drove to Tangmere airfield with the four nervous new agents. The Lysanders were ready and waiting for them, but the door of the plane was as far as Forest could go. He wished the men well and, despite poor weather, the aircraft took off on time. There was nothing Forest could do but wait for their return, hopefully with Brossolette safe and sound.

It was impossible not to have some concerns about the dangers of the operation. Every time an aircraft took off on operations during the war there was a high chance that it would not be coming back. Forest was a realist. He knew the risks, the many things, both mundane and disastrous, that could go wrong and cause the mission to abort. But he had to cling to the hope that soon his friend would be safely back in England.

Five hours passed and then the whine of an engine indicated the return of one of the Lysanders. Forest got up anxiously, but when the door opened he was disheartened to see the same agent he had wished-well only a few hours before, exiting it. The bad weather had deteriorated during the flight and it had been impossible for the pilot to make out the landing site. In the end he had had to return without landing.

There was still the hope for the second Lysander and Forest sat down to wait again. Two more hours passed, making it seven since the second Lysander had taken off. The time far exceeded the amount of fuel the aircraft had had for the journey and there was no longer any doubt that some accident had befallen it. Forest returned to London disappointed and more worried than ever about his friend.

As usual it took a couple of days for news about what had happened to filter in. The second Lysander had never even made it to the landing site. It had been shot down in a hail of anti-aircraft fire, killing the pilot and his passengers. The agents had never even had a chance to begin their work in France.

News on Brossolette was equally discouraging. While waiting at the landing site he heard that his safe house had been raided by the Germans, so when his aircraft failed to show he had to flee back to Paris. With the weather in England getting worse there was no hope of launching another mission soon and Brossolette was getting desperate.

In a message sent to London, Brossolette indicated that he was making arrangements with SIS (MI6) to get home on one of their cross-Channel naval operations. Forest was not pleased with this news and tried to convince his friend to hang on for another three weeks when the next moon period would enable him to send more Lysanders. For the time being Brossolette relented and agreed to wait.

It is hard to imagine the terror that hung over Brossolette in those last few days. Constantly on guard and with the dread that another Lysander operation might prove similarly abortive, he spent his days hiding from sight and watching his back. The burden of the fear must have become overwhelming – no surprise then that eventually he could take the situation no more and again started pursuing SIS sea routes for his escape.

Forest was unaware that Brossolette was reneging on his promise – he was working hard to have himself sent back to France to replace his friend as well as doggedly promoting the Maquis cause for greater numbers of parachute supply drops. There was nothing lacking in Forest's determination and the culmination of his efforts was an interview with Prime Minister Winston Churchill to plead his case. In fact there had already been long discussions in Whitehall about the irregular drops being delivered to the Maquis and Forest's opinion on the matter probably helped Churchill get the personal insight into the problem that enabled him to win the debate. The very next day Churchill was sending direct instructions that the amount of supplies to the Maquis should be increased and that not even bad weather should stall SOE's endeavour to arm their secret army.

It was brilliant news for Forest, but his jubilation was short-lived. Arriving for work one day he was told that Brossolette had been arrested trying to use one of the SIS sea routes. Forest later recorded: 'The blow was stunning. For a few seconds I was numbed, then my brain began to function again, thoughts came rushing through my head, in a flash I relived all our adventures.'[2]

Though angry that his friend had disregarded his advice, he was hardly surprised, knowing the dangers that Brossolette faced. More importantly his mind raced about what to do for the best. It seemed the Germans were currently unaware of the significance of their arrest, but it would only be a matter of time before the dye Brossolette used to mask his distinctive white streak would fade and his real identity would become clear. He had to do something to rescue his friend and as his conscience tortured him about leaving his comrades behind for the safety of London, he began to plan his third mission.

What really happened to Brossolette? At the beginning of February Brossolette and Bollaert managed to secure passage on a SIS vessel. As is apparent he had already waited far longer than the three weeks Forest had begged him for and with the Germans snapping at his heels he could hardly be blamed for looking for another way to escape when his promised Lysanders seemed to have forgotten him. One night in February the pair boarded the *Jouet des Flots*, a small cargo vessel working for SIS, at Brittany. The plan was that the vessel would sail them all the way to Cornwall, but what happened next was pure bad luck.

When coming into shore in the depths of night the captain of the *Jouet des Flots* misjudged the tides and the vessel struck the bottom and sprang a leak. Even so, it should be able to limp to England, so the thirty-one passengers boarded and hoped for the best. It was not to be their night. The sea was stormy and in the heavy swells the engine became flooded and then failed, and before long *Jouet des Flots* was sinking. Her captain managed to beach her at Feunteunot Creek, near Plogoff, before she was lost completely and his entire passenger list was disembarked once again.

Fortunately the local resistance were well organised in the area and they rescued Brossolette and temporarily housed him at a local inn, planning to move him inland the next day. As promised a car called for Brossolette and Bollaert and they set off inland, tired and frustrated. It was not long before they ran into a German roadblock. The car's papers and the false ones of the two agents were perfectly in order and could not be faulted, but the Germans on duty that day were clearly suspicious and after close questioning they found a crack in the men's seeming ordinariness: they had no papers granting them permission to be in the Special Coastal Security Zone.

It was an appalling oversight. Somehow missed in the panic to get away, the vital missing papers placed Brossolette directly in the Germans' hands, even if, for the time being at least, they were unaware of his significance. Whether SIS or Brossolette himself were to blame for the error, it was a foolish mistake. There was at least some consolation that the arresting Germans believed his false identity of Paul Boutet.

Rescuing him was imperative. Forest was desperate to save his friend, but loyalty would not be enough to sway his superiors into allowing him to go back to France. He had to make it clear to them how dangerous it would be to the resistance as a whole if Brossolette was identified: 'If I got caught, I knew all that there was to know about the underground but, even more dangerous,

1. American Troops – Forest's father saw to it that he was unable to join French or British troops in the First World War, so he had to wait until the Americans joined the conflict before he could sign up.

2. After the First World War Forest had numerous jobs, but he found his niche working for fashion designer Molyneux and attending the well-to-do ladies of the 1930s.

3. After the First World War General Pétain was seen as a hero and led a triumphal parade through Paris.

4. General Pétain, French hero and leader of the Vichy government.

5. With the Second World War looming, many old soldiers wanted to avoid a return to trench warfare and started to make plans for defences.

6. Trench warfare had left its scars on France, and General Pétain, among others, pushed for a defensive barricade for the French borders; this became the Maginot Line.

7. The Maginot Line was one war too late. It failed in its task of keeping the Germans out and soaked up money that could have been placed into armaments.

8. Neville Chamberlein, seen here pre-war (*back row, second from right*) founded SOE as his last political act before his death.

9. Hitler surged to power in the 1930s and was quickly clamouring for another war. Forest joined up as soon as he realised the threat.

10. By the Second World War Petain was an old man and he voted for appeasement instead of war. He founded the Vichy government, which briefly kept southern France unoccupied. He was recognised by SOE as a threat as serious as the Gestapo to their operations.

11. Place de la Concorde was one of the first ports of the city to be triumphantly taken by the Nazis. German planes landed in the square while swastikas went up on the buildings.

12. General de Gaulle opposed Petain and fled to England to set up a government in exile. Forest was an ardent Gaullist and met the man personally. De Gaulle stands here at the tomb of the Unknown Soldier after the Liberation of Paris.

13. Forest knew it was the ordinary people who would suffer most in the war and made close ties with rural communities where resistance was strong. Here, French women continue to harvest chestnuts while war rages around them.

14. The old and infirm had no place in the Nazi ideal and were often kicked from their homes or executed.

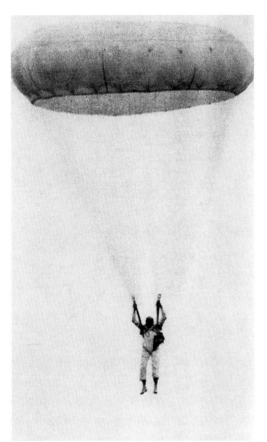

15. Forest's first attempt at parachuting scared the life out of him; it was a dangerous business and many SOE agents broke bones with bad landings.

16. France was quickly crippled by the Nazis and when Forest returned to it in 1943 his beloved country was decimated. The destruction only made him more determined to fight back.

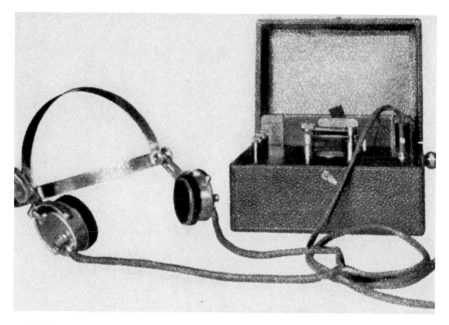

17. Wireless sets were a constant nightmare. Difficult to hide and awkward to repair, they were the bane of SOE. Forest had to use them to send back messages, but he knew the risk involved. This example is an early Marconi set.

18. Wireless-detection vans had been first designed to track pirate radios, as this British picture demonstrates. The Germans used them to track SOE agents reporting in and, over the course of the war, developed them to the point that the detection unit could be carried by a single man.

19. Barns and outbuildings proved havens for resistance men and women. Forest spent a lot of his time in rural France in such places. Unfortunately, many were raided by the Germans and their occupants murdered.

20. Jean Moulin with his good looks and charm united the early resistance, though he fell out of favour with Forest and Brossolette. When he was arrested and accidentally killed by the Gestapo, the resistance came close to falling apart and it was agreed that never again would it be united under one figurehead.

21. On his train journey from Lyons, Forest distracted the fearsome Klaus Barbie by noting the train wreckage out the windows. Teams of Germans and French civilians scrounged the debris for salvage.

22. Forest had the sense to know not all Germans were evil and when he met ordinary individuals he felt friendly towards them. He gave one German orderly some chocolate to take home to his children.

23. One of the worst tragedies for Forest was the unknown musician who was arrested by the Gestapo because his telephone number appeared on a bank note in Forest's wallet. The man was innocent, but probably perished in Gestapo hands.

24. Passy Métro station, Paris. The site of Forest's disastrous arrest. (Copyright Mbzt/Wikimedia Commons)

PIERRE BROSSOLETTE
HÉROS DE LA RÉSISTANCE

A HABITÉ CETTE MAISON
DE 1932 À 1944

25. Plaque commemorating the heroic Pierre Brossolette; he is still well remembered in French history and has a road named after him. (Copyright Mu/ Wikimedia Commons)

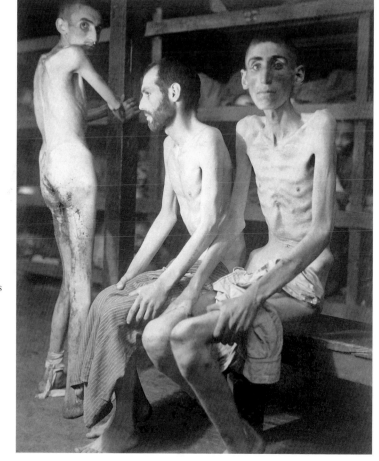

26. Buchenwald inmates – Forest's first sight of the people who he would be living with was an awful shock; they were little more than skeletons with skin. These individuals are slave labourers of multi-nationality. (By Permission of The National Archives)

27. Buchenwald Bodies – Forest's grimmest task was gathering the dead; it was often overwhelming and each corpse had to be stripped before disposal. (Copyright Zairon/Wikimedia Commons)

28. The no-man's-land Forest had to cross as the last portion of his escape attempt was all too reminiscent of the First World War. He did not make it across, being captured at the last minute by Germans.

29. Forest's final bid for freedom involved running through a minefield with gunfire all around.

SECRET & PERSONAL.
HNS/1870.   9th May, 1945.

          As we arranged at lunch, I am sending
you a copy of the letter from Squadron-Leader
Yeo-Thomas which I told you about.

          Now that we have the good news that
the writer is alive and on his way home, we will
postpone our decision about giving publicity to
this appalling document until we know Yeo-Thomas'
own views.

          In view of this, I am sure you will
not give the letter too wide a circulation.

Commander Ian Fleming,
     Admiralty.

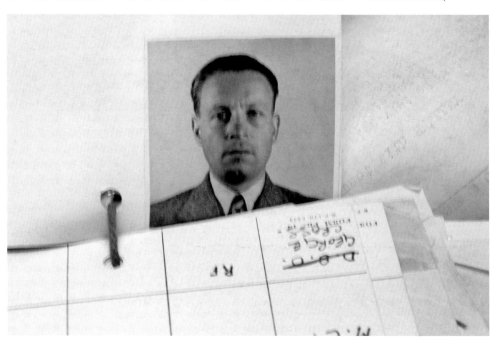

30. The Ian Fleming letter commenting on the amazing survival of Forest, and the picture of him on file. (By permission of The National Archives)

I knew a very great deal about our staff planning. Supposing I talked under torture, I could give away a tremendous lot of information.'[3]

With arguments like this Forest made it clear that Brossolette had to be extracted, no matter the risks. On 15 February the draft plan for Forest's newest operation, Asymptote, was submitted to the head of RF Section. Significantly it ignored Forest's intentions to rescue Brossolette and instead emphasised that this was another fact-finding mission designed to reinforce the security of the networks and ensure that they did not fall apart after the arrests of Brossolette and Bollaert as they had done after the loss of Jean Moulin. Forest decided that it was safest not to quibble about the wording; once in France he could do as he pleased, the important thing was getting there.

In the midst of all this, Barbara was conveniently left in the dark. She had devoted herself to Forest's work with SOE, learning French, entertaining his colleagues and even joining the BCRA, but increasingly she found it hard to accept her lover's attraction to danger. No sooner did she have him home to safety then he was yearning to be back in the action. Was it so wrong that she resented the loyalty he had for Brossolette when it seemed to completely override the loyalty he had to her?

It was no wonder then that Forest failed to tell her about Asymptote. Years later, with the war behind him, Forest realised the emotional agony he had put Barbara through, but at the time he was caught up in the whirlwind of events and nothing could deter him from returning to France. Was he right or wrong? Perhaps neither, or perhaps both. In wartime, loyalties inevitably become torn and for every serviceman that risked his life, whether at sea, in a plane or on land, there was a loved one waiting in misery at home for them to return, or not. Forest had his duty and for that he would risk Barbara's love.

The first she knew of his intention to go back to France was when the wife of a BCRA officer phoned her and asked if she would like to visit once Forest had gone abroad. Understandably Barbara was furious. Accosting Forest with the information, he played on the age-old excuse 'I was going to tell you' and did his best to avoid her wrath. Barbara could not be appeased however, and in utter fury told him that even if he returned from this mission she would not be there to welcome him back. With the arrogance that was a prevalent part of Forest's character, he told her equally bluntly that he was certain she would be waiting for him. With this discord still playing on his mind he finished his preparations for his mission.

There was an atmosphere of apprehension surrounding the preparations for Asymptote. Forest's friends made efforts to dissuade him via Barbara, but their currently tempestuous relations made her in no fit state to persuade him. It did not help her state of mind that even senior members at the BCRA were convinced that Forest was heading for his death if he journeyed to France.

They were not the only ones with concerns. Forest was riddled with his own doubts and a deep sense of foreboding enveloped him: 'For the first time, I had a feeling of impending disaster. I had a premonition that this time I would not get away with it...'

He even felt compelled to make a will, something he had not even considered before, but Forest was not usually a superstitious man and he pushed the doubts aside. Even so he asked to be issued with a Welwand, the latest in SOE's extensive catalogue of unique weapons. The Welwand, popularly known as a Sleeve Gun, looked like an uninspiring stick but was designed to be an assassination weapon or a last-resort device if an agent was captured. Attached on a lanyard up the agent's sleeve so as to be hidden, it could be easily released by detaching the lanyard from a button on an agent's belt, which enabled the Welwand to slip into his hand. Preloaded and with a silencer, the gun would fire a single shot without ejecting the bullet cartridge or making a noise. Forest acquired one of the latest models, which fired a .32 bullet, and hoped for Barbara's sake that he was never in a situation requiring its use.

There were more concerns about the outcome of his mission when continual bad weather forced SOE to consider sending Forest outside the normal moon period. This would mean he would not benefit from moonlight to guide his path or help him find his reception committee. Despite the risks he agreed to the arrangement.

He was destined to fly on 24 February, and he ate a farewell meal with Barbara. A number of his friends came to see him off, only increasing his dread that something would go wrong on his mission. He had an overwhelming desire to run back to Barbara as he got into the car, and had a terrible anxiety in his stomach that he would never see her again, but then he was on his way to the airfield and to his newest mission.

There was nothing auspicious about Forest's latest mission. Loaded into a Halifax with another agent, codenamed Trieur, the flight over the coast was the usual run of anti-aircraft flak. It would have been easy for Forest to let his mind slip back to that mission in December when the Lysander and its cargo of agents perished in the storm of German fire. But the Halifax ran into no difficulties and it wasn't long before they were circling over the landing site at Clermont-Ferrand.

Parachuting in moonlight was not exactly easy, but in the darkness of an almost moonless night it seemed impossible. Forest hooked himself to the static line and stared down at the reassuring lights of the reception committee. The despatcher on the aircraft had told him it would be a 20 second drop, which at least meant the ordeal would not last long. A hand fell on his shoulder to signal that the Halifax was in position and Forest launched himself through the hole. Seconds can seem like minutes during such a drop. Forest was counting steadily, his mind focused on preparing himself for a smooth landing. As he reached 13 seconds he smacked into the ground with a force like a car slamming into a wall. Forest was knocked unconscious by the surprise impact. The pilot had misjudged his distance and instead of flying at 500ft had clearly been much closer to the ground. When Forest came round it was to be greeted by the concerned face of the reception committee organiser and a sharp pain in his ankle. Unsure whether he had broken anything he managed to hobble with the reception committee to a secure farmhouse, half a mile away. Trieur had dropped safely in the next field and joined them shortly.

The injury to Forest's ankle proved to be a sprain and, although by the next morning it was swollen, it had not dampened his determination to reach Paris as soon as he could. Along with Trieur he was bundled into an old bus driven by a French farmer and escorted along rutted icy roads at breathtaking speed. Along the way novice agent Trieur had a heart-stopping moment when gendarmes entered the bus to check their papers. Fearing that there might be something incriminating on his SOE forged papers, or that he would be searched and his hidden revolver and sabotage plans discovered, he could barely contain his nerves as the inspection proceeded. Glancing over his shoulder at Forest he realised with envy that his fellow agent had managed to fall asleep and had to be woken to present his papers. Of course Forest was the master of catching forty winks whenever he could, knowing that any moment he might be called upon to perform some exhausting feat of espionage or escape.

Paris loomed. Forest lost no time in contacting his old colleagues. A BBC message had informed them of his imminent return and they were delighted, though apprehensive. Maud welcomed him with open arms; she was one of his bravest and most loyal followers. Jacqueline Devaux was persuaded to find a safe house for Trieur, who had entered Paris with no contacts aside from Forest. He was alarmingly unprepared for his adventure and Forest spent some time giving him hard-earned advice from his previous experiences. Finally settled in his flat at Neuilly, he began his legitimate mission objectives, while also surreptitiously planning his Brossolette operation.

Morale among the resistance had sunk again. That hardly surprised Forest, but it had less to do with the arrest of Brossolette and more to do with the lack of arms being dropped from England. There had been no new supplies in months and this had led to feelings of despondency and discouragement. How could a resistance movement remain active without the necessary weapons and money to fuel them? Forest fell into the consolation role, telling his comrades about his meeting with Churchill and the prime minister's promise for 200 planes a month to be sent on missions to France. He had no idea if SOE would stand by such orders, but he had to give his followers some hope and, at least for the time being, they were satisfied that things would improve.

That is, all but the communists were satisfied. They had other grievances to air to Forest. Why were their operators, despite being well trained and efficient, not being allowed to work on reception committees? Biting his tongue over the communists' refusal to work with SOE yet expecting everything in return, he put them in touch with some of his colleagues so that they might share in the supplies. More than ever, in this tense political minefield, he missed the cool composure and sour wit of Brossolette, who was so able to cut through all this nonsense.

For a new mission Forest needed a new identity. In fact he had several, but his most comprehensive, the one that would hopefully stand up to Gestapo inspection, was that of Squadron-Leader Dodkin. SOE always put a great deal of energy into cover stories, knowing that they could often be the key to a man's success or failure in the field. It was always advisable that an agent take on an identity he was familiar with – there was no point pretending to be a dentist when in real life the operator was a greengrocer, that would only lead to complications and blown cover at some point – so it was logical for Forest's new identity to be an RAF man.

He borrowed his cover from an actual living person. Squadron-Leader Dodkin was on the operational flying list, however he had been grounded permanently and there was no way he could end up back over France, but the Germans did not know that. So Forest spent several hours with Dodkin learning his life history, picking up his mannerisms and any useful titbits of information that would turn him into a believable replica. It was not common practice for agents to swap identity with a real person, but as Forest pointed out, if he was arrested the only way he could avoid torture and interrogation was by claiming that he was in uniform and thus had to be treated as a prisoner of war rather than a spy. This was a very complicated point in the regulations of war. In general terms, if a man was arrested in his military uniform he should automatically be deemed a prisoner of war and thus would forego the appalling treatment meted out to supposed spies. He could also not just 'vanish', and the Red Cross would have to be informed of his presence. It was a loophole in the rules of warfare that the Gestapo were constantly trying to outmanoeuvre.

Though unorthodox, the switch was accepted and new identity discs in the name of Dodkin were created for Forest.

Alongside his Dodkin persona he also had papers in the name of a French engineer. These were slightly more dangerous as Forest was no engineer and would not be able to stand up to detailed interrogation, but they gave him the advantage of being able to move freely without suspicion.

In between his official duties Forest made enquiries after Brossolette. Early news was promising: he was being held in Rennes prison, still under the identity of Paul Boutet. Brossolette was using all his ingenuity to orchestrate his own escape and had bribed a guard to pass messages out of the prison. Maud was passing messages back, hidden in his laundry and had visited him under the guise of being his mistress. Brossolette was optimistic and had begun requesting materials to aid his escape, including saws and chloroform, and was working on developing a clear mental map of the prison. Forest realised that he had some breathing space and decided to lay his plans with infinite care.

He first visited Rennes in March to reconnoitre the prison and assess his options. His initial thought was to arrange for Brossolette to be transferred to a different prison in the south of France on trumped-up charges. He even spent time with a lawyer in the resistance to discuss the possibility. During Brossolette's transfer, the plan would be to attack his escort and free him, but a host of problems quickly presented themselves. The most significant was that too many people would have to be made aware of Brossolette's real identity and there was no way of including Bollaert in the transfer, so he would have to be left behind.

Having to think again about his plan, Forest visited the outskirts of the prison to gain inspiration. Almost opposite the main gates of the building was a grocer's shop. The grocer was a member of the resistance and from his vantage point he had an unparalleled opportunity to spy on the prison. He also numbered most of the guards and officials (French and German) among his customers. Idle talk in his shop had given the grocer an incredible understanding of the workings of the prison, which he now shared with Forest. He explained that the majority of the prison was now in German hands and only a few cells remained free for French use. The main gate was the most heavily guarded, but all entrances were kept closed and watched by a sentry armed with a light machine gun. A direct line from the guard room of the prison ran to the local SS barracks no more than 600yds away, so the slightest sign of trouble would have a German division hurrying to the prison.

Forest spent some time discovering the route of the telephone line and working out the easiest location for it to be cut, but even without SS assistance the force within the prison would be too formidable for a frontal attack to have a good chance of succeeding. Subterfuge was needed. Forest hit on the idea of dressing three resistance members as personnel of the German SD division (an intelligence division) and having them present false papers to the guards ordering the transfer of Brossolette and Bollaert. The normal course of events would be for the guard who received the order to double-check it with the Gestapo before releasing the prisoners. To do this he would have to use the phone in the guardroom. His visitors would, naturally, accompany him. But once in the guardroom he would be overpowered before the call could be made.

The best German speaker among the pretend SD men would then return to the gate and ask for it to be opened so that his car could enter, and passers-by would not witness the transfer. The driver would ensure that once his car was inside, it was positioned in such a way that the guard could not close the gates. The remaining SD impersonators would enter the prison proper with the corporal of the guard who would release the prisoners to them. If he became suspicious he could be persuaded at the barrel of a gun to continue to cooperate. Once the prisoners were out of their cells and in the car they would be driven a short distance and then transferred to a different vehicle and taken to a safe house. The original car would be driven south, leaving a clear trail to fool pursuers.

It was an audacious and complicated scheme, with a lot that could go wrong, but it seemed the best plan to secure Brossolette's safety. Even so, it could not be implemented until a number of elements had been brought together, not least the finding of resistance members who spoke German without an accent and were fluent enough to pass as SD men. Forest returned to Paris, leaving the details in the hands of trusted colleagues, and continued his official Asymptote work. He was feeling optimistic and buoyant. His early dread about the mission had faded and he was thrilled to be back in the action.

He did have other thoughts on his mind than just restoring resistance morale, however. He asked Jose Dupuis if she could contact his estranged wife and request that at a pre-arranged time his daughters would be standing in the window of their apartment, so he might walk past and get a brief glimpse of them. The request was flatly turned down.

Lillian Yeo-Thomas' blunt refusal to let her husband see their girls may seem petty, but there was more behind her motives than was known to Forest. At the time of his request his eldest daughter Evelyn was gravely ill with meningitis and on 18 March 1944 she died. Jose Dupuis discovered Evelyn's illness when she paid a visit to Forest's father, who had just received a telegram informing him. Dupuis made the difficult decision to say nothing to Forest, fearful that if she did he would forget his own security and try to see Evelyn either at home or at the hospital, dangerously exposing himself. The guilt that Dupuis felt at deceiving her closest friend was only made worse by the knowledge that soon she would also be leaving him. The Gestapo were finally catching up with Dupuis and Forest instructed her to leave Paris immediately. She did so, unaware that the calamity she dreaded was about to fall upon Forest.

Meanwhile in Rennes, German ignorance of Brossolette's identity proved more fleeting than the resistance had hoped. The discovery was once again caused by a failure by Sophie and Baudet to encode a message sent to London via Spain. The message outlined Brossolette and Bollaert's arrest and while it used codenames for the two men it was not exactly difficult for the Abwehr to work out its significance when they intercepted the courier entrusted with it.

On 17 March, the day before Evelyn's death, an Abwehr officer and a member of the Paris SD interviewed the two captives. The SD man had been attached to the German consulate in Lyon prior to the war and recognised Bollaert as a former prefect of the Rhone department. Brossolette endeavoured to stick to his Boutet identity, but with Bollaert blown, the Germans were not foolish enough to think that Brossolette was not somehow involved in the resistance. Both men were soon on their way to the SD headquarters, well aware of the fate that was in store for them.

There was still an aura of uncertainty among the Germans about Brossolette's real identity, but they were convinced that they would resolve that soon, using their familiar strategies. SD torture methods followed a pattern: there was a general beating, with interludes of interrogation, then usually the bath torture, where the victim was semi-drowned and then revived only to be drowned again. Forest was mere hours away from enduring this himself as Brossolette was abused and bloodied at the avenue Foch, the beautiful tree-lined street that the SD had taken over for their own purposes.

Brossolette would have lost track of time during the ordeal, which would have seemed eternal. He would also have known that escape was unlikely: there was only one way out and that was death. He began to think that if the Germans did not kill him with their methods he would have to take matters into his own hands. Resistance members and SOE were pragmatic about the odds of surviving torture without revealing something. Unlike in Hollywood movies where the hero unflinchingly endures pain at the hands of his enemies without uttering a word, in the real world of espionage few were able to hold their tongues forever. No one could predict if they would break under torture, but most would, if not completely then partially. For many the consequences for their comrades would not be huge, but for a man like Brossolette weakening under duress could result in the destruction of all he had worked for.

With all this in mind Brossolette knew he could not risk another session with his interrogators. Before beginning his resistance career he had informed his wife, sister and Claire Davinroy that should he be captured he would take his own life. He had come to the conclusion that the risk of caving under torture would simply be too great, but his options for death were limited. His cyanide pill had been lost long ago during his captivity, and being handcuffed meant that most forms of suicide were impossible for him. As he lay in a former maid's bedroom on the fifth floor of one of the SD's picturesque houses he sized up his options. His guard was outside his locked door, not particularly concerned about the danger posed by a badly beaten and semi-conscious prisoner. The room did not offer much hope, but there was a balcony outside the window that had carelessly been left open.

With what little strength he had left Brossolette dragged himself to the balcony and tumbled over the side. In later renditions of the story he would be described as jumping through a glass window in the middle of interrogation, leaving his interviewers dumbfounded and stunned. In reality his death was a last act of desperation.

Brossolette fell five floors but survived long enough to be rushed to hospital. The verdict of the doctors was that the suicide would be complete within hours. At midnight Brossolette breathed his last. His final words were recorded as: 'Everything will be better on Tuesday.' The Germans had lost yet another of their prime adversaries.

Forest had no knowledge of the terrible tragedy that had befallen his friend and with his mind on the rescue at Rennes, he travelled to Passy Métro for that fateful meeting with Antonin. It was ironic that within hours the two best resistance organisers and closest friends would both fall into enemy hands. Forest was arrested within sight of his father's flat, by the tell-tale pointing finger of Antonin. Thinking only that he would now be unable to help Brossolette, he was bundled into a car and beaten as he was driven to the Gestapo headquarters. He would arrive at the avenue Foch an hour after Brossolette's final flight from a fifth-floor window.

....

Notes

1. Jedburghs were the only uniformed teams SOE sent to France. They were multi-national trios sent in to coordinate the various Maquis groups and take part in guerrilla warfare to distract the Germans while the British invaded.
2. Seaman, *Op cit.*
3. *Ibid.*

12

The White Rabbit and the German Wolf

THE GERMANS HAD THEIR man. Bundled into a Citroën the elated Gestapo men inflicted blows and punches to Forest's head while cheerfully singing: 'We've got Shelley. English Officer. Terrorist. *Schweinehund. Scheisskert.*'

Forest felt as though his head had swollen beyond all proportion and blood was pouring freely over his shirt. Despite this he endured the abuse with a strange feeling of disconnection. It was a remarkable skill of self-preservation that enabled him to shut himself down to the pain and humiliation, to view it almost with disinterest as though he was watching something being done to another man. It was this rare ability that would later help him survive the worse tortures his captors had in mind.

Forest later recalled that during this car journey he found himself surprisingly clear headed and able to consider his position in a rational manner. We can take this statement at face value or accept that it may in part come from a man in post-war Britain trying to think the best of himself. Forest's early personal accounts read very much like this throughout, he rarely accepted weakness in himself and he certainly would not allow it to be published publically with his knowledge. Unfortunately the first two pages of Forest's official report of the arrest, written on his return to Britain after the war, are missing from the SOE files, so we cannot tell how his official candid description of that drive tallied with what he told his biographer. Perhaps he was the incredibly calm and logical figure he portrayed, but it is too tempting to feel that the reality was far more human. Did Forest really spend his drive conjuring up ideas of how to preserve his silence under torture with indifference to his tormentors? More likely his thoughts came in random, panicked bursts. He must not let them know his real surname lest they go after his father – a shot of fear – he would pretend to be Dodkin still. He had left his identity tags at home – a stab of dread – no, no, that could work to his advantage as it would be illogical for a secret agent to publically carry tags with his real identity on them. Would anyone take on the reins of the rescue mission for Brossolette? If Forest had only known his friend was already in Gestapo hands and taking his suicide jump he never would have stood in Passy Métro and found himself in German clutches.

The ordeal was briefly paused as they arrived at Gestapo headquarters and Forest was dragged inside. His guards were still shouting excitedly about their catch and shoved him into an office where three men were seated. The men's initial bafflement at the sudden appearance of Forest was quickly lost when his guards jubilantly yelled: 'We have Shelley!'

No time was lost in beating him again and the three new Germans inflicted their own share of punches until Forest was virtually insensible. Then he was stripped naked, forced to stand on a telephone directory with his heels together and his hands handcuffed behind his back, and made to watch while the Germans searched his belongings for anything incriminating.

While Forest always had the sense to carry no paperwork other than his false identity papers, there were other objects among his belongings that left no doubt as to his role in the resistance. In his pocket he was carrying a pen containing tear-gas and, stripped naked, he could not hide the pistol still in its holster and strapped to his thigh. Upon finding these the Germans flew into another rage and beat him again, levelling several hard kicks to his groin. Somehow Forest managed to remain on the telephone directory, no doubt if he had fallen off he would have received even worse for his vulnerability.

In between the abuse the search continued. Two monocles given to Forest by SOE to help him change his identity quickly drew unexpected scorn from his captors, who threw them to the floor and ground them beneath their heels. There was something so bizarre, so petty, about the scene that Forest laughed and earned himself another beating.

The monocles were an amusing find, but the discovery of four sets of keys was deadly serious. Forest had been intending to deposit the keys back with their owners before leaving for Rennes, now he had no way of innocently explaining their presence.

The ordeal continued for over an hour, and the only consolation Forest could find was that this process of 'preparing' him for interrogation would buy his comrades time to escape. He had missed pre-arranged meetings and he trusted Maud and the other members of his *réseau* to recognise the significance of this and begin wrapping up letterboxes, safe houses and any further meetings he had planned.

There was another thought at the back of Forest's mind, the same thought that Brossolette had contemplated during his ordeal – suicide. Forest had been issued with a signet ring in which he could hide his cyanide tablet, it was the thing he had been able to retain during his interrogation. All he needed was for his guards to undo his handcuffs, even for just a moment, and he would be able to take it and be beyond their reach.

His hopes were dashed however, when a new German arrived. A towering figure, with cruel eyes and an ability to slip in and out of French and German, 'Rudi' as he was called, faced Forest with disdain. There has never been a clear identification of who Rudi really was, Forest suggested a candidate but his choice has usually been deemed a case of mistaken identity.[2] Whoever he was, Rudi was a sharp-eyed and quick-witted interrogator with a brutal streak. He spat in Forest's face and slapped him to the floor. Forced into a chair to face his abuser, Forest made a valiant, if foolish, attempt to outstare him and received another punch to his jaw.

Then Rudi called for Forest to be released from the handcuffs and for an instant he thought he would be able to escape the torments ahead, but no sooner were his hands free than the swift Rudi spotted the ring and ordered it to be removed. His last hope gone, Forest had only his resolve left to face the fierce German before him.

'You have played the game. You have lost. Now, if you are reasonable, everything will go well, or else!' snapped Rudi. There was an element of routine about his words; presumably he said something similar to most agents in his grasp. Forest held his tongue.

'So, are you going to talk?'

Silence.

'Bastard!'

Blows rained down on Forest for a moment then Rudi was yelling again.

'So, are you going to talk, yes or no?' He was greeted with more silence and reacted by punching Forest hard in the mouth.

'Bastard, scum, saboteur, spy, you will talk!'

There was one saving grace of the matter. Forest was allowed to get dressed again in Rudi's presence while a typist was sent for to transcribe anything he said. The typist was a German called Ernst, who kept his face emotionally blank as he sat down to type.

'Name?' Rudi demanded.

'Shelley,' Forest answered.

'Fool! Your real name.'

'Kenneth Dodkin.'

'Your serial number?'

'47685.'

'Rank?'

'Squadron leader.'

'Branch of the Service?'

'Royal Air Force.'

'Address?'

'I do not require to reply to that question.'

'You will reply all the same.'

'I shall not.'

Rudi struck him hard, a heavy ring on his hand slicing open Forest's cheek. More blows fell on his head until Forest's ears were ringing. His vision was swimming and only the tight grasp of Rudi's able assistants held him in the chair. But as abruptly as it had begun, it stopped and Rudi sat back in his chair. He took cigarettes from his pocket and gave one to Forest. Forest was not surprised by the switch, he had learned about German interrogation tactics from SOE and abusive treatment was always followed by a pretence of civility designed to shock the victim into speaking.

'Listen,' said Rudi, now calmly sitting in his chair. 'You've had your flutter and you've lost. Antonin has told us everything you've been doing since the beginning of the year.'

The comment was Rudi's first error and it made Forest realise his Gestapo 'friends' were not as fast on their intelligence as some mistakenly believed. Forest had been in the country for less than a month and had only been working with Antonin for a week, but it was worth playing along for his self-preservation.

'Then he's talked?' Forest said with an expression of deep shock and distress.

'Naturally.'

'So you know about my appointments?'

'Of course. You see it's no use you making a martyr of yourself. You've had your flutter and lost.' That seemed to be Rudi's favourite phrase.

'Did he tell you I had an appointment for this afternoon?'

'We know everything, I tell you.'

'In that case it won't do much good my talking, will it?'

The logical statement hardly endeared Forest to his captor.

'This is no time for joking,' Rudi barked. 'We know that you have an appointment this afternoon. All I want to know is with whom and where.'

Forest gave the impression that he had conceded defeat against Rudi's demands.

'What time is it now?' he asked.

'Half-past four.'

'In that case it's too late because my appointment is for a quarter to five.'

'Where?'

'At the Porte Maillot.'

'Whereabouts exactly?"

'In front of the ceinture railway station.'

'With whom?'

'A woman.'

'What does she look like?'

'You'll see her easily, she will be carrying a bouquet of flowers and a newspaper.

The chance of catching more resistance workers had Rudi jumping out of his chair and ordering a car. Before he left the room he spared a moment to give one last parting shot.

'If you're lying you'll pay for it.'

Forest knew he would. But for the time being he had a reprieve and was left in the room with the young typist, Ernst. Initial appearances had suggested Ernst was just another underling in Rudi's employ, but now he came up to the table where Forest's belongings had been left scattered and started examining him with keen eyes. Among them was a small keepsake handed to Forest by a Russian patron of Molyneux's when she heard of his plans to enlist in 1939.

He had worn it throughout the war with little consideration for its significance. It consisted of a brown sachet on a string that she had told him would keep him safe. The irony of his current situation did not help distract Forest from the keen interest Ernst was paying to the packet. Taking out a penknife Ernst slit open the sachet and revealed the contents that had been hidden even to Forest. It proved to contain a small slip of paper written on in neat Russian characters. It was perhaps a prayer or chant to bring good luck, but Ernst, as ignorant of Russian as Forest was, considered it to be clear proof that Forest had communist connections and the 'lucky sachet' now put Forest in even greater danger.

Ernst continued his close perusal of the items on the table. He was working through the banknotes Forest had had in his possession.

'Whose telephone number is this?'

Forest had not been aware of any telephone numbers, but now Ernst showed him a 10F note that someone had written a number on in pencil. He genuinely had no knowledge of the number, which must have been on the note before he was given it. Who was to say how long the defaced banknote had been in circulation? It was such a cruelty that it had happened to fall into his hands at the time that he fell into the Germans' clutches. Try as he might to convince Ernst that the telephone number was a genuine coincidence and nothing to do with him he was not believed, and the young German sent the digits to be traced. Before long he was grinning at Forest that he had the name and address of his accomplice and the German police were on their way to collect him.

If Ernst's misplaced accusations weren't bad enough, Rudi now returned in an utter fury. Of course he had found no woman at the meeting place and his anger was now peaked to the point where there would no more attempts at being friendly. Ernst compounded matters by showing him the incriminating documents. Rudi was irate and sent the Russian words off for translation (there is no record as to what they came back as, but presumably the innocuous nature of the contents would only have angered Rudi further).

'Where are the arms dumps?' Rudi demanded.

It was known that the resistance were being supplied by the British, though of course the Germans were under the impression that these supplies were far more generous than they actually were. Arms dumps were a constant source of concern and the Germans went to great efforts to locate them. It was logical that eventually Rudi would want to know about them, but unfortunately he had picked the wrong man as Forest had absolutely no knowledge of arms dumps. But no one was going to believe that. Infuriated by the reticence of his prisoner Rudi decided to up his game. Drawing a length of chain and an ox-gut whip from a drawer he gave instructions for the *baignoire* to be prepared.

The *baignoire*, or bath torture, was a predominantly German-used device that had gained notoriety among resistance circuits for its horrors. Forest knew its reputation. The idea of the torture was to repeatedly bring a man close to drowning in a bath of icy water. The ordeal was not only terrifying but incredibly painful, and the disorientation caused by slipping in and out of consciousness was in itself enough to make a victim talk. The Gestapo had developed the technique to a cruel perfection and rarely lost a man to drowning, taking away even that last hope from their prisoner.

Part of the process was humiliation of the victim – Rudi enjoyed an audience. As Forest was dragged down a corridor to a tiled bathroom, word was sent around of the horror about to be enacted and a gaggle of office girls in uniform were summoned to watch. They seemed rather excited at the prospect and were far from disturbed by the obvious agony another human being was about to endure. Nazi evil could come in female as well as male form.

Forest was once more stripped naked, the girls gawping and laughing at him. His arms were handcuffed behind his back and the thick chain tied around his ankles. Rudi slashed the stinging whip across his bare chest, instantly bringing up a welt and demanding to know about the arms dumps. Forest managed to grit his teeth and keep silent and anyway he had nothing that he could say. The whip came down a few more times, each slash followed by another question, but when nothing but gasps of pain could be drawn from the prisoner, Rudi finally lost his patience and slammed Forest backwards into the bath, which Ernst had kindly filled with cold water. The purpose of the chain now became apparent. By hoisting it up Forest was unable to pull himself out of the water or kick free and was entirely at the mercy of Rudi. Forest later wrote an account of his first 'dip':

> I was helpless, I panicked and tried to kick, but the vice-like grip was such that I
> could hardly move. My eyes were open, I could see shapes distorted by the water,
> wavering about me, my lungs were bursting, my mouth opened and I swallowed

water. Now I was drowning. I put every ounce of my energy into a vain effort to kick myself out of the bath, but I was completely helpless and swallowing water, I felt that I must burst. I was dying, this was the end, I was losing consciousness, but as I was doing so, I felt the strength going out of me and my limbs going limp. This must be the end.[3]

He was not to be that lucky. Rudi had had plenty of practice at this routine and as Forest lost consciousness he was quickly drawn out of the bath and laid on the floor to rouse himself. It only took a few moments for Forest's senses to return and for him to realise that he was still alive and still in the clutches of the Gestapo. The girls were laughing in the doorway and Rudi was asking his questions again. Forest barely had a moment to gasp out his lack of knowledge before he was plunged back into the water. Forest lost track of the number of times he drifted on the cusp of drowning before waking on the tiled floor before Rudi.

Splash, I was kicking again and swallowing gallons of water, not much strength left to kick. My chest was about to burst. Oblivion. Distorted faces. 'Rudi', 'Ernst', others, girls laughing, mocking 'Where are the arms dumps?' Why reply at all, let me die. Water, gulps, bursting lungs, more faces above me, more girls splitting their sides with laughter. Wish I was dead. How many times this went on, I don't know. I lay on the tiled floor, everything swaying around me, walls, bath, faces. I felt abominably sick, my tummy felt like an over-full barrel. Water kept on gushing out of my mouth, over my chest, I was numb with cold, I closed my eyes. I could hear voices, laughs, feminine laughter. What was so funny? Me, of course. I must look a fool, wilting like a doll that has lost its stuffing.

Forest's moving description of torture speaks for all those souls who never survived to tell their tale, Brossolette among them, who could not face another round with the bath and used his last strength to take himself permanently out of German hands.

But even this horror had to end. On one occasion as Forest came round, he realised the girls were gone, which suggested to him that Rudi was finally tiring of this game. He was proved right when he was dragged to his feet, sick and dizzy, and hauled back to the interrogation room. Once again he was dressed and once again the abuse began, but this time the guards used rubber truncheons to pound him violently. Perhaps their hands were tired. Eventually Forest experienced the mercy of passing out from the pain.

The bliss of nothingness did not last long though, and Forest tried to draw out his temporary reprieve by pretending to be unconscious when he awoke. His body was just one mass of pain, but even so he could pick out the individual areas that hurt. He had never been through anything like it in his life and even for him there was the temptation to talk. Somehow Forest resisted the urge; perhaps that ability to detach himself from the external world around him was his saving grace, though he would have been forgiven for giving in.

Rudi realised he was awake and propped him up in a chair so that he might discuss the keys they had found on him. For Forest this was the moment he had dreaded, as the keys were the one true link between himself and his friends. He had to stall the Germans long enough to give Maud and the others a chance to escape, but that was not so simple; to delay the Germans sufficiently he had to give them something. Reluctantly it dawned on him that one key belonged to an apartment only he, Brossolette and Maud knew about, therefore it might be the safest place to send the Germans to search.

'What do these keys open?' Rudi demanded.

Forest wanted to draw out the discussion as long as he could before giving up his one piece of information.

'They open nothing.'

'Don't lie!'

'I'm not lying, a man looks odd if he doesn't carry keys so I had these made up as cover.'

Rudi was not convinced. Taking up the keys he used them as a flail to slash across Forest's face until his blood spilled down.

'Now, what do the keys open?'

Even Forest could not endure this forever and he savoured a chance to escape the continued flagellation, if only for a short time.

'The big key is the only one of importance. It belongs to 33 rue de la Tourelle, Porte de Saint Cloud.'

'Couldn't you have said that sooner?' Rudi scowled, but he broke off from his torment to ring for another car. Repeating his earlier warning that if Forest was lying he would suffer, the Gestapo man left, leaving Ernst behind.

Ernst was looking very pleased with himself and quickly revealed that he had tracked down Forest's friend from the 10F note. A miserable-looking man, already beaten and bloody, was dragged into the room. His immediate reaction to the sight of Forest was naturally one of horror and revulsion, but unfortunately Ernst took this as a sign of recognition.

The unfortunate victim was completely unknown to Forest and he never did discover who he was or what became of him. Ernst slapped the newcomer into a chair and grinned at the pair of men.

'A pleasant surprise for you both to meet like this, isn't it?'

As pointless as he knew it was, Forest had to try and clarify that this poor man had nothing to do with him and his work.

'I've never seen this man before, he's totally unknown to me,' he insisted, but it was such a common protest in the Gestapo base that the one time it was true it fell on deaf ears.

'You're a bloody liar. Don't think I didn't see you tremble when he was brought in.'

Ernst addressed himself to his new victim.

'Even if he's not going to talk I hope you'll be a little more intelligent. You've only got to be sensible and tell us all you know and we will let you go. But I warn you that it won't be pleasant for you if you tell us any lies.'

What hope did an innocent man have in a building full of liars?

'Monsieur, I swear to you that I don't know this gentleman,' he begged. 'I swear to you that I haven't had anything to do with the resistance. I am a musician. I earn my living playing in a nightclub. I've a wife and two children. Why should I lie to you?'

There was really no hope for the unfortunate who had had the singular misfortune to have his phone number written on a franc note. Fate can be cruel and twisted sometimes. The more he protested, the more violent his captors became and soon he was as bloodied as Forest. It was too much for Forest's conscience to bear.

'Cowards! He is innocent! He has nothing to do with me. Can't you see he is such a weak fellow that if he knew anything he would tell you? You are hurting him for nothing!'

The outburst only earned Forest another beating from his guards and he fell into a faint again.

When he roused he could hear the sound of a man whimpering, but he hardly had time to consider it before he was dragged away to a small cell and left sitting on a chair, his handcuffed hands slipped over its back.

Only now, in the isolation of his cell, without Rudi or Ernst bellowing and punching him, could Forest consider himself and the many aches and pains of his body. There was not a part of him that didn't seem to throb, and his head felt swollen, his jaw ached and his teeth seemed to rattle loose in his skull. All he could taste was blood and the handcuffs were slicing into his wrists.

Through the locked door of his cell he could hear the unlucky musician screaming as his interrogators resumed their abuse. Perhaps worse than watching the torture was hearing its sounds and letting the imagination run wild about what was happening. Forest heard what sounded like a body being flung against a wall, and soft thuds and cracks, interspersed with groans and cries. At one point it sounded as though Ernst was smashing furniture. Forest forgot his pain in his anger for the poor man and began yelling his own abuse at the Gestapo from his cell, but it was unlikely that they heard him over the noise of their own violence. Certainly no one came to punish him for the outburst and slowly even Forest's energy for rage deserted him.

In the aftermath of torture there was only exhaustion. Forest's body ached for sleep, but any time his head dropped forward the handcuffs bit into his wrists and brought him round violently. No doubt this was an effect that his guards were well aware of. Added to that was a desperate desire to urinate, brought on by the large quantities of water he had been forced to drink during his 'bath'. Dreading the humiliation of wetting himself, Forest called and called for assistance, but aside from someone shouting 'English swine!' through his door, no one came.

It was long after midnight when guards eventually came to him and hauled him back to the interrogation room. Rudi had returned from inspecting the flat and was not impressed at what he had found. As Forest was thrust back into a chair he noticed a cowering figure in the corner of the room – the musician, who had finally lost Ernst's attention. Battered and shivering, occasionally moaning softly, he was a broken figure. There was no knowing how permanent his injuries were, or whether any were life threatening. He was just one more Nazi casualty who would quickly be forgotten.

'You sent me on another wild goose chase,' Rudi snapped – the flat had thankfully been abandoned by Forest's comrades. 'No one has slept there for months. Where did you sleep last night?'

'With a whore,' Forest answered quickly. 'It is what I always do, they keep their mouths shut.'

Rudi didn't believe him, but both captors were, by now, feeling almost as exhausted as their victim. They sent for food and Forest had to watch them for what felt like hours as they slowly ate. All the time his bladder was fit to burst and he could barely contain himself, despite his determination not to humiliate himself before his captors.

Abruptly Rudi and Ernst ordered him back to his cell, seemingly frustrated by their prisoner and tired of the interview. At the threshold of his cell Forest took his chance to beg his guards to let him relieve himself, informing them that if they didn't there would soon be a pool of urine trickling from under the door. Annoyed but clearly not relishing having to mop floors, the guards escorted him to a toilet and with immense relief Forest was able to empty his bladder. In the topsy-turvy world of the Gestapo prison it seemed an incomparable victory over the enemy.

Back in his cell he was once again set on the chair with his hands cuffed behind him. It was unbearable not to be able to put his head down and sleep for even a moment. With usual Forest stubbornness, he determined to free himself from the chair at least and by rocking and trying to stand he eventually flung himself forward and wriggled his arms from the back of the chair.

It was far from easy to struggle the chair back onto its feet and then to somehow position it so he could sleep on it, with his arms still firmly behind his back the whole time. Eventually he managed a position resting on the chair with his head propped against the wall, and even dozed. But his reprieve was all too short lived.

....

Notes
1. Marshal, *Op cit.*
2. Seaman, *Op cit.*
3. *Ibid.*

13

The Endless Nightmare

RUDI AND ERNST HAD tired of interrogating Forest and had relinquished their prisoner to two new officers, neither of whom felt inclined to reveal their names to him. They were new faces in the ordeal, but when Forest was brought before them he discovered that he was to endure the most horrific déjà vu as the two men repeated the process Rudi and Ernst had so generously initiated him into. First there was the firing of questions, and thankfully even a sleepy Forest could recall his cover story, but all too soon they were at an impasse, as once again he was demanded to tell them the location of the resistance arms dump.

Then it was a return to the bath, though apparently it was too late for the female personnel to attend, or perhaps they had lost interest in this particular victim. There was little that Forest could do but hold on to his stubbornness and his breath. He endeavoured to reduce the torment by kicking violently when his head was first immersed in the water and then, just as he felt himself slipping into unconsciousness, allowing his body to go limp making it seem he had blacked out a little sooner than he really had. Even so it was a nightmarish struggle: his body constantly fighting between life and death, his stomach filling with hastily swallowed water and his lungs burning from the effort to breathe. It lasted an hour, at which point he feigned complete collapse and was dragged back to the interrogation room, where he was forced to watch his anonymous questioners eating a leisurely breakfast of croissants and coffee. Despite his injuries Forest could still feel the pangs of hunger this induced, but for his breakfast all he received was another beating until he was virtually insensible, then the Germans left.

For a brief spell Forest was alone with his thoughts and his pain. Throughout the corridors of the building screams rang out as new victims received the Gestapo treatment. Forest could only close his mind to the sounds and hope there was no one he knew in those other rooms. He was still unaware that Brossolette had been a victim of the regime and had killed himself a mere hour before Forest had arrived at the house.

Then Rudi and Ernst were back and Rudi was feeling vengeful for the false errands he believed he had been sent on the day before. Perhaps Forest felt a tinge of amusement that Rudi failed to realise that he had stood in a genuine resistance safe house, before the usual round of beating and bathing continued.

By the afternoon however, his captors were getting a little desperate at the stubborn silence Forest maintained. He was driven to 84 avenue Foch with two SD men. This was one of three houses acquired in the grand residential boulevard connecting to the Arc de Triomphe by the Gestapo. They used it for various operations, including counter-intelligence and the orchestration of the 'wireless' game they played with SOE.[1] It is one of a few places in Paris synonymous with the dark secret police, but its fame was of little comfort to Forest as he was escorted to a first-floor interrogation room.

Awaiting him in the room was a bespectacled, humble-looking man at a typewriter and an SS giant, watching over him like a chained bear. They were a bizarre match, but this was a trick the Gestapo had learned from the British and tried to use to their own ends. For a long time the modest fellow at the desk studied Forest, giving the agent a chance to study him back. As no names were offered, Forest began to think of him as 'Professor', as his appearance gave him the semblance of an intellectual. Slowly, Professor inserted paper and carbon into his typewriter and the interview commenced.

'I am not like the others,' he confided in very correct French. 'I shall not hurt you. If you are sensible we shall be good friends. Come now, you will do yourself no good by obstinacy. You've had your flutter and you've lost. Now all you've got to do is answer my questions.'

The unnerving calmness of the man and the lack of the violence Forest had come to expect when he failed to answer questions disturbed him more than the torture Rudi had inflicted and with good reason. It was British intelligence that had first used the 'subtle' method of interrogation. They were helped by early German propaganda that was distributed to troops, which inflated ideas of extreme British torture. This was designed to make Germans so desperate not to be captured that they would die first. It backfired. German soldiers, sailors and airmen were taken and after they had stewed for a while over the idea of being horribly tortured they were brought before a man like the 'Professor' who would talk to them as a friend, a comrade, a fellow soldier and almost invariably they would be so relieved that they would break.

So now Forest sat before an interrogator using the 'British method' and asking quiet questions and typing up whatever was said without comment. He later wrote: 'I found his calm way of examining me much more disturbing than the brutal methods of "Rudi". His very calmness and detachment seemed much more ominous. He was more subtle, maybe less brutal, but quite possibly more cruel. It was like being in the presence of a big spider, and feeling a web being coiled around me.'[2]

It was while he was calmly typing that the Professor dropped his first bombshell.

'You know Cadillac?' he enquired smoothly.

Forest froze for a second, having thought he knew all that the Germans wanted from him (arms dumps locations and contacts), he was shaken by this new attack. Cadillac, as he was well aware (and as the Professor seemed to be) was one of Bingen's codenames. It shouldn't have surprised him, knowing the insecure methods his French colleagues were using, that the Germans should be aware of such a significant figure by his alias, but it still unsettled Forest. He feigned ignorance. The Cadillac was a type of American car, wasn't it?

The Professor, typing diligently, was unimpressed.

'And Pic? Do you know him?' he asked.

Pic was one of the less imaginative codenames for Pichard, who had also provided Forest with the services of Antonin. Knowing Antonin was in the clutches of the Germans and experiencing the same ordeal as he was, Forest was certain the young man had talked and the Professor was already well aware of the connection between himself and Pichard. Lying was pointless; instead Forest ventured to misdirect his captors.

'Yes I know Pic.'

'Describe him.'

Forest gave an imaginative and completely fictitious account of Pichard's appearance, making every detail the complete opposite of what it really was. The Professor typed quickly.

'It's just as well you told us the truth,' he said as his fingers moved. 'You see, we arrested Pichard yesterday.'

Forest had to resist smiling; if that was the truth his interrogator would have been well aware that he had just lied to him. But it was a brief triumph as the Professor turned his attention back to the 'Cadillac' issue. Once again Forest denied any knowledge and the Professor issued a weary sigh. The German patience for the 'British method' was depressingly short and with a single telephone call the Professor abandoned Forest back into the world of torture.

A giant German thug appeared, punched Forest without a word and then dragged him from the room. The relatively peaceful reprieve was over, and the next torture he was to experience was one of the worst the Germans had in their repertoire.

He was escorted to a room with a hook on a chain hanging from the ceiling via a pulley. His handcuffs were fixed to the hook and then the giant hauled on the pulley and Forest's arms were brutally pulled back and up as his feet left the floor. The handcuffs instantly bit into his wrists, but it was the agony in his shoulders that consumed his mind, and for the first time Forest let out an involuntary groan, much to his torturer's amusement. Unconsciousness came blessedly quickly, but was not total, and throughout the next few hours he hovered between reality and oblivion, the pain overtaking him far greater than he had previously experienced.

It wasn't until nightfall that he was released from the hook and collapsed onto the cell floor. As he awoke from his pain-induced daze, he could only think of the blistering agony in his shoulders, almost dislocated by the ordeal, and the burn in his wrists where the handcuffs had bitten into his arms and cut off his circulation. The long-term effects of the hanging torture could be horrendous: previous victims had lost the use of a hand or arm, sometimes both, and if nerve damage had occurred the mutilation would be permanent. Forest didn't know it, but he would be one of the lucky ones who did not suffer such debilitating long-term effects, though it was little consolation at the time.

Forest was close to defeat. There was only so much a man's body could endure and the fact that he had come this far was remarkable, but he was well aware that he was at his lowest point, and that he could not take much more. He wanted to talk and it was only because no one asked him a question at that moment that he remained silent.

Yet again his stubbornness had worn out his interrogators and a rest interval was necessary. Forest persuaded his guards to take him to the toilet, where he had to endure the humiliation of being watched while he struggled with his numb hands to perform his ablutions. Finally he was taken to another room and chained to a settee.

The long night was almost unbearable. Aside from a glass of water, his guards provided him with no sustenance and any time he dozed off a menacing NCO shook him awake. Sleep-deprivation was yet another torture and his guards knew it, though it was as much a hardship for them as for Forest, and eventually they submitted to sleep themselves, giving their prisoner a chance of forty winks. But sleep was far from easy when surrounded by the horrors of the Gestapo. Forest was cold, hungry and in bitter pain. He wished for Barbara and he wished for freedom, even if it came after the release of death. He knew he was virtually broken, and there was no point pretending to himself that he could endure any more suffering. As the darkness slowly ebbed into dawn he felt his dread of the next day almost engulfing him as his tormented imagination summoned nightmarish images of what the Germans might do to him next. There was only one solution.

Morning found Forest in another office, battered, bruised, bloodied and facing another interrogator. This one did not have the charm of the Professor and the usual round of assault and questions began. He wanted to know about Cadillac and revealed that he knew Cadillac was really Bingen. Realising there was no point maintaining a pretence that was so obvious Forest finally admitted he knew Bingen but that he did not know of his codename Cadillac. The German was surprised, but they quickly moved on to how to find Bingen. Again Forest denied that he knew. He was amazed that despite thinking he was about ready to give in, his stubbornness still wouldn't let him talk. He lied and denied, but his usually quick mind was muddled and he stumbled on his own half-truths and gave the interrogator too many opportunities. Even so he managed to keep from revealing anything important.

He was always aware that time was running out for him; he was finding it harder to play dumb and was giving too much ground. Forest's eyes slipped longingly to the window and, like Brossolette before him, he contemplated leaping out. They were on the fourth floor, so a fall might not kill him, but he would be badly injured and would have to stay in hospital for some time. Hopefully, by the time he was sufficiently recovered his comrades in the resistance would have filled the gap he had left and the Germans would have no further use for him.

It took all his remaining strength to throw himself from the chair and headlong into the window. Somehow he managed to miss the table in his dive and smashed the bottom pane of glass with his head. His shoulder slipped through the opening but his momentum had been curtailed and a pair of muscular hands grabbed his ankles and pulled him back. His interrogator only seemed amused by Forest's efforts and he was secured to the chair by chains.

'You're scared,' mocked the interrogator. 'So now you will talk.'

But Forest didn't, he didn't even dare open his mouth, because he knew if he did the words that would stumble out would be pleas for mercy and he desperately didn't want to beg from a German. The interrogation ended abruptly and Forest was driven back to the site of his first torments. Rudi was waiting for him.

'Now you are going to talk. You're scared – it's now or never.' He grinned, but Forest resolutely remained dumb.

Infuriated, Rudi sent for five Gestapo thugs. They hauled Forest onto the table, chaining his ankles apart and to the table legs, then they beat him with rubber coshes, concentrating on his exposed genitalia, though not ignoring his head and body. The new pain was horrendous and Forest screamed but to no avail, as there was no mercy in the minds of his tormentors. His only relief was when unconsciousness overtook him.

Several hours later he awoke in another unfamiliar cell. His body was racked with pain and he retched drily, only causing more stabbing agony to shoot through his system. Tears finally came to Forest's eyes and he sobbed miserably. His mind was no longer sharp or even coherent – that was a penalty of torture, victims became muddled and confused. For Forest everything was a jumble in his head, he could no longer think clearly or understand what was happening. The next few hours fell into a perpetual fog in his memory and with only snatched moments of lucid thought.

One of these moments involved the interrogator Ernst Misselwitz,[3] the man who had been with Brossolette and Bollaert on their journey from Rennes to Paris. The new Ernst was more inclined to cunning than cruelty and opened his interrogation by pointing out that he already knew where Forest lived. Forest disbelieved him.

'I'll prove it. Just circle the district of Paris you live in on this map and I will point out your address.'

Forest grudgingly outlined a circle on the map with his finger that took in a quarter of Paris. Ernst laughed.

'You live at 11 rue Claude Chahu, and you aren't the only one.'

Forest was stunned; the address was that of Suni Sandoe's flat. Tucked beneath the floorboards of that apartment were the identity discs of 'Kenneth Dodkin', and if these were found they would only implicate him further as an enemy agent.

'So you see I know a lot about you. If you tell me the names of those who sheltered you I promise no harm will befall you on my word of honour as a German officer.' Ernst spoke casually, 'Perhaps you don't believe me. There's an English prisoner here who'll tell you that we keep our word.'

Marched into the room was fellow SOE man Captain John Starr. Starr has come to be remembered as a controversial figure. After his arrest in 1943 he was a permanent resident of 84 avenue Foch, where he was regularly wheeled out to talk to new prisoners and convince them to talk. It was never obvious which side Starr favoured, and, heavily inclined towards his own self-preservation, he came dangerously close to collaborating.[4] But whatever later generations chose to believe about Starr, Forest viewed him as an ally, and while he spoke of how the Germans were pretty good to him, he interspersed his words with meaningful glances that the Nazi words of honour were not to be trusted.

How much of this was a genuine attempt by Starr, or Forest's addled mind seeing what it wanted to see has to be left to personal judgement.

Events now began to slip into a blur. Forest still refused to talk, though by now this was in part due to the deteriorating mental state that left him unable to formulate answers. He didn't recall being dragged from Ernst's presence, though he must have been because suddenly Rudi was slapping him. Then there was another sallow-faced interrogator who wanted to know about resistance sabotage plans. Once again silence was followed by a trip to the bathroom, where Forest only had vague impressions of being stripped and then immersed in the freezing water. The horror of semi-drowning was only made worse by his dazed and dream-like state.

Forest's resolve was dying; every time he was left alone to contemplate his situation he was convinced he would talk, yet every time he sat before an interrogator again his pride and stubbornness kicked in and he would remain silent despite the abuse inflicted on him. He just wondered how much longer it would be before the Gestapo got tired of him and shot him. It was the only thing he had to look forward to.

The next interrogation was conducted by a duo: a middle-aged man and a younger officer wearing glasses. It was back to sympathy and kindness to induce him to speak.

'They've been rather unkind to you, I see. It's unfortunate, but that's war for you. I expect you're rather hungry.'

The younger interrogator undid his cuffs, brought his hands forward and re-secured them, though looser so he might eat.

A tray was brought to him with sausage sandwiches and a jug of hot soup. Forest's first thought though, was to look at his arms. They were mangled-looking things. His wrists were slashed open from the edges of the cuffs, which were red with blood. The wounds were tinged purple and his left arm was swollen up to the elbow. Seeing his injuries made him realise how bad a state he was in, but he had to shove that aside and eat while the opportunity was before him.

The new interrogators had compiled a chart of the structure of the BCRA organisation from previous interrogations and now proudly showed this to Forest. Forest was alert enough to be amused that so much of the information was wrong and clearly past victims had talked quite imaginatively. Pushed to cooperate he saw no harm in adding his own inventions to the little chart and offered the names of mythical officers and their fantastical duties.

His enjoyment was short lived. Marched downstairs, he was horrified to see Suni Sandoe. She had failed to flee her safe house quickly enough and had been caught. They briefly passed each other and Forest hissed that she should say she knew nothing of his activities, particularly of any hidden firearms, then he was swept away.

More horror awaited him later that day when he was led into a room containing some of his closest associates hand-cuffed and showing obvious signs of torture. There were members of Pichard's secretariat (though luckily Pichard himself had been out of town at the time of the arrests). One woman's hair was dripping wet and sticking to her face in bedraggled strands: it appeared she had already discovered the bath torture. The men in the room were bloodied and bruised, showing they had been more traditionally treated.

The prisoners were all sitting on chairs arranged back to back to prevent subtle communications. Forest was sat behind Commandant Noel Palaud,

Artilleur, one of the most important figures of the resistance. Forest was desperate to talk to him and let him know that he had not named any resistance members, but when he turned his head he was unceremoniously slapped by a guard. For a time conversation seemed impossible, but Forest's brain had been revitalised by the shock of seeing so many resistance members captured and he suddenly had an idea.

Quietly he began humming a popular French tune, '*Tout va très bien, Madame la Marquise*'. When the guards showed no interest he started to sing the words and then carefully substitute the real lyrics with a message for his friends.

'I do not know Palaud. He does not know me. Captured at metro station.'

Then he sank back into humming and waited. After a pause Palaud joined in the song and added his own messages. Slowly, over the next 2 hours they exchanged information right under the guards' noses.

Their communication was stopped abruptly when the door burst open and the guards herded the unfortunates out into a central courtyard where a van was waiting. Rudi and the original Ernst had reappeared to check prisoners off a list as they were shoved into the vehicle. The van was divided into airless cubicles either side of a central corridor; at the end of the corridor an armed guard watched the prisoners get on and shoved them into their 'cells'. Forest found himself in the cubicle nearest the guard. There was no window and once the door was shut and locked the only light and air came through the slatted floor and a small gap under the door through which Forest could see the polished boots of his guard. There was no place to sit, so Forest stood. His only consolation was that the slats in the floor at least provided him with glimpses of his beloved Paris and as the van drove off he was able to imagine the roads they were heading down and the route they were taking. Before long he was certain of where they were going. He was off to Fresnes.

....

Notes

1. The Gestapo had infiltrated a number of resistance networks as well as capturing wireless operators and their machines and they used these to send false messages back to London. Security measures by SOE were supposedly in place to counteract this, but they were commonly ignored or missed. It is still unclear how many wirelesses were Gestapo controlled, though some were identified and used for London's own counter-counter-intelligence operations.
2. Seaman, *Op cit*.
3. Not the same Ernst as the one referred to earlier.

4. Post-war, Starr found himself being investigated by the French for collusion with the enemy, but the case came to nothing.

14

The Traitor at Fresnes

FRESNES WAS BUILT BETWEEN 1895 and 1898, the largest prison in France at that time,[1] and with the capacity to hold 1,200 male prisoners, with a smaller number of cells for women. Upon the occupation of Paris the Germans took control of Fresnes and its name quickly became synonymous with torture and horrific conditions. Intended to house British SOE agents and resistance members, it sometimes also accommodated captured Allied airmen, but these prisoners were generally spared the full horrors meted out to the rest by sadistic guards.

Whether SOE or resistance, captives at Fresnes knew that it was likely to be their last stop. Berty Albrecht, co-founder of the Combat network, died at Fresnes, as did Suzanne Spaak, who worked tirelessly for the resistance and to save Jewish children from the concentration camps. She, like so many, was shot as the Allies retook Paris.

For others, Fresnes was a mere stopping point before they were sent on to a concentration camp. For Odette Sansom, an SOE agent who operated with Peter Churchill, this meant eventual transfer to Ravensbruck women's concentration camp after torture at Fresnes. For many more Buchenwald concentration camp was their final destination, but either way it was very clear that Fresnes was the end of the line before the Germans got tired of you. As Forest realised his destination he also knew that his chances of escape or even just of survival were severely reduced.

Forest's first few days at Fresnes were not exactly pleasant. He remained handcuffed, making the most mundane tasks difficult, and was confined to a cold cell, but in comparison to the avenue Foch it was a welcome reprieve. The guards liked to emphasise their orders with slaps and kicks, but it was nothing compared to Gestapo treatment and Forest even received treatment for a nasty slice on his wrist inflicted by the handcuffs. It had begun to go septic and a German medical orderly cleaned it and gave him medicine, though the kindness was unhappily given as the orderly saw it as pointless since he would die soon anyway. Such was the reputation of Fresnes.

Gradually things began to improve and with them so did Forest's spirits. He was allowed to have his handcuffs removed, which was a massive relief, and he was even given a grubby blanket, so at least now he could warm himself and sleep a little at night.

Forest rapidly began to assess his situation and to make contact with his fellow inmates. He noticed that prisoners would shout messages out to communicate with each other, using code to fool the guards. Commonly this happened first thing in the morning and last thing at night. Forest decided to join the conversation and managed to draw the attention of his neighbour in the next cell. By removing the head of a tap in his cell he was able to whisper messages through the plumbing of the prison and got to know his new friend, Lecoq. Lecoq had been at Fresnes for three months and was a former member of Pichard's network. He passed on what little he knew, the information largely out of date, and was eager to hear from Forest what had happened since his arrest. Lecoq christened Forest 'Tartarin', so that if a guard heard a message shouted they would not know which prisoner had yelled it. The prisoners were careful only to shout at prescribed times when many would do it at once to confuse the guards and reduce their own risk of being detected.

Speaking to a friendly voice helped Forest no end and his mental state and resolve rapidly improved. His mind was once again turning to out-smarting his captors and even escaping, but his acquaintance with Lecoq was cut short when Forest was transferred to another cell on the second floor.

At least this one was cleaner, and his guard, named Korrel, was one of the few decent human beings employed by the prison. Korrel was able to get Forest odd little necessities: a toothbrush, soap and a bible. It was not much but at least meant that Forest could wash his filthy uniform in the small sink in his cell. The bloodstains were impossible to get out entirely, but the worst of the dirt was removed. In the cold cell it took a long time for the uniform to dry and in the meantime Forest had to shiver beneath his blanket, but at least it went some way to restoring his dignity and from then on he tried to maintain it by alternately washing his underwear and uniform.

Without anyone to talk to Forest's mind returned to the possibility of escape. Lecoq had made it plain that escaping from Fresnes was virtually impossible, but prisoners were regularly taken to Paris for interrogation – this could provide Forest with his opportunity. From then on he studied the movements and habits of the guards in order to work out when best to affect his escape during transfer.

There was plenty of time to take stock of his cell and Forest examined his small window in minute detail in case it offered any opportunities. He realised that the grouting around the panes of glass was not terribly thick and could be scraped away with a fingernail. Using what tools he could find, such as the sharpened handle of his toothbrush, he worked at the grout until the pane became loose. He took care that the piece of glass would still sit in the frame without the grout and then, when it was safe, removed it and took his first deep breath of fresh air. He couldn't see much through the hole, but he could hear a lot.

One evening he heard an English voice calling out to try and talk to someone. Discreetly, he called back and introduced himself as Tartarin. A small part of him was concerned he could be talking to a mole working for the Gestapo, so he was cautious in what information he revealed, but wasted no time interrogating his new contact. Through a series of evening conversations shouted through the window Forest learned that he was talking to RAF pilot Jim, in reality Sergeant E.J. Gillman, who had been shot down and captured. He shared a cell with Joe Kenny, another airman, and an American pilot, Tex. In a nearby cell there was an Australian, Flying Officer Clifton Tucker.

Forest knew the airmen would likely be sent to a POW camp soon, as they had no doubt been questioned already, but since the Germans (even the Gestapo) had a grudging respect for the Geneva Convention where it concerned military personnel it was unlikely that they had been tortured.

Forest held out a hope that sooner or later the airmen would be able to get home and take a message to Barbara. As carefully as he could he gave them her name and asked them to tell her where they had last seen him. It wasn't much, but it gave him some comfort.

If Forest had hoped the Gestapo were done with him, he was sorely wrong. As Lecoq had predicted, eventually he was transported back to the Gestapo headquarters for the usual round of interrogations. Ernst Misselwitz reappeared and tried his hand, as did Rudi, but Forest had had time to rebuild his strength and still refused to talk. It was then that Misselwitz played what he believed was his trump card.

'You know a man by the name Horace?' he asked.

Forest had to think fast. Horace was the failed *agent de liaison* he had almost shot because he doubted his loyalty.

'You mean Andre Lemonnier.' He had no loyalty to the man so was not inclined to hide his name, in fact he was intrigued to discovered what Horace had been up to.

Misselwitz was obviously pleased with his find and must have thought it a significant blow to Forest as he revealed his connection to Horace.

'Lemonnier has been working for us for some time, he has provided a great deal of information about your activities.'

Misselwitz had a list of dates and appointments that Forest had supposedly attended that had been listed by Horace. Forest had to restrain a smirk. Since he had sent the boy packing he had had no contact with him and he certainly could not have had the information he claimed. Besides, it was quite obviously all false.

'Lemonnier has been lying to you. I never went to those meetings. I knew he was a traitor and sent him away months ago.' Forest said.

'Don't try and fool me, Lemonnier has told us everything.'

'It is the truth, he can't know all this, in fact all these dates are wrong and I can prove it.'

Something about Forest's tone had clearly concerned Misselwitz, as he didn't immediately go on the attack again. He was obviously worried – perhaps even the Gestapo had had their suspicions about good old Horace.

'Let me confront him and I can prove to you he is a liar. I suppose you have paid him for all these falsehoods?'

Misselwitz had no answer to that, and instead he agreed to arrange a meeting when it would be 'proved' to Forest that Horace was a good informer. Forest returned to his cell that night feeling satisfied and gleeful that he was about to confront a Nazi collaborator and silence him forever. Long nights in Gestapo hands had made Forest more inclined towards revenge than he had ever been before. He still wasn't sure who had betrayed him at Passy Métro, but he would have them one day as well. For now he would content himself with taking down Horace the traitor.

A week later Misselwitz was waiting for him at avenue Foch. The German didn't appear entirely confident as Forest was ushered in. He was made to sit and then they were to wait.

'Horace will be late.' Forest predicted bluntly; he doubted Lemonnier had improved his punctuality for the Germans. The young man's complete careless-ness was remarkable knowing the men he was dealing with. Misselwitz ignored him, but when an hour passed with no sign of Horace he began to get agitated. It certainly wasn't improved by Forest's enjoyment of his small triumph.

He was about ready to send men out to search for the late informer when it was announced that Horace had arrived. The Frenchman sauntered in unper-turbed at the anxiety and irritation he had caused his 'boss'. He failed to show any sign of recognition of Forest as he entered, ignoring him as if he had seen this all before. Forest was not entirely surprised. The last time Horace had seen him, he had been in smart civilian clothes, clean, well fed and not covered in bruises and injuries. His time in Gestapo hands had altered his appearance dramatically. Still, Misselwitz was not happy.

'Do you know this man?' he asked Lemonnier, who nonchalantly replied that he did not. 'I want you to list the times and places you met with the man known as Shelley.'

Lemonnier happily reeled off a list of dates and times; talking about the importance of his meetings with Forest and the supposed information he had gained from him. He was clearly unaware of the danger he was in. The part that intrigued Forest the most were the supposed rendezvous they had had during the time he had been back in London, those would be the easiest to prove as lies.

'You say you do not know this man?' Misselwitz pointed angrily at Forest again.

'No.' Lemonnier replied, though now he was starting to look uneasy.

'This is Shelley and he says you are lying and that he can prove it.'

Forest was satisfied to see Lemonnier go pale.

'Have you been lying?' Misselwitz insisted.

'No.' Lemonnier could only hope that Forest would not be believed.

Misselwitz turned to Forest. 'Well, what proof do you have?'

'Those dates he claims to have met me, I wasn't even in France, I was in London.' Forest said.

By now Lemonnier was looking sick and Misselwitz's fury was evident.

'How can you prove that? You could be lying,' said the Gestapo man.

'You listen to all the BBC messages broadcasted and keep records? Have someone look at them, my codename was the White Rabbit and every time I left or returned to England a message was broadcast. You can confirm the dates.'

Misselwitz said no more but rang his colleagues to have them go through the files of BBC messages. Lemonnier was forced to wait, terrified, in the room, with Forest enjoying his predicament. A part of him wished he had shot the traitor when he had first suspected him and he still cursed himself for listening to Jose Dupuis, but that had been before this nightmare, when he was still prepared to feel merciful.

It was an awful moment for Lemonnier when the phone rang and Misselwitz spoke with his colleagues. The broadcasts had confirmed his guilt as Forest had hoped, and Misselwitz was furious that the 15,000F retainer he had paid Horace had been wasted. Lemonnier was removed to another room and Forest listened as he was interrogated and revealed first his betrayal of his resistance comrades and then the betrayal of the Germans. At least his mercenary tendencies had caused the Gestapo as much grief as they had the resistance. He was even more elated when Lemonnier was transferred back to Fresnes with him and he quickly spread the story of 'Horace the traitor' to all his friends. The foreseeable future for Lemonnier was one of isolation and suffering.

Aside from this odd excitement, life at Fresnes fell into one dull routine. Forest exercised in his cell as best he could, even taking to polishing the floor to get his muscles moving. It steadily helped his strength to return, but it could not save him from the brutality of his captors. On one occasion a Wehrmacht feldwebel came into his cell and beat him just because he was a British officer. Such abuse was commonplace and Forest kept his pride only by thinking up plans for escape.

His first serious attempt came when he was being transported between Fresnes and the avenue Foch. Dangerous prisoners were confined to the cubicles of the prison van during the journey, while more harmless prisoners were made to stand in the aisle. The only guard was one armed with a sub-machine gun, though a car with four others followed them. Forest formulated an idea of overpowering the guard, taking the gun and opening fire on the following vehicle, before escaping to a safe house he felt was still secure and where he stored papers, arms and money. It was audacious, but he was desperate.

The journey was not long, but Forest wasted no time in prising open his cubicle door. In the rattling van the noise was not noticed and when Forest peeked out he discovered the guard was facing away from him. In an instant he was out and wrestling him for his gun.

Unfortunately he had not taken into account that many of his fellow prisoners were not so eager to risk Nazi wrath and when the men in the aisle realised what was happening they intervened on behalf of the guard. Forest was forced back into his cubicle cursing them for their cowardice, though perhaps they had a point. Forest's schemes were often more adventurous than sensible and the odds of him gunning down the four pursuers and escaping were unlikely. Besides, the Germans would not have hesitated to open fire into the prison van, killing many innocents. Fortunately the guard never reported the incident, (perhaps he feared what the reaction to his failure would be) so Forest was free to plan his next move.

His second attempt was even more risky. He was at the rue des Saussaies after another interrogation, waiting to board the van with several prisoners. It was getting late and Forest snuck into some shadows near the building before making a dash for the main archway that opened into the street. He was spotted quite rapidly and a guard tripped him as he ran. With his hands still handcuffed behind his back he fell to earth like a stone and faced the full wrath of his gaolers. For the next fortnight he was only allowed food every other day. Considering daily rations only consisted of watery soup, a slice of bread and a cup of ersatz coffee, this was a severe deprivation. But it could have been worse – guards usually shot escaping prisoners.

Forest had no choice but to settle into the bleak world of Fresnes. As he had expected, his RAF chums had been transferred to a POW camp and with them had gone his message to Barbara. He made contact with other prisoners and passed his time shouting messages. Then, in early May, the Wehrmacht man returned and began to beat him for being the rebellious Tartarin who had been heard shouting anti-Nazi messages and rousing other prisoners to resist. Forest had been betrayed by his neighbour in the next cell.

Hauled downstairs to a punishment cell he found himself in complete darkness, standing on a floor that was thickly covered in a layer of fungus. The only furniture was a chair with three legs that he had to precariously balance against the wall to sleep on, but at least it meant he didn't have to lie on the floor. His starvation rations were reduced once again, so that he only ate soup every third day for three weeks, and the remainder of the time he had to sub-sist on a small piece of bread. The maniacal nature of it all flipped Forest over the edge and he started a dangerous campaign of yelling out every French and British patriotic song he could remember and slandering Hitler and Germany with every invective he could think of. It was not long before his guards came to beat him with a rifle butt, yet even this couldn't stop him. Eventually they just left him to it and he sang and chanted until exhaustion took him into a precarious sleep.

There was one ray of hope in the nightmare. Forest learned in his third week that Britain had begun the invasion of France and that sooner or later they would arrive in Paris. All he had to do was survive until then.

At the time many prisoners were unaware that the arrival of the Allies, which gave them such hope, would be the catalyst for mass executions to avoid Jews, resisters, communists, agents and political prisoners talking about the atrocities they had seen. Forest was equally in limbo about the situation.

When his punishment ended, Forest was shuffled to another cell. This one was smeared in dried blood, which did not inspire confidence. He didn't remain there long, however, before he was called before a German doctor along with several other prisoners. Forest assumed that they were being exam-ined for suitability to go to a labour camp: it was an unpleasant thought. Many who were taken to German work camps simply never returned; most people were convinced that the Germans worked them to death to avoid the expense of a bullet or the gas chamber. Forest again promised himself that he would escape before they left France.

That July he was bundled into a larger cell with several other inmates. Included among them were brothers Paul and Raoul Simons. They had been part of the team Forest had been organising to extract Brossolette from prison, and their appearance was yet another reason to be despondent. From Forest's perspective it seemed that everyone he knew in the resistance had been rounded up. His spirits fell more when they recounted the death of another friend while being arrested by the Gestapo.

Aside from the resisters the new party was comprised of black marketeers who quickly fell foul of Forest when they tried to bully the Simon brothers.

With his usual confidence, Forest singled out their ringleader and punched his lights out. It was satisfying to know that he had not entirely lost his fighting spirit during those long weeks of imprisonment.

Before long the prisoners were on the move again, but this time in a van headed for a camp at Compiègne. Forest managed to secure some paper and a fragment of pencil, which he used to scrawl a note for Barbara. Throughout his imprisonment he would produce many of these heartfelt missives and a surprising number found their target. Addressing the paper to Jose Dupuis (which was a risk in itself if the Germans spotted the note) he tossed it out of the van as they passed a group of workmen. One of them picked it up and waved. His message was on its way. It read:

> Dear Friends. Everything is fine. I am leaving for Germany – reassure Barbara – see you soon, with love to you all, especially Barbara – Cheval – Shelley – Write to Barbara for me. Tell her to be brave and patient – I will return soon. Cheval.

The air of intense optimism was a far cry from the actual desperation Forest felt, but it gave him something to think about on his long journey and, what's more, it gave him hope.

Compiègne was luxury compared to Fresnes. A former military barracks, the accommodation was rundown and running water was scarce, but the food was good and that compensated for a lot. Forest turned his mind to escape yet again, as he would later report: 'I had two cracks at it at Compiègne without success.'[2] One of these attempts involved bribing guards and having accomplices pose as Germans, but before the plan could happen news reached the inmates that they were being transferred. Forest was determined to stay at Compiègne as long as possible so that he might initiate his escape plan while still in France.

With the help of another inmate and former resistance worker who had befriended the guards and was in receipt of smuggled money from the outside world that he could use as a bribe, Forest convinced the camp doctor to give him an injection that would induce a high fever. The transport would not take a sick prisoner in case they were carrying a contagious disease, so in this way Forest missed the first transport. By regularly reporting to the camp doctor he was even able to miss a second transport and with the time he had earned himself he wrote to Jose Dupuis again:

I am at Compiegne and about to leave for Germany. My morale is good, but I am very worried about Barbara. I beg you to do everything possible to reassure her and make her understand that the war will not last for ever and that we will be together again soon. It's Barbara that concerns me so do everything you can for her and remind her that if anything bad happens to her then life will have no purpose for me – she represents everything that I hold dear in this world – tell her that I love her more than ever and I think of her constantly – I embrace her with all my heart, with all my love – it's the uncertainty about this that has caused me the greatest distress since my arrest.

But his hope was misplaced. During his time at Fresnes a clerical error had been made on his file, probably helped along by his friends on the outside. Forest had been downgraded from a 'three-star' prisoner, which would categorise him as a dangerous saboteur and terrorist and have him on a quick route to a speedy German death, to a 'one-star' minor offender. It was an error that saved his life and induced his transfer to Compiègne, but someone noticed the mistake and the file was re-graded. Forest was once again a 'three-star' prisoner and now there was no way to avoid a transfer. Surrounded by eight armed guards, he was escorted to a train and an unknown destination in Germany.

Notes

1. It is now the second largest after the construction of Fleury-Merogis prison between 1964–68.
2. Official report to SOE.

15

The Darkness of Buchenwald

'BUCHENWALD STILL SHOCKED ME when I first went there. But, of course, after all the years in the guard units at the camps, I did not come there unprepared. I over-came it. Sachsenhausen, Flossenburg and all the other [concentration camps] presented no problems after Buchenwald.'[1] So said notorious concentration camp commandant Hans Huttig during a 1970s interview. Only Auschwitz could outshine the horrors of Buchenwald and for many SS men who served as guards there, once they had adapted to Buchenwald no other camp could tweak their consciences.

Buchenwald opened its gates in 1937, initially to political prisoners and criminals, but by 1938 it was accepting its first transport of Jews. Some of these earliest inmates proved lucky, as those were the days when Nazi policy still favoured relocation over execution. There were 10,000 Jews interned at Buchenwald that were released at the end of 1938 having promised to emigrate and a similar policy was adopted with Czech Jews released at the outbreak of war. This 'generous' policy failed to last, as in 1942 remaining Jews in the camp were transported to Auschwitz while, in contrast, Polish prisoners were being sent back to Buchenwald from the infamous extermination camp.

When Forest first glimpsed his new home (the last one his captors intended for him) it was swelling to bursting point due to another new policy: Jewish slave labour intended for the armaments factories. The camp population had risen dramatically to 85,000 and the overcrowding was horrendous. In the first 100 days of 1945, 13,969 prisoners had perished simply from the horrific conditions that the overcrowding caused. When the War Crimes Committee began investigating Buchenwald prior to the trial of leading Nazi figures, they estimated that there had been 51,000 deaths at Buchenwald, of which only 33,000 were recorded and most were listed under natural causes: very few of the many executions were recorded as such.[2]

Rumours of Buchenwald had already filtered from the camp, but Forest quickly learned of the full extent of its horrors from his fellow prisoners once inside. It had been set up by Karl Koch, its first commandant, who, along with his wife Ilse, was renowned among the inmates for his sadism and cruelty. He eventually came unstuck with his own party when it was discovered that he had been embezzling camp funds, and was executed. Ilse survived the war to be labelled as the 'bitch of Buchenwald' and to be accused of making lamps and other items out of human skin.

Buchenwald's evils had not decreased with the loss of Koch. Forest learned that the Nazis were now experimenting with typhus vaccines at the camp, which meant infecting large numbers of inmates with the disease first. Many died during the experiments. Dr Schuler was in charge of the experiments and the prisoners knew him as Dr Ding.

For new arrivals life at Buchenwald began with the usual routine humiliations. Stripped naked and forced to stand outside for hours, they were eventually shorn from head to toe with blunt clippers, then jammed into a shower block to wash. The ritual was supposed to remove lice, but it seemed to Forest that it was just another way to demean him. A small towel had to be shared between four men to dry themselves, and then everyone was issued with camp clothing – cotton shirt and trousers.

A forced march had to be endured across gravel pathways in bare feet to the 'little camp', which was an external section for new arrivals that was separate from the main camp. Inmates remained in the 'little camp' for varying lengths of time; accommodation was provided in a few huts and tents, but everywhere was so overcrowded that most prisoners had to sleep in the open air, no matter the weather. Disease spread rapidly, from the more mundane environmental conditions of chilblains to rampant outbreaks of dysentery and typhus. The weakest failed to survive 'little camp' and were cremated without ceremony.

Forest had managed to maintain his health during his time in Fresnes, even avoiding serious blood poisoning in his injured arm, but now he was struck with dysentery that wracked him with agonising pains and stripped him of his strength.

There seemed no rhyme or reason to when the Germans chose to move prisoners from 'little camp' to the main building. POWs and political prisoners were kept separate from the slave labourers, but it was still a diverse population that Forest emerged into. He was surrounded by communists and Polish and French criminals, as well as those who had opposed the Nazis, while a large chunk of the camp company was made up of British and American airmen. This was clearly against the Geneva Convention, but for various reasons the Germans had removed POW rank from these men, so they could do as they pleased with them at Buchenwald. Forest felt he finally might have allies in an escape, but he had to be cautious. Internal camp politics among the prisoners were as dangerous as those of their Nazi overlords. Factions had developed and they openly warred with each other; the communists were a particular threat as they were some of the longest-serving residents and distrusted the airmen. In among them were the ever-present traitors and stool pigeons who would happily turn a 'comrade' over to the Germans. Forest had entered a hornet's nest.

He now also had the pleasure of learning about life in an SS-run camp. The Gestapo had been bad enough but at least they seemed to have reasons for tormenting their victims, even if it was just to get some minor information. The SS guards were more universal with their bullying and enjoyed picking on the weak. Mingling with the criminals and airmen were the disabled or mentally ill, yet another portion of society the Nazi regime considered pointless. They were not spared from the SS brutality and many were beaten and tortured, both mentally and physically, just for existing. It was obvious to one witness who later reported his experiences to SOE that some of the inmates had no concept of what was happening to them, 'their only crime was insanity'. A large number of these unfortunate souls perished from their wounds.

There were also rounds of extermination and executions. The same witness wrote: '250 little gypsy boys, aged between 6 and 16 years were taken out of the camp and crushed into large furniture like vans – the back was then closed and sealed, and I was told they were gassed by means of a pipe from the exhaust.'[3]

Thankfully Forest was not alone in this nightmare. On his train journey to Buchenwald he had found himself in the company of other SOE men and women. The women were destined for Ravensbruck, but the men were all headed for the same destination. Included in their number was Captain Henri Peulevé who had been captured in the same month as Forest and shared much in the way of personality and life experience. Peulevé worked for F Section as a wireless operator and had broken his ankle on his first mission during the parachute drop. He had to crawl to a nearby farm and beg for help. Fortunately the farmer's wife was sympathetic to the resistance and didn't turn Peulevé over to the Germans. He found his way back to England and was rapidly ready for his next mission.

More upsetting was Forest's recognition of Captain Desmond Hubble, an old friend from RF Section. Hubble had a family and Forest had always felt the risks he took were too great for someone with such responsibilities. He had tried to persuade him not to take on an operational mission, but like so many SOE men Hubble could not refuse the chance of getting into the action. He had been parachuted into the Ardennes and not long after was discovered and arrested by the Germans.

Among others in the group was unfortunate Christopher Burney who had been sent by SOE to join the Autogiro circuit after it had already been taken over by the Germans. He narrowly escaped walking directly into a trap and was on the run for months before the Gestapo caught up with him. Then there was Lieutenant Stephanie Hessel and 23-year-old Jewish SOE agent Maurice Pertschuk.

All told there were thirty-seven SOE men who were determined to stick together whatever the cost while in the camp. The SS were not concerned about all these agents mingling, perhaps they hoped they would share information that could then be extracted, but they did make every effort to ostracise the group from the other prisoners, even ordering them not to take part in the daily roll call. No doubt this was in an effort to generate resentment among their fellow prisoners and it certainly worked with the communists, who instantly took a dislike to the SOE men. They called the officers products of the ruling classes and whispered that they, like the capitalists, were to be disposed of first once the Soviets took control. Forest was used to this nonsense having worked alongside the communist resistance branch for so long and took no more notice than was required to avoid playing into their hands.

Anyway, he was already busy thinking about escape. While daily life was one of camp routine, interspersed with chess tournaments using a travel set that Hubble had smuggled in, and playing bridge using cards created by Captain

Frank Pickersgill of F Section, Forest's mind was diverted by assessing his chances of escape. The new agents were confined to a limited area and separated from other prisoners by barbed wire. Forest had to use the only two men he trusted who had fuller access to the camp – Burney and Pertschuk.

Forest's main interest was in the block used for housing prisoners for 'special treatment' and where it was well known that experiments were being carried out. This was the preserve of the camp doctors, a notorious bunch who could even send a shiver of fear up an SS man's spine. They were presided over by 32-year-old Dr Erwin Schuler who specialised in typhus experiments, but there was also Dr August Bender, Dr Hans-Dieter Ellenbeck (who conducted blood experiments), Dr Karl Kahr (previously a camp doctor at Dachau), Dr Erich Kather and Dr Heinrich Plaza. They were a sordid crew of hack scientists but, of more interest to Forest, their secretive experiments cast a fearful pall over their domain, which kept the SS guards at bay. Not least because Dr Schuler was working on a dreadfully infectious disease that none of the SS men wanted to get.

Only Dr Schuler and a political prisoner named Arthur Dietzech, who had been in the camp since 1922, had overall access to the special treatment centre and this potentially made it a relatively safe place for fleeing prisoners.

Forest had noted that other opportunities were limited. The barbed-wire fences were too well guarded and too many unfriendly eyes would happily reveal would-be escapees to the SS. But people who entered the special treatment centre were rather prone to 'vanishing'. It might be the only way to ship out a number of men.

Forest set his mind to not only contacting Dr Schuler, but getting him to help them. Schuler had adopted the name Ding in the camp for no obvious reason. He was a pleasant-looking young man with dark hair and eyes. He had a boyish set to his face and looked decidedly too friendly to be the sort of person to happily inject a patient with typhus. Unlike some of the tougher-looking guards there was something about Ding that suggested he might be open to manipulation. At least, that was what Forest hoped.

But getting to him was a challenge in itself. The best option was to work through Arthur Dietzech, who served as Ding's assistant and was as heavily implicated in the evil experiments as his master. He had certainly never refused an order, no matter how unpleasant. The communists had had a similar idea, but had failed to arouse Dietzech's interest, and he had flatly refused to help them. Though this was not encouraging, Forest felt that the changing war situation might be the key to securing Dietzech's help. Every day there was more news that the Allies had returned, were storming through France and would soon be in Germany. It would only be a matter of time before Buchenwald was liberated and the Nazis were scared. Any German caught inside the camp who could not prove himself a genuine prisoner would be liable to a war crimes tribunal and Ding, with his diabolical experiments, could hardly expect anything other than a long drop on a short rope. His assistant Dietzech was equally in danger.

If Forest couldn't appeal to their humanity, he would appeal to their sense of self-preservation. It felt like being back in SOE headquarters as Forest tried to negotiate a way to Ding. It began with Burney, who put him in touch with a man called Balachowski. In turn Balachowski put him in touch with two German prisoners: Eugen Kogon and Heinz Baumeister ('quite first class men').[4] Out of these Kogon proved the most useful as he was secretary to Ding and happy to help. He also had seen large numbers of papers detailing the appalling deeds of the doctor that could be used for blackmail.

During the course of his secretarial duties Kogon worked on inducing paranoia in Ding. It wasn't hard as daily news arrived that the Americans were drawing near and that Germany was suddenly fighting a defensive war. Many SS men were now trying to think how they could cover their backs and survive what was to come. With gentle prodding it wasn't long before Ding came up with the idea one day that perhaps if he was to help a couple of prisoners escape it would be his insurance for the day the Allies knocked on the gate.

The news that Ding was slowly cracking could not have come at a better moment. Things within the camp were taking a nasty turn. A further 168 Allied airmen had been martialled into the camp three days after Forest had arrived; they should have been in a POW camp but the SS had manoeuvred around this by accusing them of being 'terror fliers' – airborne terrorists – and they were not to be treated as genuine prisoners of war.

Their lives were quickly made unbearable at the camp. Many of the men had to sleep outside and developed pneumonia and pleurisy. When an Allied air raid destroyed the factory attached to the camp, killing 300 prisoners and eighty SS men, the situation only got worse for the POWs.

They were fortunate that Burney was actively working to save them and managed to smuggle a message to a nearby Luftwaffe station about their situation. The Luftwaffe immediately saw to it that the airmen were transplanted into their care, except for eleven men who were too sick to be moved.

It was a lucky break but it worried Forest that if genuine airmen could be treated so badly what would happen to him and his fellow SOE men?

Then in the early afternoon of 9 September the usual roll call began. Forest and his colleagues had been ordered not to attend so it was a surprise when, over the speakers, a supplementary order came that sixteen men from Forest's little group were to attend. Among the names was that of young Pickersgill and Desmond Hubble.

No one was particularly concerned about the summons; it just seemed like another of the random things the SS thought up. Perhaps they wanted to check for escapees. While Hubble made sure that Forest looked after his chess set during his absence, he was not worried that he wouldn't be back. Henri Peulevé later commented that he was under the 'assumption that if the SS had wanted them dead they would have killed them in France.'[5]

Even so, as Forest stood with a few others to watch the men off he noticed the bleak expression on the face of the prisoner who controlled their block and heard him mumble that 'it was a bad business'. Forest was alarmed and exchanged glances with Peulevé and the others, but it was quietly agreed that they would not say anything to the others to upset them unnecessarily.

When night came there was no sign of the sixteen and Forest feared the worst. He quietly hid Hubble's chess set with his belongings, doubting there would ever be any future camp tournaments.

The next morning a Polish prisoner brought news that the sixteen had been badly beaten but were still alive and others reported they had been seen exercising outside, but it didn't appease Forest's suspicions. The SS rarely did things without sinister motives and he wasn't convinced they had removed the men so carefully simply to beat them. They preferred such punishment to be public.

The following day Forest's fears were confirmed when the Polish prisoner returned to them again, this time looking particularly gloomy. A fellow prisoner had reported seeing the bodies of all sixteen, it appeared they had been executed the previous night. Panic swept through the group, but some tried to remain hopeful, after all it was just a rumour. Forest, however, was inclined to believe the story, it sounded far too similar to others he had heard.

Later, Balachowski appeared with the full story. After going to the roll call the sixteen men had been removed to another building where they were savagely beaten and then hung from meat hooks in the ceiling. This was around 5.30 p.m. and the process of slow strangulation from the hangings had taken at least 5–10 minutes. It was a popular method of execution among the Nazis and some of the conspirators in the plot to assassinate Hitler had died in a similar method. The bodies had been passed on to the crematorium, where the Polish informer had seen them. Balachowski was distraught to have to tell them the news, not least because they now had an idea of their own fates. Or at least some did.

'So these sixteen were condemned, then perhaps we are not, because if we are, why haven't they taken us too?' asked some, but Forest did not share their optimism.

Balachowski was still willing to help and arranged for Forest and Peulevé to hide in one of the camp laboratories for a while so they could write letters undisturbed. Forest was quite convinced that these would be his last messages and expressed as much in his notes. They were the bleakest he had written during his entire confinement:

These are 'famous last words' I am afraid, but one has to face death one day or another so I will not moan and get down to brass tacks.

I will not attempt to make a report on my journey, except to say that up to the very moment of my arrest it had been a success and I had got things cracking and woken up a number of slumberers (*sic*). I was quite pleased with things – I took every precaution and neglected nothing – my capture was due to one of those incidents one cannot provide for – I had so much work that I was overwhelmed so I asked PIC to provide me with a sure dependable agent de liaison, and he gave me a young chap called Guy whom I renamed Antonin. He worked for me for a week, and then he got caught; how I do not know, but in any case, he had an appointment with me at 11am on Tuesday 21st March by the metro Passy and brought the gestapo with him. He was obviously unable to withstand bullying and very quickly gave in to questioning. I was caught coming around a corner and had not an earthly chance, being collared and handcuffed before I could say 'knife'. I was badly beaten up in the car on the way to gestapo HQ, arriving there with a twisted nose and a head about twice its normal size. I was then subjected to 4 days' continuous grilling, being beaten up and also being put into a bath of icy cold water, legs and arms chained, and held head downwards underwater until almost drowned, then pulled out and asked if I had anything to say. This I underwent six times – but I managed to hold out and gave nothing away. Not a single arrest was made as a sequel to my capture. The only trouble was that the party who was lodging me got arrested and will have to be compensated for losing liberty and home. The name is Mlle Sandoe…

I was interrogated for about 2 months, but dodged everything – I was offered freedom if I would hand over Bingen – some hopes – I nearly lost my left arm as a result of the tortures, as I got blood poisoning through my wrist being cut to the bone by chains and remaining unattended with handcuffs biting into the wound for about 6 days. Apart from that I was kept in solitary confinement for 4 months at Fresnes…

I was pretty weak when I came out, had lost about 2½ stone in weight. I was sent to Compiegne on July 17th, whilst there recuperated a bit and had arranged an escape together with a chap well-known to … BCRA, whose name is Roberty – and got sent to Weimar on the eve of escaping. Roberty succeeded. Bad luck for me. The journey here [Buchenwald] was an eventful one, it took 8 days.

We had to stop at Saarbrucken for 3 days in a punishment and reprisals camp, and were beaten up on arrival – as usual I seemed to attract particular attention and was well and truly slapped and cuffed. We were confined for 3 days and nights, 37 of us in a hut 9 feet by 7 feet by 7 feet. It was Hell. We then came on to this place Buchenwald – on the way our escorts plundered and stole practically all our affects. Never believe a word about German honesty, they are the biggest thieves, liars, bullies and cowards I have ever met. In addition they delight in torturing people and gloat over it.

Men die like flies here – I sent a message to you thru (*sic*) Geneva. I hope you received it, but have no means of telling. The bearer of this message will give you all the details so I will not say more – whatever he tells you is Gospel truth, he is no romancer, and he will never be able to really do justice to the horrors perpetrated here. For God's sake Dizzy [Lt Col Dismore], see to it that our people never let themselves be softened towards the German people, or there will be another war in 15 years' time and all our lives will have been sacrificed in vain. I leave it to you and others to see that retribution is fierce, it will never be fierce enough.[6]

Forest also made it clear that there was a great deal of material on bacterial warfare and other research held at the camp that should be seized at all costs. While Forest pitied those who had been subject to the tests it seemed illogical to let the material collected be wasted. He signed off sadly, but for the most part he felt numb to the terror that should have been gripping him.

'I seemed to have lost all feeling and become a machine' he commented later. 'I had no fear of death in any shape or form, and I felt absolutely no apprehension. Never during those days did I worry for myself; it was not a matter of courage, I just cannot explain it.'[7]

It was in this atmosphere that the Ding plan progressed.

Kogon had been working steadily on his boss, and when Ding had come to the conclusion that he must help some prisoners his secretary was quick with suggestions.

'What about men from block 17?' (Forest's group).

'Perhaps, but it could only be a maximum of three, any more and it would look suspicious.'

Ding had other concerns: 'And what about Dietzech? They would need to go into block 46 where he is *kapo*.'

'I am sure we can find a way to persuade Dietzech to cooperate,' Kogon said, but in fact he feared that the thuggish Arthur Dietzech might be their biggest stumbling block.

Dietzech was certainly not an easy character to deal with. He might have been a prisoner but that was all that divided him from the Nazis who guarded and ran the camp. He was ruthless and even cruel, had no compunction about doing anything to the guinea-pig prisoners who came before him and tolerated no disobedience or nuisance. If the communists could not illicit his help then Kogon would have to be extra cunning. Fortunately in his duties for Ding he had also gathered quite a bit of evidence on Dietzech and now he moved to blackmailing his second victim.

Dietzech might be a thug but he was not stupid. He recognised that he would not escape a criminal court should he fall into Allied hands and, unlike the SS men who could flee the camp if they needed to, he did not have that option. So when Kogon suggested a way to mitigate the damage his work at Buchenwald had caused he was curious enough to listen.

'We'll have the three prisoners sign papers before you help them as evidence of how good you were to them. That will go a long way with the Allied authorities.' Kogon explained.

'And the credit will go all to me? I don't want anyone sharing it and reducing its impact.'

'Of course, the papers will say you helped them entirely on your own.'

It was a necessary deception to get Dietzech on board, but from now on it was imperative that no one mentioned Ding's role in the escape lest the *kapo* went back on his word.

Kogon returned to Forest with this news, but he was not happy. He had wanted all twenty-one remaining men saved, not just three.

'Ding will only agree to three and that is better than nothing. He also insists you must be one of them as the commanding officer, because your evidence has the most weight.'

Forest was distressed. He had already given up on his own escape, he still wanted freedom of course, but he would not put his life before others. If he had to choose three to live he certainly wouldn't have put himself among them, but now he had no choice. If he argued too much he would ruin everything for the other two men he could save. It was a terrible dilemma, yet Forest had to agree.

The next few days were agonising as he made his decisions about who to take with him in isolation and secrecy. Revealing the plan could result in dreadful despondency among those who were not going, so he plotted alone. His final decision was to take Peulevé and the young Hessel from BCRA. Forest never gave a deep explanation for why he picked these men over the others, in many respects perhaps he could not define the reasons for himself. In the heavy camp atmosphere, decisions were never easy or entirely logical.

Even after his decision was made Forest dared not mention it to the two chosen until the plan came to fruition. He was also still uncertain whether he could trust Dietzech and decided he would have to be a sacrificial victim to test the man's reliability. With everything settled, one day Forest was smuggled to Dietzech who gave him an injection to induce the symptoms of typhus. Forest quietly returned to his hut and waited for his symptoms to develop. It was only now that Forest pulled Hessel and Peulevé aside and told them the gist of the plan. They were to remain silent, tell no one and wait for further instructions from Balachowski.

That night Forest descended into a prickly fever and, in the morning, reported to the block commander, asking to go see the camp doctor. Typhus was a deadly fear within the camp and the block commander was all too keen to get Forest out of his domain and sent him to the camp hospital where, as arranged, Dietzech was waiting to diagnose him with typhus and have him transferred to the guinea-pig block, 46.

The fever lasted three long days and there was no doubt that at times Forest wondered if Dietzech had proved treacherous. Then on the third day he began to improve and as the effects of fever left him he sent word to Kogon to fetch Peulevé and Hessel.

On 19 September, ten days after the deaths of Hubble, Pickersgill and the others, Dietzech appeared at block 17 looking for guinea pigs for his experiments. It was not uncommon for Dietzech to seek out healthy victims without SS knowledge and no one thought much about it when Peulevé and Hessel were unceremoniously selected. Their colleagues miserably wished them farewell, while Peulevé and Hessel had to control their emotions and not reveal that it was actually those they were leaving behind who were in the greatest danger.

Dietzech marched them through the barbed-wire cordon and into block 46 with no hint of sympathy for the conspirators. It must have been a hair-raising moment as Peulevé and Hessel wondered if they were going to meet Forest or an SS welcoming committee. It would have been so easy to be betrayed, but Dietzech had a lot riding on the plan and kept his side of the bargain.

Forest was waiting for them in a room on the first floor. There were two other occupants who had been initiated into the conspiracy: English-speaking orderlies who had sworn to keep the secret. The room was luxury compared to the huts. There were four individual beds for the men (as opposed to one bunk per two men in their prison accommodation) and the room was divided in two by a line of cupboards. Windows looked out onto the camp and for the first time in many months the men felt relief and a fragile sense of safety. Forest was elated to see them and now hoped for their plan to move forward.

The next step to ensure their escape from instant execution was to use Ding to swap their identities with typhus patients, thus faking their deaths. Then they would work on actually getting out of the camp. But as Forest well knew, nothing was ever that simple.

With no new executions being ordered for block 17 Dietzech and Ding started to relax and believed they had plenty of time to arrange for the swap. Their newest 'patients' were safely housed in the hospital room above the wards. No SS guards would dare risk passing the typhus-ridden patients to inspect the room and the three men were even kept busy filling in hospital paperwork. Yet Forest was anxious they should be moving as fast as they possibly could.

A few days after the arrival of the escapees a group of ailing labourers arrived from a work camp in Cologne where there had been a bad typhus outbreak. They were all French and Hessel had the grisly task of interviewing them and assessing which would make suitable candidates for an identity switch. It was not a pleasant chore, but when he was done and could talk with his comrades it was decided that three men – Michel Boitel, Maurice Chouquet and Marcel Seigneur – would prove ideal matches. Now all they had to do was wait until the men died.

It was a morbid situation to have one's fate hanging on the death of another man. It was one of those things that could never be resolved easily in a person's conscience. They also knew that Dietzech would not be averse to hastening a death to ensure his own safety. They all expressed their own desire that nature should be allowed to take its course and, if it should be that one of the men got better, than that was how fate wanted to play it and they would not take that from him. Dietzech was less than impressed by this selflessness, but apparently seems to have obeyed their request.

After all, there seemed no imminent danger.

Two weeks passed without incident, and boredom was the only thing that interfered with the men's days. Forest retrieved Hubble's chess set and took to playing again. The bond between the escapees gradually strengthened as the time passed, and their thoughts revolved around typhus and freedom. Then came 4 October, and a new supplement was added to the usual roll call. Just as before eleven prisoners from block 17 were being specially summoned and one of the names on the list was Peulevé.

It was an awful moment. Peulevé felt sick that not only were his colleagues walking to an atrocious death but, by not being with them, he could risk the lives of Forest and Hessel. He could hardly walk out of the hospital and present himself, as that would ruin everything when he was supposed to be dying of typhus, but if the SS came looking what would happen?

The SS did come looking, even though their usual terror of the sickness that hung around block 46 made them hesitate. But the camp commandant wanted to know where Peulevé was and he had heard he had been transferred to the hospital. Dietzech made himself scarce and the SS men left empty-handed.

They came back however, and this time Dietzech could not feign absence. The camp commandant was determined to carry out his orders and even when Dietzech protested that no one was allowed to enter the hospital without his express permission, as arranged by Ding, the guards were not persuaded. They told Dietzech that a stretcher was on its way for the patient. Express orders from Berlin had said that Peulevé must be executed, no matter his condition, and if that meant shooting him on the stretcher, so be it.

Dietzech was deeply worried that the plan was about to crumble around them; the consequences of which were not to be contemplated. Above all else Peulevé must have every appearance of suffering from typhus when the guards next returned, so he was given an injection to mimic the symptoms and within a few hours he was burning with fever.

When the stretcher finally arrived Peulevé was on the ward boiling with a temperature of 105 and a worried Dietzech was close by. Peulevé's fake symptoms were now proving as dangerous as if he really had typhus, but at least it convinced the SS men that he was truly sick. Still they wanted to remove him.

Ding made a hurried appeal to Commandant Pister, explaining that a patient running such a high fever was a serious contamination risk if moved from the hospital. Pister was unmoved – he wanted Peulevé dead sooner rather than later.

'I could give him a lethal injection,' suggested Ding, desperate to buy time.

'I just want him dead, I don't care how it's done. But not by you Ding, I want someone else to give the injection.'

Was this a sign that the commandant was already having concerns about Ding's ruthlessness? Ding tried not to think about it as he offered another solution.

'What about Dr Schiedlausky?'

SS Hauptsturmführer Gerhard Schiedlausky had performed large numbers of experiments on the female patients at Ravensbruck, so to Pister he would have seemed an obvious candidate, but Ding knew he was another doctor who was feeling his conscience prickling under the threat of the Allies – he would eventually be sentenced to death after the war.[8] Ding suspected he would send a subordinate to complete the order.

Ding's assessment was entirely correct. Good Dr Schiedlausky delegated the execution to an elderly NCO from block 61. This was white-haired Friedrich Wilhelm, a man not known to have any qualms about executing prisoners, but who did have a weakness for schnapps.

Dietzech greeted him at block 46 with a purloined bottle and offered him a drink. It didn't take much to persuade Wilhelm to accept the glass, nor the next, and very rapidly he was satisfactorily drunk. Dietzech then led him onto the ward and pointed out one of the other patients who was as seriously ill as Peulevé. Wilhelm hovered over the sick man like a drunken grim reaper, swaying so much on his feet he could barely remain upright.

'It seems a waste of Phenol to inject the man when he will be dead in hours,' Dietzech mused as Wilhelm tottered dangerously. 'And a waste of your time too. Look, leave the injection with me and if he is still breathing by the morning I'll give it to him myself.'

Everything hung on how conscientious of his duty Wilhelm was: if he insisted on performing the execution now then Peulevé could not allow an innocent man to be hastened to his death. He would have to reveal himself and that would reveal them all. Whether Dietzech would have allowed such a thing to happen (what he had at stake was just as huge) is another matter. He would have no concerns about ushering another victim off quickly to save his own skin.

Fortunately for them all Wilhelm was too drunk to really care who killed who and happily handed the injection over to Dietzech, then wandered away to sleep off his schnapps. He later reported to Schiedlausky that the deed had been done.

Once again it was a narrow escape, but still a corpse was needed to prove that Peulevé was dead, and his chosen double, Marcel Seigneur, was proving to have a fighting spirit. He had clung to life through his illness for far longer than anyone could have expected, though it seemed as if he had now taken a turn for the worse. Dietzech kept trying to persuade the agents to let him quicken his death, but still they refused. Amazingly he obeyed them: perhaps twenty years in a concentration camp under Nazi rule had instilled an almost pathological inability to disobey his superiors! But on the morning of 9 October Seigneur finally succumbed and, with Peulevé's number painted on his thigh, he was sent off to the crematorium.

Peulevé had successfully switched identities and his elation could be hardly contained. He wrote a note to Kogon thanking him in vague terms for his help.

This left Forest and Hessel hanging in a limbo of fear. They did not know for certain the fates of the men who had been called forward on the 5 October. As far as they were aware they must have been executed by slow strangulation and it was a thought that played on their minds (in fact, one of the officers in the party had been granted his request that they be executed by firing squad). It could only be a matter of time before Hessel and Forest (still known to the SS as Dodkin) were also summoned to their deaths.

As the days before the next execution order sped by, Maurice Chouquet (Forest's double) suddenly took a turn for the worse and died on Friday 13 October. Never had such an ominous day seemed so lucky to Forest. Kenneth Dodkin was officially recorded as yet another victim of typhus and Forest could relax a little. Now the only person left was Hessel.

He was frightened that the delay on his behalf would betray everyone, and the longer they hid at block 46, the more people learned about their presence and the deception. How long before they were betrayed? Hessel was a bundle of nerves, and as he feared the approaching of another execution order, he started to doubt the plan. He asked Kogon to make arrangements to ship him from the camp in one of the work parties, anything to put himself at a distance from the SS men, but Kogon refused. Hessel could hardly contain himself, the confinement and waiting seemed yet another torture, then on 20 October, his 27th birthday, news arrived that Michel Boitel had died. Suddenly Hessel was saved.

Notes

1. Segev, T., *Soldiers of Evil*.
2. SOE official files 'Information required on Buchenwald Concentration Camp' 29 June 1945.
3. SOE official files, untitled report on Buchenwald, 17 November 1945.
4. F Section letter, 1/11/1945.
5. Perrin, N., *Spirit of Resistance: The Life of SOE agent Henri Peulevé*.
6. Excerpts taken from typescript of original letter kept in Yeo-Thomas' SOE personnel file.
7. Seaman, *Op cit*.
8. Schiedlausky's official SS records do not list him at Buchenwald in 1944. It appears that he transferred there in 1943, but his record does not indicate when he left. He served at Ravensbruck between 1941 and 1943.

16

A Final Adventure

Every man in the camp knew that Block 46 was a dreadful place. Only a very few people in the camp had an exact idea of what was going on in Block 46. A dreadful horror seized anyone who was brought into any kind of connection with this block. If people were selected and taken to Block 46 through the sick bay, then they knew that the affair was a fatal one. The untold horror, which was attached to this block, made things even worse.[1]

So said Kogon at the Nuremburg War Crime Trials where he served as a witness for the prosecution. It was the sort of testimony Ding was desperately trying to insure himself against with the saving of Peulevé, Hessel and Forest. Even so, he lost faith in the effectiveness of their statements and killed himself before he could be brought to trial.

Ding's fate was the last thing on Forest's mind as he waited in that house of horror and adapted to being Maurice Chouquet, a 35-year-old carpenter and native of Rouen. What Forest knew about carpentry could be noted on a single sheet of paper. SOE rule no.1: don't impersonate someone who has a skilled knowledge of a subject you have no idea about, but Forest had had no choice and, as he watched Hessel and Peulevé being dispatched to a working party, he knew he would soon need to be convincing with a hammer and nails.

Just being transplanted into a new identity was not enough to save the men. They had to get out of the camp, and that need became greater each day. Too many people in block 46 knew about the agents who had been switched with dead Frenchmen, and it was fortunate that no one was inclined to turn traitor, but it was not a situation Forest wanted to prolong. Kogon had been working hard to secure places for the men in work kommandos (labour gangs) now that they had 'recovered' from their sickness. Peulevé and Hessel were headed for Schonebeck where Kogon knew the manager. When they left it was bittersweet for Forest, who wished them the best and hoped to see them again after the war. Once again alone in block 46 he had too long to contemplate the friends he could not save, his own precarious future, and the frequent bouts of dysentery that still tormented him.

Then, in early November, he learned that he was headed for Gleina, where another friend of Kogon's would be waiting for him and it was be unlikely that he would be recognised. Relief and worry about his next step consumed him, but he remembered his friends from his short stay in block 46; he had even become fond of the thuggish Dietzech. On 9 November 1944, bundled up heavily against a snowstorm and hiding food and clothing and Hubble's chess set, he boarded a truck and looked forward to freedom.

Forest was taken from one grim hospital to another. Gleina was as much a death camp as Buchenwald, though in this case the victims were not shot but worked into oblivion. Kogon's contact at the camp was Walter Hummelsheim, but Forest very rapidly fell in with another doctor, Jean Dulac, the head of the camp hospital. He assured Forest that he would get him listed as an orderly at the hospital (avoiding any need to display carpentry skills) and took him to the building where the sick were supposedly tended.

Forest quickly realised that the horrors of block 46 could be easily equalled at Gleina. The wards were full of living skeletons, so starved and emaciated that they barely resembled humans at all. Dulac was doing his best for them with limited resources. Many wore pathetic paper bandages that could barely contain the blood and pus seeping out of their wounds and most dressings were filthy. Forest later described it as feeling like stepping into Dante's 'Inferno'. The atmosphere was full of soft moans and mumbled prayers and the stench of sickness and death. Those that were still aware looked at the newcomer with dull eyes; there was nothing of hope left in them as they lay wasting away in their bunks. Forest was stunned by the horror of it all.

But there was a flip side to the hospital. In the corner was a small room where a group of Frenchmen resided, all former members of the resistance.

Forest instantly decided to take charge of this little group; he was still planning his big escape after all and would need help. He introduced himself as Colonel Maurice Chouquet – the humble carpenter had been promoted, but Forest knew that to get these men to help he had to 'pull rank'. He was treated with instant suspicion, not surprising as he had been led into the room by Hummelsheim, a German, and had been discussing the camp with him. At first it seemed that no one would trust him.

The next day Dulac set to work getting Forest assigned to the hospital as an orderly, and he was instructed to wait with another inmate who had been introduced to him as Pierre Kaan. Pierre had a familiar look about him, but Forest could not place him, which worried him. They slipped into conversation and it seemed Pierre was equally trying to work out where he had seen Forest before. Suddenly he asked: 'Are you Shelley?'

Forest was surprised and a little unsettled, as he had worked too hard to have his real identity discovered now. After a moment he answered.

'Shelley is dead, but Chouquet lives.'

Pierre nodded his understanding.

'In Paris I was known as Biran,' he said, and realisation dawned on Forest. Biran had been the diligent secretary for the Comite Militaire.

'No one must know I am Shelley. I am Chouquet now,' he explained.

'I understand, but it would help the others to trust you if I could tell them you were a respected member of the resistance?'

'Yes, you may tell them that.'

Forest settled into his new life at Gleina, but it wasn't easy. The camp was the medical centre for the larger working camp at Rehmsdorf, though Forest failed to see anything medical about its operation. There were no supplies and the patients were so ill that he soon discovered his main job was to remove the dead from the building. SS orders stated the dead had to be stripped of the thin rags they were wearing. Carrying the frail, filthy bundles and removing the last of their dignity made Forest violently sick on more than one occasion, but slowly he got used to that as well. It was amazing what a person could adapt to, as so many SS and Gestapo men would testify to when stood on trial.

One revelation that took Forest by surprise was that the prisoners were allowed coffins. He couldn't fathom this strange act of dignity in the otherwise degrading procedure of removing the dead. It turned out that the factories that 'employed' the workers had to pay for their funerals and the mistress of the camp commandant owned an undertaker's. Commandant Kenn was in on the deal and was making a healthy profit on every victim he had buried in a cheap coffin supplied by his mistress. The undertakers produced thirteen coffins a day at a cost of 15 marks each, the profits from which fed straight back into Kenn's pockets.

The only problem arose when the death toll outnumbered the coffins. On one occasion Forest was forced to double-up corpses, but the cheap and insubstantial coffins were not designed for even the light weight of two emaciated bodies and as luck would have it the bottom of one such coffin gave way and deposited its cargo at the Kenn's feet. The commandant was irate as he saw his profit margin infringed upon and gave strict orders that the doctors at the camp should ensure that the death toll did not go above thirteen a day. The idiocy of the order and the complete disregard for life only stirred up a deeper hatred of the Nazis in Forest's mind.

So Forest's daily routine consisted of nursing the dying, watching SS doctors sell what few medical supplies were provided, avoiding the many brutes and sadists among the guards, and carrying the dead. He also had the job of collecting the bread ration, but as his dysentery continued even this became a harder and harder chore.

It was a thin and gaunt Forest that got his first whiff of freedom one day when Hummelsheim, who was allowed the privilege of going to Leipzig to get supplies, arranged for Forest to come with him. It was, of course, a grand opportunity for escape, but Forest knew that if he did so Hummelsheim would invariably be cruelly executed and he had no intention of getting his new friend punished for his actions. He had to content himself with whispering a message to some British POWs he found working at a factory. He gave them a stilted report of Buchenwald and his life since and a message of hope to Barbara. They promised that when they could they would pass on his words.

It was only a glimmer of freedom, however, and life was due to get a lot worse before it got better.

Christmas 1944 was misery for Forest. The other prisoners tried to maintain the celebrations and even smuggled in a small Christmas tree and made gifts for each other. But the jolliness of the event seemed bitter and stupid to Forest when they were surrounded by the dead and dying. Even his continued optimism had faded: the horrors of Gleina had eroded him more than anything that had happened at Buchenwald. It was around this time that Forest, never much of a religious man, came to the conclusion that there could be no god.

Pierre felt sorry for him and quietly came over and whispered 'Merry Christmas' in English, but it was hard to penetrate the isolation and loneliness that had built up around the SOE man. It seemed an eternity ago that he had walked through Paris as a free man and taken pleasure at fooling the Nazis.

It was that same month the prisoners learned that the Germans wanted to turn Gleina into a British POW camp and all the current inmates would be transferred to Rehmsdorf. Forest wondered if this would improve his chances of escape or worsen them, though with his strength flagging due to his dysentery, his ability to plot escapes had been compromised. There was also the depressing news that Hummelsheim had been caught smuggling a message out of the camp and was to be sent to Buchenwald for execution. Forest didn't know until later that Kogon had once again proved a heroic rescuer and ensured that Hummelshein was spared. At that time however, all he knew was that his friend was heading for his death. And then they were all moving to Rehmsdorf, the sick and dying bundled into lorries with the relatively healthy. It was just after the new year that all of Gleina was moved to the bigger camp.

Forest was at a stage where he didn't think any new horror could touch him, but this proved to be wrong when he discovered the hospital facilities at Rehmsdorf were even worse than at Gleina. Set in its own compound at the centre of the camp, buildings that were designed to hold 300 now had to accommodate 1,250. Overcrowding was horrendous, internal toilets non-existent (patients had to make do with oil drums arranged by the staff if they could not make it outside). The sick lay three to a bunk, corpses mingled in with the living. It became so hard to tell who was dead and who was still alive that the only definite method was to take temperatures with a thermometer. Even so, starving patients would try to fake the temperature of a dead bunk mate so they could eat his ration.

But, despite it all, there was still hope. The British POWs had been successfully transferred to Gleina and work parties were being sent from Rehmsdorf to the camp. Forest was not yet on a work party, but he knew someone who was and could be trusted, Hans Gentkow.[2] Gentkow replaced Hummelshein in smuggling Forest's messages and managed to get one to a senior British NCO at Gleina. There was some scepticism among the POWs about Forest's identity and it took some careful negotiations before they were prepared to believe that here was an RAF man who had served with SOE. Forest was invited to Gleina by the British and Gentkow arranged for him to be placed on a work party due to dig vegetable beds at the camp. Once at Gleina, Forest was pulled aside to the cookhouse by Corporal John Stevenson and treated to a decent meal and mugs of tea with milk. It was like a strange dream being presented before British airmen who stood to attention and saluted Forest in his pyjama-like prisoner clothes. He was hardly the dashing, strong figure of Paris, but something about his presence still impressed itself on these men. There was little they could do for him however, aside from promising to pass messages and reports about his whereabouts to whoever they could, and they swore that if the Allies took Leipzig they would do what they could to take Gleina and rush to Rehmsdorf to help the inmates there.

It was little, but it was something.

January brought death transports. Forest saw yet another Nazi evil as those deemed too sick to recover were shipped to extermination camps. What he could not be aware of was that this sudden drive was sparked by the increasing proximity of the Allied advance. The same transports were occurring in many concentration camps, in order to get rid of as many living testimonies to Nazi brutality as possible before the Allies descended. If Forest had known, it may have added macabre hope to the transports, but it was still abhorrent to see the sick and dying herded into train carriages, many to die of cold, thirst or exhaustion along the way.

At one point the entire hospital was cleared of its patients, but within a matter of days it was filled with new ones again. Some were only suffering from prolonged exhaustion and the hospital offered the bare essentials of respite and recuperation to build up their strength before they returned to work. They were the lucky ones; those that required medication or surgical treatments might as well have been in a medieval hospital and even then they would probably have been better supplied. Gleina boasted the paltry provisions of a few paper bandages, a single pair of scissors and a small amount of iodine substitute. Operations had to be performed without anaesthetic because there was none and the appalling scenes this created sickened everyone except the SS guards.

On one occasion Allied aircraft bombed the camp and destroyed a prisoner hut. Forest and the teams of orderlies and doctors were helpless to do much. One man required his leg to be amputated and all they had to hand was a surgical knife with a 1½in blade. He survived several days in agony before succumbing to shock.

After another raid on a nearby town the camp doctors were summoned to help the victims. They arrived while Allied aircraft were still strafing the area with bullets. A Jewish Hungarian doctor who was a prisoner at Gleina was caught in the crossfire and died several hours later at the camp.

It was difficult to assess the feelings of the prisoners when they heard the news that they were being killed by the men who were supposedly on their side. Forest, knowing the inaccuracy of navigation and releasing of bombs, could retain the generous view that bombing the camp was an unpleasant accident. He could think of less to justify the gunning down of civilians in the town, but this was war and he knew that such things happened in the heat of the moment. At least he knew the Allies were getting closer, which was some comfort in his current, horrific surroundings. 'At times, I wondered if I was still alive, or even if I was dead and in Hell. How we managed to remain sane, I don't know.'[3]

As April and the warmer weather of spring approached, it also brought rumours that the Nazis had begun to massacre inmates in other camps. It seemed they were determined to wreak as much havoc and misery as they could right until the end.

Forest was not about to be gunned down at the last moment and set about making defensive plans. He got permission to dig trenches under the pretext of turning them into air raid defences, but in fact he intended them as bunk holes if the guards should turn on them. The prisoners managed to hoard a surprisingly large collection of arms as well, including hand grenades, rifles and pistols. Yet the immediate danger came from their fellow inmates. The various divided groups of the camp were segregating themselves even further to ensure their survival and regular fights broke out, especially over food, which was becoming even scarcer. Forest was barely able to fend them off when he collected the bread ration for his patients. He knew now that the camp was at breaking point.

At midnight on 13 April the order was issued that the entire camp was to be evacuated. Forest was not surprised at this turn of events, nor was he shocked to learn that even the sick and dying were to be loaded onto trains headed for an unknown destination. He was certain they were headed for a mass grave. As the train seemed to take an almost random route through the countryside Forest predicted they were heading for Czechoslovakia and he warned Dulac that there would only be one chance for escape and when the time came they must take it.

Two days of travel in cramped conditions was too much for some and over 100 inmates died. The SS guards initially took amusement in simply throwing their bodies off the train, but this soon became tiresome. An SS commander had the train halted in a clearing in a large expanse of woodland and ordered the healthy prisoners to climb down and dig a mass grave. Forest knew that this was their chance; there might be no other on this transportation to death. He arranged things as quickly as he could among his resistance comrades. They would carry bodies to the grave then pretend to turn back to the train before making a dash for the woods. With luck the SS guards would be busy watching the remaining inmates on the train and would take a moment to realise what was happening. It was risky, they could be gunned down easily and they were not men in their prime, sickened by illness and deprivation, but it was better than just sitting and waiting to die. Those that were chosen agreed eagerly.

Chances were still slim though, and Forest hoped to even the odds by speaking with one of the few SS guards who had shown a modicum of sympathy and consideration for the prisoners. Otto Moller was a low-level SS man who had not been of the same cruel and brutal calibre as his cohorts. Forest later said about him: 'This German SS NCO was one of the very few Germans who did not deliberately ill-treat prisoners, and prior to my escape I had him under my thumb... He is the type of man who will give everything away to save his skin...'[3]

He approached Moller and put his own safety on the line. He explained he was actually a British officer in the Secret Service, there was no time to explain his identity change, but he assured Moller that he had managed to smuggle reports to his superiors about life in the camps and the treatment by guards. However, he had noted the kindness Moller at times had shown and his restraint, so he would be prepared to make a statement on his behalf expressing this. Unfortunately if he was executed that could not happen and nothing could be done to put a barrier between Moller and the wrath of the Allies when they saw what had been going on. It was in Moller's own self-interest to see that Forest escaped.

It was a dangerous ploy, as Moller could so easily have remembered his SS oath and turned the whole escape party in, but for some reason he didn't. It was obvious at that point to all but the most deluded of Nazis that Hitler's regime was doomed. Some might contemplate slipping away and working towards World War Three, but others were in too deep and their retreat was all about the simplest motive – survival. It seems likely it was this thought that swayed Moller, in any case he agreed to help Forest.

Thus twenty brave souls carried bodies to the mass grave then turned and, on a shout from Forest, ran as fast as they could into the woods. It was not the most athletic of escapes as the men were too worn down for that. Even Forest, who had so prided himself on his physical fitness, was appalled to find himself stumbling from a run to a trot as he reached the treeline. It was not a mad dash, it couldn't be, and they were fortunate that the SS had been distracted and their gunshots wide.

Forest threw himself into the first bush he spotted and landed on another resistance man. Panting and gasping, they huddled into the foliage, listening uneasily to the sound of German voices coming closer. Then there was a shout, which Forest knew was Moller. He tensed, knowing he was doomed if the SS man broke his word. The shout was followed by a shot and then Moller was calling his men off in the wrong direction. There was little time for relief. When everyone was rounded up there were only ten remaining of the twenty who had fled. Forest had no idea what had become of the others. In fact, nine had been easily recaptured and swiftly executed. Pierre Kaan was the tenth, but he was lucky to be found by Moller and escorted back to the train without anyone knowing. He would die in hospital a few weeks after being rescued by the Allies.

For those that had got this far the next step was vital. Along with gathering arms the resistance men had made a conscious effort to gather whatever civilian clothing they could. Forest had spare clothing that was given to him by his friends at Buchenwald and had smuggled it off the train during the escape. Now everyone removed their inmate clothing, which would have given them away in seconds, and pulled on a mismatch of clothes. Forest wore grey trousers and a corduroy jacket and boots that the strange character Dietzech had given him. Nothing fitted properly and at any other time he could have been mistaken for a tramp or vagrant, but the war had gone on for a long while and the countryside was littered with displaced persons, few of whom would look any better than he did. Slowly the men regained their bearings, waited 3 hours in case Moller took the opportunity to join them, and then split into three groups. Forest teamed up with his old friend Dulac and a Belgian named Georges Piot[5] and they set out mid-afternoon.

No one was entirely sure where they were, nor the best direction in which to head. The Allied advancing lines were their best bet, but even so, finding them was a matter of stumbling on them in the dark. They walked through the woods slowly, conserving strength and only resting when it was too dark to navigate. Forest's dysentery was playing up again. He was frequently cramped with agonising pains in his guts, any food he ate tended to make it worse for the next few hours, so perhaps it was just as well he had only brought one piece of bread with him (he had sacrificed a second piece so he could bring Hubble's chess set, which he intended to return to Desmond's family).

Every step of the journey was fraught. They came across a woodcutter's camp and were challenged, but managed to get away. When they came to a river they discovered the bridge too well guarded and had to wade across, Forest in the lead. He stumbled in a hole and was almost swept away, but was saved by Dulac. At another point they reached a road guarded by the German Home Guard, who had been created to supplement the rapidly diminishing home forces. To make matters worse the three escapees heard footsteps behind them and assumed they were trapped between two German forces. It was some relief when the approaching footsteps proved to be another of the escape parties. Individually they made dashes across the road when the Germans had their backs turned and split up again into their respective groups.

For Forest this victory was a chore and he wondered how much more he could take. His dysentery had become acute, perhaps due to drinking freezing river water, and he was gripped by stomach pains all the time to the point where he had to double up and remain still until they dispersed. He was out of food as well – soon his strength would fail him.

It was not long before he faced a trial that was too much for him. They reached an open expanse of land with only a small clump of trees to act as cover. They had no choice but to cross it, but their luck had run out: they were some distance from the trees when three men appeared to their left. Dulac and Piot made a dash for the clump and vanished into the trees, but Forest could not run long before his dysentery tortured him and forced him to slow down. He could only make it to one solitary tree that stood away from the rest and there he slumped down on his belly and hoped. What could he do but trust in his luck and hope that the men would miss him?

He heard them walk past and then, to his horror, they stopped. They had seen him. One called out to him in German. Forest feigned a heavy sleep;

perhaps they would think him drunk. They were closer now and someone else shouted at him, but he didn't move. There was a pause and then one man said something to his friends that made them laugh loudly. Forest had the impression they were commenting on his laziness, and now he just hoped they would move on as if they tried to shake him awake he was doomed. His German was too limited to talk himself out of the situation. He waited miserably.

The Germans watched him for several moments then abruptly turned and walked away. As soon as it was safe he got to his feet and headed for the main clump of trees, but when he got there Dulac and Piot were gone. He reflected that had he been in Dulac or Piot's place perhaps he too would have assumed that when he fell he was doomed to discovery by the passing Germans. Still, he liked to imagine that he might have hung around to see what happened. But the end result was simple, he was on his own.

Now the weather deteriorated. Forest encountered another river but found an unguarded bridge and, soaked to the bone by heavy rain, made it into the refuge of woodland once again. He was exhausted, but there seemed nowhere to settle, then suddenly the world fell away from him. He had stumbled into a pit lined with branches. The fall shook him, but in the next instant he realised that he had found his bed for the night. Thanking his luck he pulled branches around him and doing his best to block out the pain and the cold, he slipped into sleep.

When he woke it was still raining and he was famished. He found a potato field and rooted around for something to eat without success. He fell behind a woodpile and drifted into sleep again. When dawn came he was at least a little rested and carried on towards a road. He had a vague idea of heading to Chemnitz and reaching the Allied line, but beyond that he was just walking. He was less alert than before and when he reached a road he was spotted by armed Germans who challenged him.

Some reservoir of adrenaline spurred him back into the trees despite shots whizzing past. He collapsed into the undergrowth – his body was spent. When he tried to lift his legs he simply couldn't. His head throbbed and stabbing pains shot through his eyes. He wanted to be sick, but retching only hurt his empty stomach. It was then he realised that his dysentery had struck during the run and his legs were wet with his own bodily waste. He confessed to himself that he was in a sorry mess.

Somehow he eventually gathered his strength together and carried on. He had lost his sense of direction and before long stumbled into another pit. This one was deeper and he panicked when he realised he did not have the strength to climb out. He tried to remain calm, but there was no option left but to sleep and try to conserve his flagging energy.

He awoke to the smiling face of a Yugoslav prisoner of war. The friendly figure tried to explain something to him, but Forest was ignorant of Yugoslavian. Fortunately the POW knew French and when he switched to this language they were able to communicate. Forest told him he was an escaped prisoner of war and had to get moving. He endeavoured to stand but his body collapsed in protest. Gently his new friend lifted him up and carried him into the shelter of some woods. Forest sunk into unconsciousness again.

When he awoke it was to see that the Yugoslav POW had brought him bread and a little wine in a bottle. Forest could not express his gratitude at the small gift, but the first bite of bread on his sick and hollow stomach made him violently ill. Unperturbed, the Yugoslavian offered him the wine and that at least stayed down. The POW had brought some food for Forest, which he insisted he took. He then allowed Forest to rest while he kept a watch for enemy patrols.

Finally Forest felt strong enough to carry on. He thanked the kindly stranger and walked away, after a short distance he turned back and waved and the POW waved back. He could only wonder where this generous and compassionate man had emerged from: was he part of a working party in the woods or was he an escapee too? Forest had not asked and he would never know. He was just grateful for the miracle of stumbling upon a friendly face in these vast and enemy-filled woods.

Though he was still ailing and his legs were heavier with each step, Forest felt a new-found hope and decided to push his luck and follow a main road for a time in the hope of finding a signpost to give him a clue where he was. It wasn't long before he came upon a crossroads and, to his amazement and joy, he discovered he was only 2km from Chemnitz. The elation of seeing the town, despite its bomb-damaged buildings and ruinous appearance, was overwhelming for the footsore Forest. Better still, he realised that the Germans were using French POWs and civilians to clear rubble and carry water, so for the first time he was in no danger if someone heard him speaking French. His luck seemed eternal when he even managed to hitch a lift on a horse and cart driven by a French POW. It was the fastest 25km he had travelled during his entire escape and now he was on course for the Allied lines.

That was when his luck ran out. He was so close to the Allied lines that he could hear the machine guns and artillery. Refugees fleeing the fighting streamed past him; he was so near that he could hardly restrain himself. Perhaps it was this last feeling of relief that let his usually coy senses down. As he headed out into a field that had become no-man's-land, he heard a guttural German voice behind him shout 'halt'.

Later, Forest wrote: 'It all appeared so unfair.'[6] Metres from safety he had been spotted by a German patrol. He wanted to run, but his body refused and when bullets hit the ground around him he collapsed, finally overcome with hopelessness. Surely this was not how it would end, a bullet in the back of the head from an unknown German?

Fortunately the soldiers who had found him were more interested in taking him alive. They hauled him back behind German lines and to their unit. At least they were pure army and inclined to treat prisoners fairly. Forest gave himself the name of Adjutant-Chef Maurice Thomas and stuck to his story of being an escaped French POW who had been living off the land for some time. At least his appearance convinced them of that. They supplied him with as much potato soup as he could eat and a bed for the night in a hut. To Forest it seemed the epitome of luxury, the only thing that spoiled it was the resurgence of his dysentery.

The decent army officers unfortunately handed him over to a band of little thugs from the Hitler Youth at Chemnitz. They enjoyed spitting at him, slapping him, slamming their rifle butts into him and generally torturing him as he endured a 10-mile march to another town. It seemed he would never be free of this torment.

He spent an unpleasant night in a prison cell and then was returned to Chemnitz to wash, which at least was a welcome relief. Before long he was being moved again, this time to a transit camp. Briefly he was reunited with some British servicemen, but then he was on another forced marched to a French POW camp.

Forest had not come this far to give up now, and remarkably, within two days of his arrival, he had not only convinced ten other prisoners to escape with him but had agreed upon a plan and created forged documents and passes to enable it to happen. Despite the speed of its organisation the plan proved successful.

At 10 p.m. one evening Forest and the others slipped from the camp. At the nearest train station they booked tickets to Chemnitz and, once there, split into pairs and headed west for the front line. So far so good, but Forest had forgotten how badly his body had deteriorated: 'All my old pains came back even more acutely than before. My feet felt like open stumps, my legs were stiff and appeared to be receding into my guts. Dysentery kept wringing my innards, I could hardly place one foot in front of the other.'[7]

Forest had to rely on the support of the NCO who had paired with him to walk the relatively short distance. Even so it was agony and when finally all the escapees reunited in sight of the front line, he collapsed.

Hope and freedom were so close. Forest could see the outline of camouflaged tanks and could hear the shrill bursts of gunfire. Yet he couldn't move. He lay on the ground and yelled to be left, promising to follow the others when his strength returned. No one moved, and with a generosity others had not shown, the escapees all refused to leave Forest's side. He grumbled and ordered them to leave, but by now they were well aware that he was actually a British officer and so, being French, they ignored his orders. They hauled him up while Forest grouched and complained: he didn't like to think of himself crossing the Allied lines in the arms of others. But he had no choice, and off they headed towards the sound of guns.

They later would discover that they had crossed a minefield to reach the American troops, who looked at them mildly astonished. It was a peculiar moment as the dishevelled men explained they were French POWs and emphasised Forest's importance. It was like a dream come true when he found himself sat before an American officer, sipping coffee and explaining his story in detail. He was too exhausted to truly give in to his feelings; he was almost numb to them after all this time. Yet here he was back in the land of the living, being treated as a human being once again. As he took in the civility of his surroundings and the men questioning him he felt a sharp pang of happiness – he was home.

The White Rabbit had returned to his hutch.

Notes

1. Spitz, V., *Doctors from Hell: The Horrific Account of Nazi Experiments on Humans*.
2. Forest reports that he was a prisoner due to his habitual drunkenness.
3. Seaman, *Op cit*.
4. Letter to SOE, 10/8/1945.

5. A barber in Buchenwald, who Forest later reported as being a useful witness for the American War Crimes branch.
6. Seaman, *Op cit.*
7. *Ibid.*

17

And then the War was Won

IN LONDON, NEWS QUICKLY spread that the White Rabbit was on his way home, but no one could be more relieved and elated than Barbara, though plenty of people within SOE and the departments it liaised with were ecstatic at the news.

Within rooms 39 and 40 of the NID (Naval Intelligence Division) one man was particularly intrigued by the news. This was a kooky NID officer who had created the 30AU (his 'Red Indians' as he liked to call them): an elite troop of commandos. Somehow this man, who was both loved and loathed by his contemporaries, had learned about the reports Forest had had smuggled home to Britain, in particular his letter about what was happening at Buchenwald. He had plans to publish the letter in order to inform the public about what was really happening in the depths of Germany, but when news reached him that Forest was on his way home, he hesitated:

As we arranged at lunch, I am sending you a copy of the letter from Squadron-Leader Yeo-Thomas which I told you about.

Now that we have the good news that the writer is alive and on his way home, we will postpone our decision about giving publicity to this appalling document until Yeo-Thomas' own views are known.

In view of this, I am sure you will not give the letter too wide a circulation.

Commander Ian Fleming
Admiralty[1]

Ian Fleming (future creator of the eponymous spy James Bond) had always shown a great deal of respect for the agents he had come to know both directly and indirectly. His role with the NID was largely one of liaison between the various secret intelligence units. SOE occasionally needed the assistance of the navy (though not as often as the air force) and it was useful for there to be an official contact. Fleming's brother, Peter, worked for SOE and was involved in a number of high-profile missions, so it was hardly surprising that Ian knew much of the workings within the organisation.

In later years his memories of the brave and unique individuals who worked for SOE in their various divisions filter into his novels; at least two SOE female agents are reputed to have been inspiration for characters in the James Bond stories. It doesn't seem that Forest ever knew Fleming personally, but his daring adventures, lucky escapes and, ultimately, his survival, caught Fleming's attention to the extent that he became personally interested in Forest's story.

Ian Fleming was a backseat spy, and there are various legends about great plans he concocted and missions he went on, including a story about training at SOE's Camp X in Canada. However, the facts behind these legends are missing: they are a combination of wishful thinking and purposeful misdirection on Fleming's part – he was always the natural storyteller.

Fleming's career in NID was largely a desk job; he did make a trip to France to try and persuade Admiral Darlan to move his fleet to England in the early days of the war when the Nazis had taken Paris, but he was unsuccessful and his mission was one more of diplomacy than espionage. From his position in room 39, orchestrating and listening to the various intelligence missions the British were running, he could live the life of a spy vicariously. It was the closest he could get to the action; no one really considered him secret agent material, but as an organiser and creative individual he stood out.

Somewhere along the line he learnt about Forest Yeo-Thomas. It's probable that had the two ever actually met they would have got along quite well. Both had a well-ingrained stubborn streak and an independent nature. Neither had been particularly fond of school or academic achievements, despite being intelligent men, and had preferred instead to excel at sports, though not team games (Forest was keen on boxing, while Fleming was exceptional in athletics). Neither had a peaceful relationship with their parents and both felt the burden of being compared to a favoured sibling: in Ian's case his older brother Peter, in Forest's his dead younger brother Jack.

Both were men of action deemed unsuitable for the field, Ian because of his independent streak and difficulty to control, Forest because of his age. But while Forest had managed to overcome these obstacles and become an active agent for SOE, Ian remained stuck at his desk. That is where their similarities end. Ian was glorified as an ideal spymaster, had he only had the opportunity to sit further up in the NID. His work with 30AU, which he initially controlled, demonstrated this. Forest on the other hand was much more typically a spy: he found organising necessary but frustrating and his temper could make him far from diplomatic.

Emotionally the two men had a lot in common, especially their creativity. Forest had come up with some audacious and completely unworkable ideas during his time in SOE and Ian had certainly matched him with schemes for underwater concrete observation posts and daring raids. Both had individually concocted plans for kidnapping a high-ranking German officer. There seems little doubt that Ian would have liked a man like Forest working on espionage for him, though Forest may have found the budding novelist's need for control rather taxing on his patience.

This leads smoothly to speculation about the ultimate spy and ladies' man, James Bond. Was Forest one of many inspirations for 007?

Over the years there has been a great deal of speculation as to who the real Bond was, and the consensus is now that there was no single individual who formed the character, but that he was an amalgamation of several people, both known and not known personally to Ian Fleming. Fleming rather enjoyed spreading rumours about who the real Bond was, sometimes doing it for publicity, sometimes for a joke. But his time in NID and his connections to other secret organisations certainly gave him plenty of inspiration for the ultimate secret agent.[2]

SOE in particular contained a lot of brave and heroic individuals whose stories stuck in Fleming's memory. Agents went undercover for months, even years, and faced horrendous torture and death if captured. There was something extraordinary and dashing about these men and women who slipped into the Nazi world, many never to return.

Two significant SOE names that have been linked to Fleming are Vera Atkins and Christine Granville. Atkins was an executive officer in the F Section of SOE and known for her work after the war of trying to trace the fates of the hundreds of SOE agents who never returned from missions. She was originally employed as a secretary, but quickly proved an exceptional intelligence officer. In her obituary in the *New York Times* she was credited with being the inspiration for Miss Moneypenny, the formidable secretary to Bond's boss 'M' and a staple of the novels. It is reasonable to suspect that Atkins might have preferred a more dynamic fictional role.

Christine Granville caught Fleming's attention just after the war. An amazing and audacious agent, Christine managed to talk her way out of many difficult situations partly because of her dramatic and inventive imagination and partly because of her innate sex appeal. In his 1993 book, Donald McCormick makes a case for her being the original Vesper Lynd, Bond's love interest in his first adventure *Casino Royale*. There is no conclusive proof, as in all Bond speculations, that she was the genuine inspiration, but she was a friend of Fleming's and it is possible that he carried on a quiet affair with her. In 1947 he wrote to a friend: 'I see exactly what you mean about Christine. She literally shines with all the qualities and splendours of a fictitious character. How rarely one finds such types.'[3]

In 1952 Fleming wrote his first Bond novel as a mental escape from his pending marriage. The same year, Christine was murdered. She was stabbed to death in a hotel at the age of 37.

The list of Bond inspirations is forever growing, but Forest Yeo-Thomas' name has not cropped up with a Fleming connection before. The letter that links them and proves that the novelist had at least some interest in the man and his escapades, is tucked away in a thick personnel file. It is small slip of paper, all too easy to overlook if the name 'Ian Fleming' was not spotted on the bottom.

What could have been the reason for Fleming's fascination with Forest? Well, he was a rarity among SOE agents – he fell into the hands of the Nazis and came out alive. His amazing escapes (switching identities, jumping from trains, fleeing through no-man's-land) would be enough to draw any budding thriller writer's attention, but Forest's connection with James Bond went deeper than that.

Forest was not just a good secret agent, he was a great one. SOE was swamped with the mediocre, the mundane and even the dangerously careless. There were not many men like Forest who had the skill to stay undercover and the caution to maintain their security. There were even fewer who survived the war to tell their story. Forest was also a relatively high-ranking agent: he took charge of situations and was not just another wireless operator or messenger boy to be bossed around. He demanded respect and he usually got it. Fleming could identify with such a man.

Then there was Forest's life. He was charming and attractive to women, not necessarily because he was stunningly handsome, but because he was good company, and in a war situation, gave worried helpers the impression that he could take care of them. Forest was surrounded by women: the main members of his personal cell were all female. While Bond would have struggled to put such faith in female agents, he certainly would have appreciated being surrounded by loyal women. Jose Dupuis could even be considered reminiscent of the formidable Miss Moneypenny.

Aside from his female connections, Forest was an impressive master of disguise. He had a whole host of tricks that would have appealed to Bond, who also knew the value of a good cover. From faked walks to a range of hats that changed his appearance, Forest could blend in anywhere. He also always carried a gun; this was not general SOE policy, but for once Forest broke the rules and was not afraid to get his hands dirty if the need arose. If he had to kill he could do so, armed or unarmed.

His eventual capture was due to an act of betrayal, the same method that usually results in Bond's downfall. His torture held all the dark torments that Fleming would inflict on his personal spy. The beating of Bond's genitals in *Casino Royale* is all too familiar of the Gestapo techniques that Forest endured.

Lastly there is the daring and incredible escape, the bravery to the last and, when trying to survive, still that desire to fulfil a mission. For Forest, that was getting details of medical experiments out of Buchenwald, something he achieved despite the terrible odds against him. It was probably his 'letter from Buchenwald' describing these experiments that Fleming refers to in his own letter.

Finally there was the fact that Forest survived. He came home, he made it. There is an element of thriller fiction in Forest's story, a suggestion that some of the incidents he was involved in may have been exaggerated slightly.

Fleming would have liked that: he was fond of inviting legends about himself. But what was ultimately important was that Forest returned a hero, even if it was only a hero to his closest friends and those he saved. Bond could identify with that.

So was Forest an inspiration for Bond? He certainly has as many credentials and Fleming connections as other accepted contenders. His story was known to Fleming and intrigued him. Is it unreasonable to think he would not have stored away memories of Forest's adventures that would resurface when he began creating a new spy? All novelists are inspired by the people around them and the stories they hear and lock away inside their minds. Forest was a true-life hero and he was as close to Bond as any real agent could possibly be.

But the post-war period for Forest was far removed from Fleming's world. When he arrived in London it was to be greeted by Barbara, who had been tormented with the idea that she would never see him again. Forest was not the man she remembered: gaunt, shaven-headed, ailing and with too many dark and grim memories to enable him to settle easily back into normal life.

Forest's mind was consumed with one overriding desire: revenge. He wanted to find the man who betrayed him, he wanted to make the Germans who had tortured him suffer and he wanted to make the camp doctors and commandants stand before a courtroom and try to defend themselves. As he arrived home his thoughts revolved around the friends he had lost: Brossolette, who he now learned was long dead, and Hubble, whose chess set he had sacrificed bread for, to name but two. Life would never be the same.

Meanwhile SOE was singing its swan song. There would be no need for it in peacetime and the various sections were rapidly reduced to leave enough space for the tying up of loose ends only. De Gaulle was back in France and scorning his British allies as only he could, and the Americans were fast preparing for the pending war crimes trials at Nuremburg. Then there were the Russians, but that was business for MI6. In the muddle of post-war confusion, one sick and frail rescued agent was greeted warmly and then forgotten.

Forest's first stop was a military hospital at Millbank, where a preliminary diagnosis was a tad depressing. The physician noted:

1. Diminished airway right side of nose.
2. Persistent headache confined to right side of head.

This officer is referred for the E.N.T. specialist's opinion to exclude nasal cause for his persistent headaches.

He appears to have a deflected septum with a reduced airway on the right side. I should be grateful for your opinion about his nasal condition and possible presence of a chronic infected antrum or sinuses.[4]

After a more thorough examination the ENT specialist felt there was no reason to suspect that Forest's nose problems were the cause of his headaches. He remarked that the reduced airway was probably due to an allergy problem. There are no further medical documents in the file, but it would later become apparent that they had missed something vital.

On the other hand, Forest's psychological evaluation was much more intense. Post-traumatic stress was not a term bandied around, but the war office had learned enough from the First World War to realise that they couldn't expect badly war-damaged individuals to just walk back into a normal life. At least not without first cataloguing their condition.

In August 1945 SOE was advised that Forest's 'psychological condition is, naturally enough, very bad indeed' and they should not allow him to be interviewed about his war experiences for the Nuremburg trials until he was more recovered. Forest, however, had other ideas. Moves were afoot in SOE to track down missing agents and to make contact with former resistance colleagues. Forest wanted to be part of it, but for his own reasons: he wanted to see if he could find the traitor who had sent him to the Gestapo and the two men who had earned his greatest hate, 'Rudi' and 'Ernst'. They would be hard to find, as he had no knowledge if those were their actual names, and even if they were, there were plenty of Rudis and Ernsts in Germany. But Forest never let low odds defeat him and now the thought of bringing his torturers to justice absorbed his thoughts.

He began to pressure SOE to let him go to Germany and conduct his own, personal, investigations. His superiors were naturally reluctant, but agreed to submit him to another psych exam to see if he was mentally fit. This was conducted in September.

I interviewed [Yeo-Thomas] again this morning. He certainly has made very good progress during the past ten days. His physical condition is now practically back to normal. Mentally he states that he feels much more settled and that he has regained some of his former confidence.

He is very anxious to take the proposed trip to Germany. In view of the improvement of his general condition I think it would be alright from a medical point of view for him to proceed for a few days. However, I think it advisable that someone should accompany him on this trip.[5]

In light of modern thinking the above seems debatably optimistic. Forest was 'practically back to normal' despite his blazing headaches and the potential brain damage he had suffered. As for what he stated about his mental condition, Forest was always good at bending the truth to suit himself. His ardent desire to get to Germany and seek out his enemies should have been enough to raise warning flags about how he was feeling. But this was 1945, and psychology, especially within the military, was a very different thing. Besides, there were lots of cases to be dealt with and, in comparison to some, Forest did appear to be quite normal.

SOE was also feeling some consternation as to what to do with Forest. To be blunt, they didn't need him anymore, and nor did the RAF, and to clear their books, they ideally would have liked to demobilise him and send him back to civilian life. The only thing holding them back was the Air Ministry neuropsychiatrist, who insisted that Forest remain on their books until he had finished his treatment, though he optimistically predicted this would only take about six weeks.

The problem was that SOE was not going to exist for much longer. There was talk of handing Forest's case over to the French services completely, but that was not ideal, and then there was this German mission they had agreed to. What was to be done with Forest? Should he be invalided out of the service? Offered a position with the Home Office (if his medical reports felt him fit)? In the end it was felt that his best option was to be demobbed from SOE and, considering the suffering he had endured in his work for the service, he should receive terminal benefits and gratuity suitable to his rank as a wing commander, and a pension.

Forest's first post-war mission was codenamed Outhaul, but it was a failure from the start. The War Office had grave concerns about the mission, not least because of Forest's precarious mental balance (on 5 September 1945 he had been declared 'unstable') and that the amount of weapons he chose to take on

his trip suggested that his proposed endeavours to find and take into custody
the men who had tortured him were slightly misleading. It was felt he was out
for blood and he was hastily recalled.

Outhaul II got the go ahead because its criteria were less controversial. Its
main aims were to:

1. Wrap up his personal *réseau.*
2. To clarify the circumstances of his and Brossolette's arrest.
3. To track down a stool pigeon who had been at Compiègne and was thought
   to report to the Gestapo.
4. To trace war criminals in Fresnes.
5. To find any documents or accounts relating to the late Hubble.

The mission only lasted a week when Forest was forced to return to Britain,
probably due to failing health. At the end of 1945 Forest was having an operation on his nose that, it was hoped, might alleviate some of his symptoms. In
December his demob was announced: from 1 January 1946 he would officially
be back in civilian life. In February he received the George Cross and now all
he had to do was adapt to normal life.

In *The White Rabbit,* written by Bruce Marshal a few years after the war,
but largely based on Forest's own work, Forest's mental and physical problems
are carefully brushed aside. In Marshal's book Forest is the fictional hero who
comes out of the worst situations unscathed. He is equivalent to Fleming's
James Bond, who brushes off psychological harm and bodily abuse ready to
start his next adventure. The reality for Forest though, was not so clear-cut.

The months of abuse he had suffered left scars. Regular nightmares and
overreactions to war stories were just two symptoms. Forest, like so many victims of starvation, now found himself eating to excess and gaining weight.
He savoured food in a way he had never done before and couldn't face the
thought of empty cupboards.

Returning to his old line of work with Molyneux quickly proved unsat-
isfactory. He resented the customers, some of whom he suspected of being
collaborators or successful black market operators. There was something
wrong about selling fine clothes when he could still picture those poor souls
at Gleina stripped of their rags to be buried. A brief appearance at Nuremburg
to testify about his experiences only brought a small amount of satisfaction. So

many had escaped the Allied noose and were now free to continue their lives, and no punishment could truly compensate for what they had done.

Then there was Dr Ding. Forest was having his doubts about keeping his promise to him, while his old friend Peulevé was far more tolerant: 'A doctor Von Schuler, known by the inmates ... as Dr Ding, gave very great assistance to Wing Commander Yeo-Thomas ... and to Major H.L.T. Peulevé. Peulevé is anxious to implement the bargain that he made.'[6]

On the other hand he remained moved by the risky aid that Dietzech had provided him. Dietzech recognised a friend and wrote to him when life in post-war Germany became hard:

> After the entry of the Soviet Army ... the general conditions of life were of such a nature [that I] faced the future full of apprehension ... I cannot turn to the German authorities who, by the way, are far from being cleansed of Nazis. Unwilling as I am, dear Mr Yeo-Thomas, to worry you with personal matters, I can think of no other course then to ask whether you can somehow help me out of my present predicament. You may rest assured that I will never cease to be grateful to you for the rest of my life. Yours very truly, Arthur Dietzech.[7]

Was this the same thug who had tortured thousands of patients? Forest responded by doing what he could to assist him and ensuring necessary correspondence was translated into English and reached the relevant departments.[8]

Even so, Forest returned to Molyneux a troubled man. Whatever the military doctors had said about his problems being a minor fractured nose and nothing else, there was something far worse going on with Forest. In 1948 he started to have blackouts, and his health was clearly deteriorating; the headaches were still a feature of his life. A job as a country estate manager in Ireland seemed like the ideal change Forest needed to restore himself, but it was not to be and he was soon back in France.

In the meantime Barbara had accepted her role as Forest's common-law wife, his first wife Lillian was still refusing a divorce so there was no other option. Barbara went to France with Forest. Then in late 1949 it seemed things were on the up, as Forest was offered the role of Paris representative of the Federation of British Industry (the former representative had been found murdered, which cannot have comforted Barbara, but suggested an element of danger Forest missed from the war).

For a time life settled into a normalcy that was appealing. Forest and Barbara's relationship (always a little stormy) grew stronger. They resided in his father's old apartment and Forest started to relish his work for the Federation of British Industry. The memoirs of his adventures in France, partly encouraged by Barbara to try and exorcise wartime ghosts, appeared in 1952 and there was talk of a movie or TV series. But it was only a brief reprieve.

In 1960 a decrease in his manual dexterity and occasional losses of balance suggested that Forest's condition was worsening. Whatever damage he had sustained at Nazi hands was now taking its toll. He started to struggle to drive; he hit a set of gates when with Barbara and within a short space of time had given up driving altogether. He also began to have kidney problems. During his time in the camps he had suffered from kidney stones, which had gone untreated and thus damaged his kidneys permanently. He was admitted to hospital and found to have high blood pressure. Before long he was living on a daily cocktail of eighteen different drugs.

In 1963 Forest was presented with the Commandeur of the Légion d'honneur. At the ceremony he wept, had to be helped to stand and struggled to remember his time in the war. His friends were struck by how much thinner he looked and by his exhausted appearance. He was no longer the fit and extraordinary Shelley, he was a prematurely old man.

Forest's deterioration now became rapid. He was bedridden, and his mental state was so poor that he only occasionally slipped into lucid moments. Barbara was his full-time nurse.

On 26 February 1964 Forest suffered a massive haemorrhage and died. Barbara was by his side to the last.

In the end he could not match James Bond's final, remarkable quality. He could not make himself immortal.

Notes

1. Secret and personal letter HMS/1870, written 9 May 1945, contained in Yeo-Thomas' SOE personnel file.
2. An interesting look at possible 'Bonds' and other character inspirations can be found in Macintyre, B., *For Your Eyes Only: Ian Fleming and James Bond*.
3. McCormick, D., *17F: The Life of Ian Fleming*.
4. Major Ireland's report from Millbank military hospital, 2/8/1945.
5. Medical memo, 24/9/1945.
6. Letter from the War Crimes branch, US forces, 7/11/1945.

7. Letter from Arthur Dietzech dated 20/7/1945.
8. Letter to the War Office dated 20/8/1945.

Select Bibliography

Beevor, J.G., *SOE Recollections and Reflections 1940–45* (The Bodley Head, 1981)

Boyce, F. and Douglas, E., *SOE: the Scientific Secrets* (Sutton Publishing, 2003)

Crankshaw, E., *Gestapo: Instrument of Tyranny* (Wren's Park Publishing, 2002)

Dank, M., *The French Against the French: Collaboration and Resistance* (Cassell Ltd, 1974)

Dear, I., *Sabotage and Subversion: Stories from the files of the SOE and OSS* (Arms and Armour Press, 1996)

Delarue, J., *The Gestapo: A History of Horror* (Frontline Books, 2008)

Distel, B., *Dachau Review I: History of Nazi Concentration Camps, Studies, Reports, Documents* (Berg Publishing Ltd, 1988)

Foot, M.R.D., *SOE in France* (1966)

Howarth, P., *Undercover: The Men and Women of SOE* (Phoenix Press, 1980)

Mackenzie, W., *The Secret History of SOE: Special Operations Executive 1940–45* (St Ermin's Press, 2000)

Maclean, F.L., *The Camp Men: The Officers who ran the Nazi Concentration Camp System* (Schiffer Publishing Ltd, 1999)

Marshal, B., *The White Rabbit* (The Riverside Press, 1952)

Murphy, C.J., *Security and Special Operations: SOE and MI5 during the Second World War*, (Palgrave Macmillan, 2006)

Perrault, G., *Paris Under the Occupation* (Andre Deutsch Ltd, 1989)

Perrin, N., *Spirit of Resistance: The Life of SOE Agent Harry Peulevé, DSO, MC* (Pen and Sword, 2008)

Seaman, M., *Bravest of the Brave* (XXX)

Segev, T., *Soldiers of Evil: The Commandants of the Nazi Concentration Camps* (Grafton Books, 1990)

Spitz, V., *Doctors from Hell: The Horrific Account of Nazi Experiments on Humans* (Sentient Publications, 2005)

Turner, D., *Aston House, Station 12: SOE's Secret Centre* (Sutton Publishing, 2006)

Winstone, M., *The Holocaust Sites of Europe: An Historical Guide* (I.B. Taurus & Co. Ltd, 2010)

Escape from Germany: True Stories of POW Escapes in WW2 (The National Archives, 2009)

SOE Syllabus: Lessons in Ungentlemanly Warfare, World War II (The National Archives, 2001)

Index